taste of home

A TASTE OF HOME/READER'S DIGEST BOOK

®2011 Reiman Media Group, LLC
5400 South 60th Street
Greendale WI 53129

Taste of Home and Reader's Digest are
registered trademarks of The Reader's Digest Association, Inc.

Editor in Chief: Catherine Cassidy
Vice President/Executive Editor, Books: Heidi Reuter Lloyd
North American Chief Marketing Officer: Lisa Karpinski
Food Director: Diane Werner, RD
Creative Director: Howard Greenberg
Senior Editor, Retail Books: Faithann Stoner
Editor: Sara Lancaster
Associate Creative Director: Edwin Robles, Jr.
Art Director: Rudy Krochalk
Content Production Manager: Julie Wagner
Project Layout Designer: Kathryn Pieters
Cover Design: Courtney Lentz
Recipe Asset System Manager: Coleen Martin
Proofreader: Victoria Soukup Jensen
Recipe Testing and Editing: Taste of Home Test Kitchen
Food Photography: Taste of Home Photo Studio
Administrative Assistant: Barb Czysz

The Reader's Digest Association, Inc.
President and Chief Executive Officer: Mary G. Berner
Executive Vice President, RDA, and President North American Affinities: Suzanne M. Grimes

---

International Standard Book Number (10): 0-89821-896-9
International Standard Book Number (13): 978-0-89821-896-1
Library of Congress Control Number: 2011924980

For other *Taste of Home* books and products, visit **www.shoptasteofhome.com.**

For more Reader's Digest products and information, visit
rd.com (in the United States) or **rd.ca** (in Canada).

PRINTED IN CHINA
3 5 7 9 10 8 6 4 2

halloween
party favorites

Getting into a spooky spirit on October 31 will be a snap if you turn to this wickedly good collection featuring three creepy cookbooks in one.

In *Ghoulish Food & Fun, Spirited Shindigs* and *Bewitching Bashes*, we've scared up 243 ghoulish goodies guaranteed to frighten away your fears of hosting a haunting Halloween bash.

You won't need hocus-pocus to concoct these simple-to-fix foods because they've all been tested and approved by the Taste of Home kitchen staff.

Mummy Man Cheese Spread, Scarecrow Veggie Pizza, Serpent Tongue Potatoes and Magic Potion Punch will jump start your eye-popping party.

For a fiendish feast, turn to Witch's Hat Soup, Ham 'n' Cheese Spiders, Spooky Monster Sandwiches, Slimy Red Goop Salad and Pumpkin Chili.

Little goblins will do tricks for treats like Scaredy-Cat Cupcakes, Halloween Caramel Apples, Pretzel Pumpkin Grahams and Dracula Cookies.

Other to-die-for desserts include Ghostly Pirate Cake, Great Pumpkin Brownie, Spiderweb Cheesecake, Mousse-Filled Witches' Hats and Pumpkin Trifle.

Your eerie event will come together like magic when you rely on our spooky-but-easy party ideas, creepy crafts and clever costumes.

It's all here in *Ghoulish Food & Fun, Spirited Shindigs* and *Bewitching Bashes*. So turn the page and "enter"...if you dare!

Ghoulish Food & Fun

CONTENTS Ghoulish Food & Fun

snacks &BEVERAGES

Keep the party going with a spread of these easy-to-make finger foods. Just add a ghoulish beverage or two, and you'll have the best monster bash of them all!

Snacks & Beverages CONTENTS

FUNNY BONE!
Did you hear about the skeleton who couldn't go to the party? He had no body to go with.

Real Vampires!

Vampire bats really feed on blood, but it's mostly that of farm animals, so don't worry. Contrary to popular belief, they're not from Transylvania. Native to Mexico, Brazil, Chile and Argentina, these little creatures are wired to detect the regular breathing of their sleeping prey—that way, they can attack at night without being detected!

blood 'n' guts dip

Taste of Home Test Kitchen
Guests will love this dip that gets its bold zip from the Dijon mustard. It pairs perfectly with Pretzel Bones!

2	cups chopped fresh *or* frozen cranberries
1	cup packed brown sugar
1/2	cup honey
1/4	cup water
1	cup Dijon mustard

1 In a small saucepan, combine the cranberries, brown sugar, honey and water; bring to a boil. Cook and stir for 5 minutes or until thickened. Remove from the heat; cool slightly. Stir in mustard. Refrigerate until serving.

Yield: 2 cups.

pretzel bones

Taste of Home Test Kitchen
Just grab a bag of pretzel sticks, season them and you'll have tasty bones in no time at all! These sweet and savory treats are perfect for Halloween gatherings.

1/4	cup honey
2-1/2	tablespoons butter
2	tablespoons chili powder
1	tablespoon onion powder
1	package (15 ounces) pretzel sticks

1 In a Dutch oven, melt honey and butter; stir in chili powder and onion powder. Add pretzels; toss to coat. Spread in a single layer in 15-in. x 10-in. x 1-in. baking pans coated with cooking spray. Bake at 300° for 5 minutes, stirring once. Cool in pans on wire racks. Store in an airtight container.

Yield: 12 cups.

nutty caramel apple dip

Darlene Brenden, Salem, Oregon

Looking for a standout appetizer that could double as a dessert? Try this no-fuss favorite that you can whip up for family and friends. It's a fun change of pace for your munchies menu and an easy way to get folks to snack on apples instead of junk food.

1	package (8 ounces) cream cheese, softened
1/2	cup apple butter
1/4	cup packed brown sugar
1/2	teaspoon vanilla extract
1/2	cup chopped salted peanuts
3	medium apples, sliced

1 In a small bowl, beat the cream cheese, apple butter, brown sugar and vanilla until combined. Stir in the peanuts. Serve with apple slices. Refrigerate leftovers.

Yield: 2 cups.

Editor's Note: This recipe was tested with commercially prepared apple butter.

pumpkin cheese ball

Suzanne Cleveland, Lyons, Georgia

Everyone will get a kick out of this creamy, savory spread. The zippy cheddar ball can be made a day ahead.

1	package (8 ounces) cream cheese, softened
1	carton (8 ounces) spreadable chive and onion cream cheese
2	cups (8 ounces) shredded sharp cheddar cheese
2	teaspoons paprika
1/2	teaspoon cayenne pepper
1	celery rib *or* broccoli stalk

Sliced apples and assorted crackers

1 In a small bowl, beat cream cheeses until smooth. Stir in the cheddar cheese, paprika and cayenne. Shape into a ball; wrap in plastic wrap. Refrigerate for 4 hours or until firm.

2 With a knife, add vertical lines to the cheese ball to resemble a pumpkin; insert a celery rib or broccoli stalk for the stem. Serve with apples and crackers.

Yield: 2-1/2 cups.

FUNNY BONE!
What kind of mistakes do ghosts make? BOO-BOOs.

pumpkin snack mix

Shirley Engstrom, Genoa, Nebraska

Mix all these great snack items together and then add the candy pumpkins and you'll have a perfect October treat. Be sure to have extra pumpkins on hand, though, because you'll probably have people picking those out of the bowl!

3	quarts popped popcorn
4	cups Cheerios
4	cups Corn *or* Rice Chex
2	cups salted peanuts
1	cup packed brown sugar
3/4	cup light corn syrup
1/4	cup butter, cubed
2	teaspoons vanilla extract
1/2	teaspoon baking soda
1	package (16 ounces) candy pumpkins

1 In a large greased roasting pan, combine the popcorn, cereal and peanuts. In a large saucepan, combine the brown sugar, corn syrup and butter; bring to a rolling boil. Boil for 6 minutes, stirring occasionally. Remove from the heat; quickly stir in vanilla and baking soda until mixture is light and foamy.

2 Immediately pour over the popcorn mixture; toss to coat. Bake, uncovered, at 250° for 1 hour, stirring every 15 minutes. Stir in the candy pumpkins. Cool completely.

Yield: about 5-1/2 quarts.

toasted pumpkin seeds

Dawn Fagerstrom, Warren, Minnesota

To enjoy the seeds from a pumpkin you hollow out, spice them and bake them for a fun snack using this easy recipe. It's quick to make and so tasty.

2	cups fresh pumpkin seeds
3	tablespoons butter, melted
1	teaspoon salt
1	teaspoon Worcestershire sauce

1 Line a 15-in. x 10-in. x 1-in. baking pan with foil and grease the foil. In a small bowl, combine all ingredients; spread into prepared pan. Bake at 250° for 45-50 minutes, stirring occasionally.

2 Increase heat to 325°. Bake 5 minutes longer or until seeds are dry and lightly browned. Serve pumpkin seeds warm, or cool before storing in an airtight container.

Yield: 2 cups.

FUNNY BONE!
Why was the vampire race a tie? They were neck and neck.

pumpkin pie latte

Taste of Home Test Kitchen

Enjoy this espresso drink during the holidays or all year-round! With just the right amount of spice, it tastes just like the popular version found at gourmet coffee shops.

2	cups milk
2	tablespoons canned pumpkin
2	tablespoons sugar
2	tablespoons vanilla extract
1/2	teaspoon pumpkin pie spice
1/2	cup hot brewed espresso

Whipped cream, pumpkin pie spice and ground nutmeg, optional

1 In a small saucepan, combine milk, canned pumpkin and sugar. Cook and stir over medium heat until steaming. Remove from the heat; stir in vanilla extract and pumpkin pie spice. Transfer to a blender; cover and process for 15 seconds or until foamy.

2 Pour into two mugs; add espresso. Garnish with whipped cream and spices if desired.

Yield: 2 servings.

brie with apricot topping

Taste of Home Test Kitchen

Folks will think you fussed over this pretty appetizer that glows with harvest color, but it takes only minutes to prepare! Just top a round of smooth and creamy Brie cheese with warm sweet apricots. It's one of the easiest appetizers you can make.

1/2	cup chopped dried apricots
2	tablespoons brown sugar
2	tablespoons water
1	teaspoon balsamic vinegar

Dash salt

1/2	to 1 teaspoon minced fresh rosemary *or* 1/4 teaspoon dried rosemary, crushed
1	round Brie cheese (8 ounces)

Assorted crackers

1 In a small saucepan, combine the apricots, brown sugar, water, vinegar and salt. Bring to a boil. Reduce heat to medium; cook and stir until slightly thickened. Remove from the heat; stir in rosemary.

2 Remove rind from top of Brie cheese. Place in an ungreased ovenproof serving dish. Spread apricot mixture over cheese. Bake, uncovered, at 400° for 10-12 minutes or until the cheese is softened. Serve with crackers.

Yield: 6-8 servings.

Salem's "Witches"

From June through September of 1692, hundreds of men and women were accused of witchcraft near Salem Village, Massachusetts. Nineteen of these were hanged. Another elderly man was pressed to death with heavy stones because he wouldn't declare himself guilty or innocent. Dozens languished in jail for months without trials until the hysteria subsided.

chip 'n' dip bread witch

Taste of Home Test Kitchen

Who needs tricks with a treat as bewitching as this appetizer that's sure to steal center stage on your table? Our home economists created this ghoulish beauty—right down to the raisin wart on her nose!

2	loaves (1 pound *each*) frozen bread dough, thawed
3	egg whites

Black, green and red paste food coloring

1	sliced almond
1	pimiento-stuffed olive slice
1	raisin
1/4	cup shredded Parmesan cheese
1	to 2 jars (15-1/2 ounces *each*) salsa con queso dip

Tortilla chips

1 Let dough rise according to package directions. For witch's face, on a lightly floured surface, roll one loaf into an 8-in.-high x 6-in.-wide oval. Cut a 3-in. piece off the top and set aside. Place rolled piece on a large greased baking sheet. Pull lower left side of dough down and to the left, forming a chin.

2 For hat, roll remaining loaf into a 9-1/2-in.-high x 6-1/2-in.-wide triangle; place above face. Divide reserved dough into thirds. Roll two pieces into 12-in.-long ropes; twist together. Place over bottom of hat for brim.

3 Shape two-thirds of remaining dough into nose. Cut a 1-in. slit at an angle 1 in. below brim; insert nose. Roll remaining dough into 4-in. piece; fold in half for lips. Cut a 2-in. slit below nose; insert lips.

4 Divide egg whites among three custard cups; with food coloring, tint one portion black, one green and one red. Brush black over hat. Brush green over face and nose. Brush red over lips.

5 For witch's eye, place almond and olive between nose and brim. For wart, lightly press raisin into nose. Sprinkle Parmesan cheese over dough for hair.

6 Let rise in a warm place for 20 minutes. Bake at 350° for 15-20 minutes or until golden brown. Remove from pan to a wire rack to cool.

7 Hollow out center of hat; fill with dip, adding more as needed. Serve with tortilla chips.

Yield: 1 witch (1-1/2 to 3 cups dip).

spiced green tea

Sandra McKenzie, Braham, Minnesota

It's fun to cozy up to the campfire with a mug of this tangy tea, which is a unique blend of green tea, fruit juices and spice. The pumpkin pie spice adds autumn flavor to each sip.

5	cups boiling water
5	individual green tea bags
1/2	cup sugar
1/3	cup lemon juice
1/4	teaspoon pumpkin pie spice
5	cups unsweetened apple juice
2	cups cranberry juice

1 In a large kettle, bring water to a boil. Remove from the heat; add tea bags. Cover and steep for 8 minutes. Discard tea bags.

2 Add sugar, lemon juice and pumpkin pie spice to tea; stir until sugar is dissolved. Stir in apple juice and cranberry juice. Serve warm or cold.

Yield: 12 servings (3 quarts).

pumpkin pie dip

Laurie LaClair, North Richland Hills, Texas

I came up with this rich, creamy dip when I had a small amount of canned pumpkin left in the fridge after my holiday baking. This is also good served with sliced pears and apples, or as a spread on zucchini bread or any other nut bread.

1	package (8 ounces) cream cheese, softened
2	cups confectioners' sugar
1	cup canned pumpkin
1/2	cup sour cream
1	teaspoon ground cinnamon
1	teaspoon pumpkin pie spice
1/2	teaspoon ground ginger

Gingersnap cookies

1 In a large bowl, beat the cream cheese and confectioners' sugar until smooth. Beat in the pumpkin, sour cream, cinnamon, pumpkin pie spice and ginger until blended. Serve dip with gingersnaps. Refrigerate leftovers.

Yield: 4 cups.

FUNNY BONE!
How do you make a skeleton laugh? Tickle his funny bone.

mad scientist punch

Taste of Home Test Kitchen

You can concoct this potion with convenience items such as juice concentrate, soft drink mix, soda and sherbet. It appeals to kids of all ages! For extra fun, serve it in chemistry-type beakers found at science stores.

2	cans (12 ounces *each*) frozen pineapple-orange juice concentrate, thawed
2	cups water
1	envelope unsweetened orange soft drink mix
2	liters lemon-lime soda, chilled
1	pint orange sherbet, softened

1 In a punch bowl, combine the juice concentrate, water and soft drink mix; stir in soda. Top with scoops of sherbet. Serve immediately.

Yield: 16 servings (4 quarts).

warm ham 'n' cheese spread

Pattie Prescott, Manchester, New Hampshire

I'm always looking for creative yet family-pleasing ways to stretch my tight grocery budget. I usually make this delectable dish with ham "ends," available inexpensively at the deli counter.

4	pita breads (6 inches), split
1/4	cup olive oil
4	cups ground fully cooked ham
1	cup (4 ounces *each*) shredded Swiss, American and cheddar cheeses
1/4	cup mayonnaise
1/2	teaspoon ground mustard
2	tablespoons minced fresh parsley

Additional shredded Swiss cheese, optional

1 Cut each pita half into eight wedges; brush rough sides with oil. Place on ungreased baking sheets. Bake at 350° for 10-12 minutes or until golden brown, turning once. Remove to wire racks.

2 In a large bowl, combine ham, Swiss and American cheeses, mayonnaise and mustard. Transfer to a shallow 1-qt. baking dish.

3 Bake, uncovered, at 350° for 15-20 minutes or until edges are bubbly. Sprinkle with parsley and additional Swiss cheese if desired; serve with pita wedges.

Yield: 3-1/2 cups.

Editor's Note: Reduced-fat or fat-free mayonnaise is not recommended for this recipe.

FUNNY BONE!

What did the monster eat when he went to the dentist? The dentist.

Candy corn has been around for over 120 years! Its invention is most commonly attributed to George Renniger from the Wunderle Candy Company. By 1900, the Goelitz Candy Company (now known as Jelly Belly) started mass-producing the kernel-y confection. The National Confectioners Association estimates that 20 million pounds of candy corn is sold each year.

candy corn cheese spread

Taste of Home Test Kitchen

This yummy cheese spread is perfect for Halloween gatherings. It can be served warm, at room temperature or even chilled. This has lots of Tex-Mex flavor which is sure to please your guests.

3/4	cup finely crushed yellow tortilla chips
2	tablespoons butter, melted
1	package (8 ounces) cream cheese, softened
4	tablespoons sour cream, *divided*
1	egg, lightly beaten
1	garlic clove, minced
3/4	teaspoon chili powder, *divided*
1/4	teaspoon ground cumin
1	can (4 ounces) chopped green chilies
1	cup (4 ounces) shredded Mexican cheese blend

Assorted crackers

1 Press parchment paper onto the bottom of a 1-qt. round baking dish. In a bowl, combine crushed chips and butter; press into prepared dish. Bake, uncovered, at 325° for 10 minutes.

2 Meanwhile, in a small bowl, combine the cream cheese, 2 tablespoons sour cream, egg, garlic, 1/4 teaspoon chili powder and cumin. Stir in chilies and cheese blend. Spoon evenly over warm crust.

3 Bake at 325° for 40-45 minutes or until the top is lightly browned and a thermometer inserted in the center reads 160°. Let stand 10 minutes. Run a knife around edge and invert onto a serving platter. Carefully remove parchment paper.

4 Place the remaining sour cream in a heavy-duty resealable plastic bag; cut a small hole in a corner of bag. Pipe a large candy corn shape; sprinkle with remaining chili powder. Serve with crackers.

Yield: 2 cups.

buffets

Cook up a mesmerizing party spread when you make these simple and impressive recipes designed to be buffet-ready in a snap. From sweet treats to savory main dishes, you'll please the crowd with the goodies found here.

Buffets CONTENTS

FUNNY BONE!
Who goes to a vampire family reunion? All the blood relatives.

chocolate macaroon critters

Taste of Home Test Kitchen

Kids love to help make these yummy treats. They will especially enjoy using the M&M's to make the faces into a variety of expressions—silly, happy and yes, eve[n] scary!

1-1/2	cups semisweet chocolate chips
1	package (14 ounces) flaked coconut
1-1/4	cups sugar
3/4	cup egg whites (about 6)

M&M's miniature baking bits

Red decorating frosting

1 In a microwave, melt chocolate chips; stir u[n]til smooth. Cool. In a large bowl, beat the c[o]conut, sugar and egg whites until combine[d] Beat in melted chocolate. Refrigerate for [] hours.

2 Drop by tablespoons 2 in. apart onto parchme[nt] paper-lined baking sheets. Bake at 350° f[or] 25-30 minutes or until tops feel dry. Remove [] wire racks to cool.

3 Using baking bits and frosting, create face[s] on cookies.

Yield: 4 dozen.

dated eyes

Taste of Home Test Kitchen

These spooky-looking appetizers are the perfect balance between sweet and salty. Easy to serve and hold, they're a good buffet appetizer. Shape the dates as round as you can.

2	ounces cream cheese, softened
1/3	cup crumbled blue cheese
2	tablespoons heavy whipping cream

Dash salt

15	large unpitted dates
15	hazelnuts, toasted and peeled (about 1/2 cup)

1 In a small bowl, beat cheeses until smooth. Ad[d] cream and salt; mix well. Cut a small hole i[n] the corner of a plastic bag; fill bag with chees[e] mixture.

2 Cut a 1-in. slit along the length of each date[;] discard pit. Fill with cheese mixture; top wit[h] a hazelnut. Repeat.

Yield: 15 stuffed dates.

FUNNY BONE!
What kind of coffee does Dracula like? De-coffin-ated.

witch's hairy finger breadsticks

aste of Home Test Kitchen

With a bright green color and shredded cheese that ooks like hair, these creepy breadsticks are just right for Halloween fun. Serve directly from the oven when the heese is still warm and soft. Don't forget the marinara ipping sauce.

3	teaspoons active dry yeast
1/4	cup warm water (110° to 115°)
1/2	cup warm milk (110° to 115°)
1	egg
1/4	cup grated Parmesan cheese
1/4	cup butter, softened
1	tablespoon sugar
3/4	teaspoon salt
3/4	teaspoon Italian seasoning
1/4	teaspoon garlic powder
1/4	teaspoon green food coloring
2	to 2-1/2 cups all-purpose flour
1	egg white, lightly beaten
1/4	cup shredded Parmesan cheese
1/3	cup sliced almonds

Marinara *or* spaghetti sauce

1 In a large bowl, dissolve yeast in warm water. Add the milk, egg, grated Parmesan cheese, butter, sugar, salt, Italian seasoning, garlic powder, food coloring and 1 cup flour.

2 Beat on medium speed for 2 minutes. Stir in enough remaining flour to form a soft dough.

3 Turn onto a floured surface; knead until smooth and elastic, about 6-8 minutes. Place in a greased bowl, turning once to grease top. Cover and let rise in a warm place until doubled, about 45 minutes.

4 Punch dough down; let stand for 10 minutes. Turn onto a lightly floured surface. Divide into 16 pieces. Shape each piece into a 10-in. rope. Cut in half. Place 2 in. apart on greased baking sheets. Cover and let rise for 30 minutes.

5 Brush egg white over breadsticks; sprinkle with shredded Parmesan cheese. Place an almond slice at the tip of each. Bake at 375° for 8-10 minutes or until lightly browned. Serve warm with marinara sauce.

Yield: 32 breadsticks.

The Skinny on Bones

Did you know that not everyone has the same amount of bones? Babies actually have more bones than adults do. Babies are born with around 270 bones, and as a child grows and develops, many small bones will fuse together to form larger bones, resulting in an average number of 206 adult bones.

spicy skeleton ribs

Taste of Home Test Kitchen
These ribs are sure to add kick to the party thanks to the haunting combination of spices.

4	cups diced cooked chicken breast
1-1/4	cups water
1/4	cup tomato paste
2	tablespoons *each* paprika and lime juice
1-1/2	teaspoons *each* onion powder, garlic powder, dried basil and dried oregano
1	teaspoon *each* salt, dried thyme, celery seed, pepper and cayenne pepper
1	bay leaf
12	ounces cream cheese, softened
1	tablespoon grated lime peel
2	tubes (11 ounces *each*) refrigerated crusty French loaf
2	cups (8 ounces) shredded Monterey Jack cheese

1 In a large saucepan, combine the diced chicken, water, tomato paste, paprika, lime juice and seasonings. Bring to a boil. Reduce heat to low. Simmer, uncovered, for 20 minutes or until all liquid is evaporated, stirring occasionally. Discard bay leaf.

2 Combine cream cheese and lime peel. On a large piece of foil, roll one tube of bread dough into a 14-in. x 10-in. rectangle. Spread with half of cream cheese mixture to within 1/2 in. of edges; sprinkle with half of the chicken mixture and shredded cheese.

3 Starting with a long side and using foil, fold in to thirds. Form a 14-in. x 4-in. loaf with a seam along one side. Pinch edges to seal. Transfer to a baking sheet. Repeat. Bake at 325° for 45-50 minutes or until golden brown.

4 Remove to wire racks. Let cool for 10 minutes before cutting into 1-in. slices. Arrange on a large serving platter to resemble ribs with a plastic skull if desired.

Yield: 2 loaves (14 slices each).

witch's cauldron tortellini

Taste of Home Test Kitchen

Orange peppers add Halloween flair to this easy salad that's perfect for your gathering. For a fun presentation, use a plastic cauldron for serving. You can also make this into appetizers by cutting the peppers into 1-inch cubes and threading them and the other ingredients onto skewers.

1	package (9 ounces) refrigerated cheese tortellini
1/2	pound fresh mozzarella cheese (1-inch balls), drained
1	jar (7-1/2 ounces) marinated quartered artichoke hearts, drained
1	can (6 ounces) pitted ripe olives, drained
1	medium sweet orange pepper, chopped
1/4	cup prepared pesto
3	tablespoons white wine vinegar

1 Prepare cheese tortellini according to package directions. Meanwhile, in a large bowl, combine the remaining ingredients. Drain tortellini. Add to cheese mixture; toss to coat. Serve warm or refrigerate until chilled.

Yield: 9 servings.

ghoul-ade

Taste of Home Test Kitchen

This is a delicious, refreshing punch for everyone at your Halloween gathering, and it's not too sweet. The lychee eyeballs are an unexpected surprise. (Lychees can be found in the Asian food section of the grocery store.)

1/2	cup fresh or frozen unsweetened blueberries
1	can (15 ounces) lychees, drained
1	bottle (46 ounces) V8 V-Fusion peach mango juice, chilled
1	envelope (.15 ounce) unsweetened orange soft drink mix
2	drops orange food coloring
46	ounces lemon-lime soda, chilled

1 For floating eyeballs, insert a blueberry into the center of each lychee. Place in a single layer in a freezer container; freeze.

2 In a 3-qt. punch bowl, combine the juice, soft drink mix and food coloring. Just before serving, add soda and frozen lychees.

Yield: 15 servings.

FUNNY BONE!
What should a mummy do when he's stressed? Unwind.

bone-crunching meatballs

Taste of Home Test Kitchen

Water chestnuts are the secret ingredient in these unique meatballs. Kids will love the "bone-like" crunch the chestnuts add when they bite into each meatball!

1	can (8 ounces) sliced water chestnuts, drained
1	egg, lightly beaten
3	tablespoons soy sauce
1/2	cup chopped green onions (green part only)
1/4	cup dry bread crumbs
2	tablespoons minced fresh cilantro
1-1/2	teaspoons grated lime peel
1-1/2	teaspoons minced fresh gingerroot
1	garlic clove, minced
1/4	teaspoon salt
1/4	teaspoon pepper
1-1/2	pounds lean ground turkey
2	tablespoons canola oil

Plum sauce

1 Cut enough water chestnut slices in half to make 60 pieces; set aside. Save the remaining water chestnuts slices for another use.

2 In a bowl, combine the next 10 ingredients Crumble turkey over mixture and mix well Divide into 60 portions and shape each portio around a water chestnut piece.

3 In a large nonstick skillet, saute meatballs i oil in batches for 5 minutes or until browned Transfer to a 13-in. x 9-in. x 2-in. baking dish Cover and bake at 350° for 10-15 minutes o until meat is no longer pink; drain. Serve with plum sauce.

Yield: 5 dozen.

pecans diablo

Taste of Home Test Kitchen

The spices in this recipe showcase pecans in a whole different light. This is a great snack for any party, but their heat suits the cool and crisp evenings during the Halloween season.

1/4	cup butter, melted
3/4	teaspoon dried rosemary, crushed
1/4	to 1/2 teaspoon cayenne pepper
1/4	teaspoon dried basil
5	cups pecan halves
2	teaspoons kosher salt

1 In a large bowl, combine the butter, rosemary cayenne and basil. Add pecans and toss to coa Spread in a single layer in a 15-in. x 10-in. x 1-in. baking pan. Sprinkle with salt.

2 Bake, uncovered, at 325° for 17-20 minutes o until pecans are crisp, stirring occasionally Cool completely. Store in an airtight container

Yield: 5 cups.

FUNNY BONE!

How many vampires does it take to change a lightbulb? None. They like the dark.

Lunar Truths

Crescent moons are either in the waxing phase (getting bigger) or waning phase (getting smaller) to those of us here on earth. Of course, the moon stays the same size and shape—it only looks like it's changing because of the shadows caused by its orbit around the earth. The moon is actually egg-shaped with the large end pointed toward Earth.

fudgy cheesecake moons

Taste of Home Test Kitchen

These little cakes are deceiving because despite how thin they are, they are rich and filling. Instead of crescent moons, you can also cut them into circles to celebrate the Harvest Moon.

3/4	cup butter, cubed
6	squares (1 ounce *each*) semisweet chocolate, chopped
2	eggs
3/4	cup sugar
3/4	cup packed brown sugar
1	teaspoon vanilla extract
1	cup plus 2 tablespoons all-purpose flour
6	tablespoons baking cocoa
1/2	teaspoon salt

TOPPING:

2	packages (8 ounces *each*) cream cheese, softened
1/4	cup sugar
1	tablespoon cornstarch
1	egg
1	teaspoon vanilla extract
1/3	cup caramel ice cream topping

1 In a small saucepan, heat the butter over medium heat until golden brown, or about 7 minutes. Remove from the heat. Add the chocolate; stir until smooth.

2 In a large bowl, combine the eggs, sugars and vanilla; whisk in chocolate mixture. Combine the flour, cocoa and salt; add to egg mixture and stir until smooth. Line a 15-in. x 10-in. x 1-in. baking pan with waxed paper and grease the paper; spread the batter evenly into the prepared pan.

3 In a small bowl, beat the cream cheese, sugar and cornstarch until smooth; beat in egg and vanilla. Gently spread over chocolate layer. Drizzle caramel topping over cream cheese layer in vertical lines about 1 in. apart. Use a toothpick to draw right angles across the drizzled lines, about 1/2 in. apart.

4 Bake at 325° for 15-18 minutes or until a toothpick inserted near the center comes out clean (do not overbake). Cool on a wire rack for 1 hour. Refrigerate for 1 hour before removing from pan. Discard waxed paper. Cut with a 3-in. x 1-in. crescent-shaped cookie cutter. Store in an airtight container in the refrigerator.

Yield: 20 bars.

Creepy Crawly Folklore

Some people believe that if caterpillars' brown stripes are thick, the upcoming winter will be mild. If the brown stripes are narrow, the winter will be severe. Caterpillars were once used to "cure" whopping cough. Sick folks tied a caterpillar in a bag, wore it around the neck, and as it wasted away, so did the illness (or so they thought).

fuzzy caterpillars

Taste of Home Test Kitchen

Kids and adults will all love this unique way to prepare chicken. The coconut coating provides a crunch and the dip has a tropical flair. Using a food processor makes it easy to chop the cashews.

3/4	cup plain yogurt
1	carton (6 ounces) pina colada yogurt
1-1/2	teaspoons grated lime peel
1-1/4	teaspoons salt, *divided*
2	pounds boneless skinless chicken breasts
1	cup sesame ginger marinade
2	tablespoons lime juice
2	cups flaked coconut
1/2	cup finely chopped cashews
3	eggs
2	tablespoons milk
1	cup all-purpose flour
1/2	cup canola oil

1 In a small bowl, combine the yogurts, peel and 1/4 teaspoon salt; cover and refrigerate.

2 Cut chicken into 30 thin strips. In a large resealable plastic bag, combine marinade and lime juice; add chicken. Seal bag and turn to coat; refrigerate for 30 minutes.

3 Meanwhile, in a shallow bowl, combine coconut and cashews. In another shallow bowl, combine eggs and milk. In a third shallow bowl, combine flour and remaining salt. Drain and discard marinade from chicken.

4 Coat chicken with flour; dip into egg mixture, then roll in coconut mixture. In a large skillet over medium heat, cook chicken strips in oil in batches for 2 minutes or until lightly browned, turning once.

5 Place a wire rack in a 15-in. x 10-in. x 1-in. baking pan; place chicken on rack. Bake chicken, uncovered, at 350° for 10-15 minutes or until chicken is no longer pink. Serve warm with dipping sauce.

Yield: 2-1/2 dozen (1-1/3 cups sauce).

corn maze munch

Taste of Home Test Kitchen

All hail to the Corn King with this sweet, crunchy and savory treat. The "corny" combination of ingredients sure says "Harvesttime!"

2	tablespoons butter
3	cups Corn Chex
1/2	teaspoon salt
3	cups cheese popcorn
1	package (18-1/2 ounces) candy corn
1	package (14 ounces) Halloween-colored milk chocolate M&M's
2	packages (4 ounces *each*) corn nuts
1	cup raisins
1	package (3-1/2 ounces) caramel popcorn with peanuts

1 In a large skillet, melt butter; add Corn Chex and toss to coat. Cook and stir on medium heat until the Corn Chex is lightly browned, about 5 minutes. Sprinkle with salt; set aside to cool.

2 Meanwhile, in a large bowl, combine remaining ingredients. Add Corn Chex and toss to coat. Store in an airtight container.

Yield: 3-1/2 quarts.

stuffed potato ghosts

Taste of Home Test Kitchen

These hearty and yummy treats are easier to make than most stuffed potatoes and are a perfect appetizer.

2	pounds fingerling potatoes
1	large baking potato
1/3	cup sour cream
2	ounces cream cheese, softened
1	tablespoon butter
1/4	teaspoon salt
1/8	teaspoon pepper
7	thin slices Monterey Jack cheese
1	tablespoon chopped ripe olives
2	green onions, thinly sliced

1 Bake fingerling potatoes at 350° for 40-45 minutes or until tender; set aside.

2 Meanwhile, pierce baking potato several times with a fork. Microwave for 6-7 minutes or until tender. Cut in half and scoop out pulp; discard shell. Place pulp in a small bowl; mash. Stir in the sour cream, cream cheese, butter, salt and pepper until smooth.

3 Cut each fingerling in half lengthwise. Spoon about 1 tablespoon mashed potato mixture over each potato half. Place stuffed potato halves on a foil-lined baking sheet.

4 Cut each cheese slice into six rectangles; place one on each stuffed potato. (Save remaining cheese for another use.) Bake at 350° for 10-11 minutes or until cheese is melted and potatoes are heated through. Position olives and green onions on each for eyes and mouths.

Yield: 40 appetizers.

Editor's Note: This recipe was tested in a 1,100-watt microwave.

FUNNY BONE!
What do ghosts eat with meatballs? SPOOK-etti.

sweet TREATS

Halloween wouldn't be the same without sweet treats! Whether you need a school treat or a party-perfect dessert, look no further. Here's an array of easy and oh-so-good confections that are sure to impress.

Sweet Treats CONTENTS

FUNNY BONE!
What do ghosts say to each other on Valentine's Day? "BOO my Valentine."

mounds of bugs

Taste of Home Test Kitchen

If you have lots of little hands begging for a few minute in the kitchen, this is a perfect recipe for you. Kids will squeal with delight when they make these cute bugs, decorated with candies.

1	package (11.3 ounces) snack-size Mounds candy bars
20	pretzels
1/4	cup chocolate frosting

Assorted candies: Nerds, Candy Buttons, Dots and/or sprinkles

1 Using a skewer, poke three holes in both lon sides of each candy bar. Break rounded pretze sections into 1-in. pieces; insert into holes fo legs. Use frosting to attach candies.

Yield: about 1-1/2 dozen.

frightfully good cakes

Taste of Home Test Kitchen

If there is one word to describe these one- or two-bite cakes, it is EASY! Use different Halloween candies to make different cakes, such as "Boo" or Frankenstein.

1	loaf (10-3/4 ounces) frozen pound cake, thawed
1	can (16 ounces) vanilla frosting

Green, orange and black paste food coloring, optional

4	ounces white candy coating, chopped

Halloween candies and miniature marshmallows

1 Level top of the cake; cut into 1/2-in. slices. Place on a wire rack over a baking sheet.

2 Spoon the frosting into a microwave-safe bowl; microwave, uncovered, on high for 20 seconds. Stir; repeat until frosting no longer holds a peak. (Do not overheat.) Tint some frosting with green and/or orange food coloring. Slowly pour frosting over cakes, coating top and sides. If necessary, use frosting drippings and reheat. Let stand for 30 minutes or until set.

3 For words, melt white coating in a microwave-safe bowl; stir until smooth. Tint with food coloring. Transfer to a pastry or plastic bag; cut a hole in the corner of bag. Pipe words onto waxed paper. Let stand for 15 minutes or until set. Carefully remove words from the paper and position on cakes. Add faces, candies and marshmallows as desired.

Yield: 14 servings.

Editor's Note: This recipe was tested in a 1,100 watt microwave.

FUNNY BONE!
Why did the witches cancel the baseball game? The bats flew away.

26

dracula cookies

Christy Hinrichs, Parkville, Missouri

These sweet treats are very easy to make and a must-have on the table at your Halloween gathering. The truffles must be cold and dipped in cooled chocolate to prevent the icing from melting into the white candy coating. Since assembly is the only thing required, it is a perfect recipe for little kids!

6	hazelnut truffles
5	ounces white candy coating, chopped
1	green *or* red Fruit Roll-Up
6	cream-filled chocolate sandwich cookies
1	can (6.4 ounces) black decorating icing
6	slivered almonds, cut in half

1 Place truffles on a waxed paper-lined pan. Freeze for 10 minutes or until chilled. Meanwhile, in a small microwave-safe bowl, melt the candy coating; stir until smooth. Dip truffles in coating to cover completely; return to pan. Refrigerate until hardened.

2 Cut Fruit Roll-Up into 2-1/2-in. x 1-1/2-in. strips. Reheat candy coating if necessary. Dip truffles in candy coating again; immediately place one on each cookie. Wrap a fruit strip around base of truffle for cape. Let stand until set.

3 Using decorating icing and a round tip, pipe hair, eyes and mouth on each. Insert almonds for fangs. Store in an airtight container.

Yield: 6 cookies.

Editor's Note: This recipe was tested with Ferrero Rocher hazelnut truffles.

hosts of ghosts

Taste of Home Test Kitchen

This is a simple, four-ingredient recipe that can create a wide variety of ghosts, each with a different personality! The filling is very easy to work with, too.

10	chocolate cream-filled chocolate sandwich cookies
1	package (3 ounces) cream cheese, softened
6	ounces white candy coating, chopped
1	teaspoon shortening

1 In a food processor, cover and process chocolate cream-filled cookies until mixture resembles coarse crumbs. Cut cream cheese into three pieces; add to food processor. Cover; process until mixture forms a soft dough.

2 Using 2 teaspoons of dough for each ghost, form 26 ghost shapes. Place the ghosts on a waxed paper-covered baking sheet.

3 In a small microwave-safe bowl, melt candy coating and shortening; stir until smooth. Slowly spoon over each ghost shape to cover.

4 Use a toothpick to create the eyes. Store the ghosts in the refrigerator.

Yield: 26 servings.

Grave Reading

A rose or calla lily symbol on a gravestone symbolizes beauty, while a broken bud, daisy or lamb symbolizes a child's death. Corn is meant to represent fertility or rebirth, and a cornocopia represents a fruitful, abundant life. Dogs symbolize loyalty, lions symbolize strength and owls show the wisdom of the deceased.

coffin pumpkin cake

Kathy Michel, Dubuque, Iowa

The maple flavoring in the frosting makes this spooky cake taste delicious. And the gingersnap crumbs make the "coffin" look like a pine box to suit the Halloween season perfectly.

3/4	cup butter, softened
1-1/2	cups sugar
3	eggs
1-1/2	cups canned pumpkin
1-1/2	teaspoons vanilla extract
3	cups all-purpose flour
1-1/2	teaspoons ground cinnamon
1	teaspoon baking powder
1	teaspoon baking soda
3/4	teaspoon ground nutmeg
1/2	teaspoon salt
1/4	teaspoon ground ginger
1/4	teaspoon ground cloves
1	cup buttermilk

FROSTING/FILLING:

2	packages (8 ounces *each*) cream cheese, softened
1/2	cup butter, softened
3-1/2	cups confectioners' sugar
2	to 3 teaspoons maple flavoring
1/2	cup heavy whipping cream
2	cups crushed gingersnap cookies (about 40 cookies)

1 In a large bowl, cream butter and sugar until light and fluffy. Add eggs, one at a time, beating well after each addition. Beat in canned pumpkin and vanilla extract. Combine flour, cinnamon, baking powder, baking soda, nutmeg, salt, ginger and cloves; add to the pumpkin mixture alternately with buttermilk, beating well after each addition.

2 Line a greased 13-in. x 9-in. x 2-in. baking pan with waxed paper and grease the paper; spread batter into pan. Bake at 325° for 40-45 minutes or until a toothpick inserted near the center comes out clean. Cool for 5 minutes before removing from pan to a wire rack to cool completely.

3 In a large bowl, beat the cream cheese and butter until smooth. Add confectioners' sugar and enough maple flavoring to achieve a spreadable consistency. For filling, in a small bowl, beat 1 cup frosting with whipping cream until soft peaks form.

4 Cut cake into a coffin shape (discard scraps or save for another use). Cut cake horizontally into two layers. Place the bottom layer on a serving plate; spread with filling. Top with the second layer.

5 Set aside 2 tablespoons frosting for writing; frost cake with remaining frosting. Sprinkle top with cookie crumbs. Cut a small hole in the corner of a plastic bag; fill with the reserved frosting. Pipe "RIP" onto cake. Store cake in the refrigerator until ready to serve.

Yield: 20 servings.

midnight mice

Taste of Home Test Kitchen

...t these on a plate and they'll be gone in no time! Kids will love decorating the mice with assorted candies.

- 1   cup creamy peanut butter
- 1/4   cup butter, softened
- 1/2   teaspoon vanilla extract
- 1/2   cups confectioners' sugar
- 1/2   cups crisp rice cereal
- 3/4   cup sliced almonds
- 12   ounces dark chocolate candy coating, chopped
- 1   tablespoon shortening
- 36   pieces black shoestring licorice (2 inches *each*)

Assorted candies: red cake decorator dots, &M's semisweet miniature baking bits and ...ack sugar

1. In a small bowl, beat peanut butter, butter and vanilla until blended. Gradually beat in the confectioners' sugar. Stir in cereal. Shape into 1-in. balls, tapering one end to resemble a mouse. Position almonds on heads for ears. Refrigerate until chilled.

2. In a large microwave-safe bowl, melt candy coating and shortening; stir until smooth. Dip mice into coating; place on waxed paper-lined baking sheets. Immediately insert licorice for tails. Add red dots for the eyes and M&M's miniature baking bits for noses. Sprinkle with black sugar. Refrigerate until set.

Yield: 3 dozen.

maple ginger fudge

Steve Westphal, Milwaukee, Wisconsin

...combine two fall favorites—maple and ginger—in this sweet, smooth fudge. One piece just isn't enough!

- 2   teaspoons plus 2 tablespoons butter, *divided*
- 2   cups sugar
- 2/3   cup heavy whipping cream
- 2   tablespoons light corn syrup
- 1/4   teaspoon ground ginger
- 1/2   teaspoon maple flavoring
- 1/2   cup chopped walnuts

1. Line a 9-in. x 5-in. x 3-in. loaf pan with foil and grease the foil with 1 teaspoon butter; set aside. Butter the sides of a small heavy saucepan with 1 teaspoon butter; add the sugar, cream, corn syrup and ginger. Bring to a boil over medium heat, stirring constantly. Reduce heat; cook until a candy thermometer reads 238° (soft-ball stage), stirring occasionally.

2. Remove from the heat. Add maple flavoring and remaining butter (do not stir). Cool to 110° without stirring, about 1 hour. With a portable mixer, beat on low speed for 1-2 minutes or until fudge begins to thicken. Using a clean dry wooden spoon, stir in walnuts until fudge begins to lose its gloss, about 5 minutes.

3. Spread into prepared pan. Refrigerate until firm, about 30 minutes. Using foil, lift fudge out of pan. Discard foil; cut fudge into 1-in. squares. Store in an airtight container in the refrigerator.

Yield: 1-1/4 pounds.

Editor's Note: We recommend that you test your candy thermometer before each use by bringing water to a boil; the thermometer should read 212°. Adjust your recipe temperature up or down based on your test.

FUNNY BONE!
What do ghosts eat for dessert? BOO-berry pie and I-scream.

pumpkins on parade

Taste of Home Test Kitchen

Let the kids help make these festive, fun and colorful cupcakes. The quick bread mix makes the cupcakes nice and moist. The footed cupcake holders shown in the photo are available at www.wilton.com.

1	package (14 ounces) banana quick bread and muffin mix
1/2	cup miniature semisweet chocolate chips
11	ounces yellow candy coating disks
28	brown semisweet M&M's miniature baking bits
3/4	to 1 cup vanilla frosting
6	drops orange paste food coloring
4	green medium gumdrops

1 Prepare muffin mix batter according to package directions; stir in miniature chocolate chips. Fill paper-lined muffin cups two-thirds full.

2 Bake at 350° for 20-25 minutes or until a toothpick comes out clean. Cool for 10 minutes before removing to wire racks to cool completely.

3 Meanwhile, in a small microwave-safe bowl, melt candy coating. Transfer to a pastry bag or plastic bag; cut a hole in the corner of bag. Form the eyes, noses and mouths for 14 jack-o'-lantern faces on waxed paper. Add M&M's baking bits for pupils. Let stand until set.

4 Tint frosting orange; frost cupcakes. Carefully peel off eyes, noses and mouths; position on cupcakes. Cut gumdrops into small triangles for stems; attach to top of pumpkins.

Yield: 14 servings.

eye spy cookies

Taste of Home Test Kitchen

These cookies are reminiscent of old cartoons where eyes pop out in a dark room! They're a cinch to make and doubly fun to decorate!

1-1/2	cups butter, softened
1/2	cup confectioners' sugar
1-1/2	teaspoons vanilla extract
2-1/4	cups all-purpose flour
3/4	cup cornstarch

FROSTING/DECORATING:

1/4	cup butter, softened
3	cups confectioners' sugar
2	to 3 tablespoons lemon juice
3	teaspoons grated lemon peel

Neon purple *and/or* green food coloring

Miniature milk chocolate kisses

1 In a large bowl, cream butter and confectioners' sugar until light and fluffy. Add vanilla. Combine flour and cornstarch; gradually add to creamed mixture and mix well.

2 Roll into 3/4-in. balls. Place 1 in. apart on ungreased baking sheets. With fingers, flatten to 1/4-in. thickness, forming eye shapes. For variety, shape some balls into logs, then flatten. Bake at 350° for 9-10 minutes or until edges begin to brown. Remove to wire racks to cool.

3 For frosting, in a small bowl, beat butter and confectioners' sugar until smooth. Add enough lemon juice to achieve a spreading consistency. Beat in lemon peel. Tint frosting purple and/or neon green; frost cookies. Add kisses for pupils.

Yield: 8 dozen.

FUNNY BONE!
Where do ghosts go fishing? On Lake EERIE.

Spider Myths Revealed

Spiders aren't insects, they're arachnids, which in the animal world, is as different as a bird from a fish. Putting a house spider outside isn't kind—most (95%) do not survive outdoors. And think twice when you're considering getting rid of them. They are harmless and feed on other insect "pests" in your house!

~~D~~ark side chocolate ~~c~~aramel tart

~~T~~aste of Home Test Kitchen

~~T~~his is a rich, sweet and oh-so-delicious after-dinner ~~tr~~eat. The decorating can make it fun or elegant. ~~It~~ tastes like a turtle candy.

1	cup sugar
3/4	cup water
1	tablespoon light corn syrup
1/4	teaspoon salt
1	cup heavy whipping cream

~~P~~astry for single-crust pie (9 inches)

1/2	cup *each* chopped pecans, milk chocolate chips and semisweet chocolate chips
2	eggs

~~D~~RIZZLE:

1/4	cup semisweet chocolate chips
1	tablespoon milk

1 In a small heavy saucepan over medium heat, bring the sugar, water, corn syrup and salt to a boil. Cook, stirring occasionally, until mixture turns an amber color, about 15 minutes. Remove from the heat; slowly stir in cream (mixture will appear lumpy). Cook and stir over low heat until mixture is completely smooth, about 5 minutes. Remove from the heat; cool for 30 minutes.

2 Meanwhile, press pastry onto the bottom and up the sides of an ungreased 9-in. fluted tart pan with removable bottom; trim edges. Prick the bottom with a fork. Bake at 350° for 20 minutes or until golden brown.

3 Sprinkle pecans and chocolate chips into crust. Whisk eggs, one at a time, into warm caramel mixture. Pour over chocolate and pecans.

4 Bake at 350° for 30-35 minutes or until top is bubbly and crust is golden brown. Cool completely on a wire rack.

5 In a microwave, melt chocolate chips with milk; stir until smooth. Cut a small hole in the corner of a plastic bag. Fill with chocolate mixture; pipe a web over tart. Store in the refrigerator.

Yield: 12 servings.

buried surprise cupcakes

Taste of Home Test Kitchen

Most kids will love the gruesome gummy body parts they find in the center of these cupcakes, but if it is too much for you, use any kind of autumn-motif gummies for the same sweet taste.

1	package (18-1/4 ounces) red velvet cake mix
1	package (3.4 ounces) cook-and-serve chocolate pudding mix
1-1/4	cups water
1/3	cup canola oil
3	eggs
1/2	cup seedless raspberry spreadable fruit
24	Halloween gummy candy body parts *or* gummy candy finger rings
1	can (16 ounces) cream cheese frosting
6	to 12 drops purple neon food coloring
Purple sugar	

1 In a large bowl, combine cake and puddin[g] mixes. Beat in the water, oil and eggs on lo[w] speed for 30 seconds. Beat at medium speed fo[r] 2 minutes.

2 Fill paper-lined muffin cups two-thirds ful[l.] Bake at 350° for 18-22 minutes or until a tooth[-] pick comes out clean. Let cool for 10 minute[s] before removing from pans to wire racks t[o] cool completely.

3 Using a sharp knife, cut a 1-in. circle 1 in. dee[p] in the top of each cupcake. Carefully remov[e] tops and set aside. Fill each with 1 teaspoo[n] spreadable fruit and a gummy candy; replac[e] tops. Tint frosting; spread over cupcakes an[d] sprinkle with purple sugar.

Yield: 2 dozen.

caramel apple trifle

Joanne Wright, Niles, Michigan

Trifles are terrific desserts because they're made in advance and feed a crowd. This caramel-apple version appeals to kids of all ages.

3	tablespoons butter
4	cups chopped peeled tart apples (about 5 medium)
1	cup chopped walnuts
1/2	cup packed brown sugar
1	teaspoon apple pie spice, *divided*
1	package (8 ounces) cream cheese, softened
1	jar (12-1/4 ounces) caramel ice cream topping, *divided*
1	carton (12 ounces) frozen whipped topping, thawed, *divided*
2	loaves (10-3/4 ounces *each*) frozen pound cake, thawed and cut into 1-inch cubes
Additional apple pie spice, optional	

1 In a large skillet, melt butter over medium hea[t.] Stir in the apples, walnuts, brown sugar an[d] 1/2 teaspoon apple pie spice. Cook and stir f[or] 8-10 minutes or until apples are tender.

2 In a large bowl, beat cream cheese until smoot[h.] Beat in 1/2 cup caramel topping and remainin[g] apple pie spice. Fold in 2 cups whipped toppin[g.]

3 In a 3-1/2-qt. trifle bowl or glass serving bow[l,] layer a third of the cake cubes, cream chees[e] mixture and apple mixture. Repeat layer[s] twice. Dollop with remaining whipped toppin[g] and drizzle with remaining caramel toppin[g.] Sprinkle with additional apple pie spice if de[-] sired. Cover and refrigerate for at least 1 hou[r] before serving.

Yield: 14 servings.

halloween night cookie puzzle

Taste of Home Test Kitchen

A Halloween sleepover can't be complete without this cookie puzzle. It is easy to make and decorate...and even more fun to eat. The kids will never stop talking about the puzzle they ate at your house!

1	tube (18 ounces) refrigerated sugar cookie dough, softened
1/2	cup all-purpose flour
	Unblanched almonds
3	cups confectioners' sugar
1/3	cup light corn syrup
2	to 4 tablespoons water

Assorted food coloring, decorating gels, sprinkles and candies

1 In a large mixing bowl, combine cookie dough and flour. On a parchment paper-lined surface, roll dough into a 14-in. x 11-in. rectangle. With Halloween cookie cutters, cut out puzzle shapes but do not remove them. Slide a baking sheet under the parchment paper and dough. Chill for 5-10 minutes.

2 Remove shapes; place shapes on an ungreased baking sheet. For handles, press the side of an almond into the center of each puzzle shape. Bake shapes at 350° for 7-9 minutes or until edges are golden brown. While still warm, recut shapes with the same cookie cutters to form neat edges. (If cookies cool too quickly, return to oven until softened.) Remove to wire racks; cool.

3 Bake large rectangular puzzle on a parchment paper-lined baking sheet for 12-13 minutes or until the edges are golden brown. Immediately recut the shapes inside the puzzle to form neat edges. Cool completely on a wire rack.

4 In a small bowl, combine the confectioners' sugar, corn syrup and water until smooth. Tint frosting with food coloring as desired. Frost puzzle and shapes; decorate with decorating gel, sprinkles and candies as desired. Place puzzle shapes inside puzzle.

Yield: 1 cookie puzzle (24 servings).

FUNNY BONE!
What did the witch mommy say to her screaming child? "Don't fly off the handle."

spooky cookie cottage

3/4	cup butter, softened
3/4	cup sugar
2	eggs
1	teaspoon vanilla extract
2-3/4	cups all-purpose flour
2	teaspoons baking powder

ICING AND ASSEMBLY:

4-1/2	cups confectioners' sugar
3	tablespoons meringue powder
1/2	teaspoon cream of tartar
6	tablespoons warm water
1	teaspoon vanilla extract

Orange, regal purple, black and yellow gel food coloring

Pastry tips—round #6 and #3

12	white candy coating disks, cut in half

Clean paintbrush

Red sprinkles

Additional confectioners' sugar

Cream-filled oval vanilla sandwich cookies

Black-covered board

2-1/2	cups chocolate wafer crumbs

Candy pumpkins

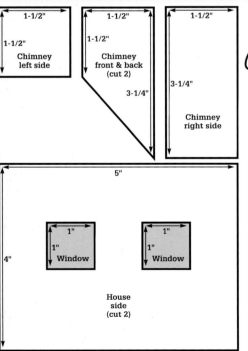

1-1/2"
1-1/2"
Chimney left side

1-1/2"
1-1/2"
Chimney front & back (cut 2)
3-1/4"

1-1/2"
3-1/4"
Chimney right side

Bat

3-3/8"
House front & back (cut 2)

2"
1-3/4"
Window

1-1/2"
2-1/2"
Door front only
4-1/2"

4"

5"
1"
1"
Window
1"
1"
Window
4"
House side (cut 2)

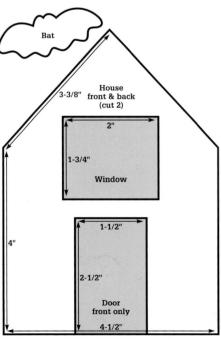

TO USE PATTERN, ENLARGE ON A PHOTOCOPIER 200%.

1 In a large mixing bowl, cream butter and sugar until light and fluffy. Add eggs, one at a time, beating well after each addition. Beat in vanilla. Combine flour and baking powder; gradually add to creamed mixture and mix well. Divide dough into thirds. Chill for 1-2 hours.

2 On a lightly floured surface, roll out one portion of dough to 1/4-in. thickness. Position house side pattern on dough. With a sharp knife, cut one side piece. Reroll scraps; cut another side piece. Score and cut out window outlines; set window pieces aside. Transfer side pieces to an ungreased baking sheet. Bake at 400° for 10-12 minutes or until edges are lightly browned. Cool for 10 minutes before removing from pan to a wire rack to cool completely.

3 Roll out the second portion of dough. Position house front pattern on dough. Cut out house front; remove scraps. Cut out door and window pieces; set aside. Reroll scraps; cut out house back. Cut out window piece; set aside.

4 Roll out remaining dough to 1/4-in. thickness; cut into two 6-in. x 4-1/2-in. rectangles for roof pieces. Transfer front, back and roof pieces to ungreased baking sheets. Bake at 400° for 10-12 minutes or until edges are lightly browned. Cool for 10 minutes before removing from pans to wire racks to cool completely.

5 Reroll scraps; cut out chimney pieces. From reserved front window piece, cut out two 1-1/2-in. x 1/2-in. strips for front shutters; set aside. Discard remaining dough. Cut the reserved side and back window pieces in half for shutters. Place the chimney pieces, shutters and door on an ungreased baking sheet. Bake at 400° for 5-8 minutes or until edges are lightly browned. Cool for 10 minutes before removing to a wire rack to cool.

6 **To make icing:** In a mixing bowl, combine the first three ingredients; add water and vanilla. Beat on low speed for 1 minute. Beat on high for 4-5 minutes or until stiff peaks form. Set aside 3/4 cup white icing. Tint two-thirds of remaining icing orange; thin with 2 tablespoons water. Tint remaining icing purple; thin with 1 tablespoon water. Place a damp cloth over bowl and cover tightly between uses.

7 **To decorate:** Place house front, back and sides and chimney pieces on a waxed-paper lined work surface. Insert #6 tip into a pastry bag; fill with 1/2 cup orange icing. Pipe icing over pieces; let dry overnight. Repeat for roof pieces, using purple icing. Working quickly, attach halved candy disks at random for shingles, leaving space on one roof piece for chimney. Brush halved disks with purple icing; let dry completely. With a paintbrush and orange gel, add brick designs to house and chimney pieces; let dry. Assemble chimney with orange icing; let dry.

8 **To make decorations:** Divide the reserved white icing into thirds. Tint one portion black and one light yellow; leave remaining icing white.

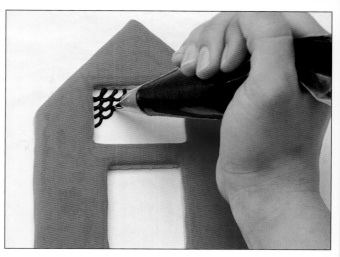

On waxed paper, pipe a web in the corner of the front window with black icing (as shown above); let dry. Use the black icing to make the bat. Let dry.

9 With yellow icing, make a 3-1/2-in. moon; let dry completely. Use a toothpick and white icing to attach red sprinkles for bat's eyes; let dry.

10 Thin white icing with 1 to 2 teaspoons water. Using #3 tip and white icing, outline three or more 3-1/2-in.-long ghosts on waxed paper; let dry. Fill in ghost outlines. Let dry completely. Thicken remaining black icing with 1 to 2 teaspoons confectioners' sugar; pipe faces onto ghosts. Pipe outlines and "RIP" or other designs onto oval cookies. Let dry completely.

11 **To assemble:** Transfer remaining orange icing to a mixing bowl. Beat in 1 to 2 tablespoons confectioners' sugar until stiff peaks form. Pipe icing along sides of house front and one side section. Position at right angles to each other on work surface. Press into place; prop with cans.

12 Pipe icing along inside edge for added stability. Repeat with second side piece and back; let dry. Pipe white icing along top edges of house walls. Position one roof piece; repeat. Pipe purple icing along roof seam. Let dry completely. Attach the chimney.

13 **Finishing touches:** Thin remaining purple icing if necessary with water, then spread over shutters and door; let dry. With white icing, pipe "BOO" on the door and stripes on the shutters; let dry completely. Attach the door, shutters and ghosts to house with white icing. Attach bat to moon; attach moon to back of house.

14 Place house on a black-covered board; add wafer crumbs, tombstones and candy pumpkins.

Yield: 1 haunted cottage.

Editor's Note: Meringue powder is available from Wilton Industries. Call 1-800/794-5866 or visit *www.wilton.com*. Use of a coupler ring will allow you to easily change pastry tips for different designs when decorating.

fall
FARE

Celebrate the bounty of harvesttime
with hearty comfort food. This
collection of warming recipes is sure to
bring compliments at your table when
the cool autumn winds start to blow.

Fall Fare CONTENTS

FUNNY BONE!
Why do vampired need mouthwash? They have bat breath.

apple cranberry crumble

Teri Roberts, Hilliard, Ohio

When I first took this fruity dessert to my family's Thanksgiving dinner, it quickly became a tradition. We enjoy it for breakfast, lunch, dinner and snack time, and it is especially good in autumn!

3	cups chopped peeled apples
2	cups fresh *or* frozen cranberries, thawed
3/4	cup sugar
1	cup old-fashioned *or* quick-cooking oats
1	cup packed brown sugar
1/3	cup all-purpose flour
1/2	cup butter, melted
1/2	cup chopped pecans, optional

1 In a greased 8-in. square baking dish, combine apples and cranberries; sprinkle with sugar. In another bowl, combine the oats, brown sugar, flour and butter; sprinkle over cranberry mixture. Top with pecans if desired.

2 Bake, uncovered, at 350° for 55-60 minutes or until browned and bubbly. Serve warm.

Yield: 6 servings.

2	tablespoons water
1/2	cup balsamic vinaigrette
2	tablespoons jellied cranberry sauce
1	package (5 ounces) spring mix salad greens
1/2	cup dried cranberries
4	ounces crumbled Gorgonzola cheese

1 Wash beets; trim stem and leave root intact. Wrap beets in aluminum foil. Place on a baking sheet. Bake at 400° for 1 hour or until tender. Remove foil and cool.

2 In a microwave-safe bowl, combine the sweet potato and water. Cover and microwave on high for 4-5 minutes or until tender. Cool.

3 In a blender, combine vinaigrette and cranberry sauce; cover and process until smooth. Peel the beets and cut into slices. On six salad plates, arrange the greens, beets and sweet potatoes. Sprinkle with cranberries and cheese. Drizzle with dressing.

Yield: 6 servings.

Editor's Note: Use plastic gloves when peeling beets to avoid stains. This recipe was tested in a 1,100-watt microwave.

harvest green salad

Beth Royals, Richmond, Virginia

This salad always gets rave reviews. Guests say that it fills them up without weighing them down.

3	whole medium fresh beets
1	large sweet potato, peeled and cubed

FUNNY BONE!

What do you get when you cross a vampire and a snowman? Frostbite.

hearty rye melts

Melanie Schlaf, Edgewood, Kentucky

When we moved from the Midwest to Kentucky, we were invited to a neighborhood gathering, where this appetizer was served. It is traditionally served at Derby Day parties, but at our home it's become a year-round favorite.

1/2	pound lean ground beef
1/2	pound bulk pork sausage
1-1/2	teaspoons chili powder
8	ounces process cheese (Velveeta), shredded
24	slices snack rye bread

Fresh parsley springs, stems removed

1 In a large skillet, cook the beef and sausage over medium heat until no longer pink; drain. Add chili powder and cheese; cook and stir until cheese is melted. Spread a heaping tablespoonful onto each slice of bread. Place on a baking sheet.

2 Bake at 350° for 12-15 minutes or until edges of bread begin to crisp. Garnish with parsley. Serve warm.

Yield: 2 dozen.

creamy alfredo potatoes

Lissa Hutson, Phelan, California

With turkey and broccoli, this special scalloped potato dish is a meal in itself. Using a jar of Alfredo sauce makes the preparation time minimal.

1	jar (16 ounces) Alfredo sauce
1	cup milk
1	teaspoon garlic powder
3	pounds potatoes, peeled and thinly sliced
5	tablespoons grated Parmesan cheese, *divided*

Salt and pepper to taste

2	to 3 cups cubed cooked turkey
3	cups frozen chopped broccoli, thawed
2	cups (8 ounces) shredded Swiss cheese, *divided*

1 In a large bowl, combine the Alfredo sauce, milk and garlic powder. Pour a fourth of the mixture into a greased 13-in. x 9-in. x 2-in. baking dish. Layer with a fourth of the potatoes; sprinkle with 1 tablespoon Parmesan cheese, salt and pepper.

2 In a large bowl, combine the turkey, broccoli and 1-1/2 cups Swiss cheese; spoon a third over potatoes. Repeat layers twice. Top with remaining potatoes. Sprinkle with remaining Swiss and Parmesan cheeses. Spread with remaining Alfredo sauce mixture.

3 Cover and bake at 400° for 45 minutes. Reduce heat to 350°. Bake, uncovered, 30 minutes longer or until potatoes are tender. Let stand for 15 minutes before serving.

Yield: 6-8 servings.

autumn pot roast

Deby Kominski, Honesdale, Pennsylvania

Good old-fashioned pot roast has a new mouth-watering flavor in this colorful dish. The cranberries mixed with horseradish give the beef terrific taste. You can add any vegetables you like to make it more unique.

1	boneless beef rump roast (about 3 pounds), tied
1/4	teaspoon salt
1/4	teaspoon pepper
2	teaspoons canola oil
3/4	cup fresh *or* frozen cranberries
1/2	cup water
1/4	cup sugar
1	cup reduced-sodium beef broth
1/3	cup prepared horseradish, drained
1	cinnamon stick (3 inches)
3	whole cloves
16	pearl onions
2	medium sweet potatoes (about 1-1/2 pounds), peeled and cut into 3/4-inch cubes
16	baby carrots
4	teaspoons cornstarch
2	tablespoons cold water

1 Sprinkle meat with salt and pepper. In a Dutch oven, brown meat in oil. Drain and remove from the heat. In a large saucepan, combine the cranberries, water and sugar. Cook and stir over medium heat until cranberries pop and liquid is slightly thickened, about 8 minutes. Remove from the heat.

2 Add the broth and horseradish; pour over meat. Place cinnamon stick and cloves in a double thickness of cheesecloth; bring up corners of cloth and tie with kitchen string to form a bag. Add to Dutch oven. Cover and bake at 325° for 2 hours.

3 Meanwhile, in a large saucepan, bring 6 cups water to a boil. Add pearl onions; boil for 3 minutes. Drain and rinse in cold water; peel and set aside. Add sweet potatoes to Dutch oven. Cover and cook 15 minutes longer. Add carrots and onions; cover and cook 30-40 minutes more or until vegetables and meat are tender. Remove meat and vegetables; keep warm. Discard spice bag.

4 Cool pan juices for 10 minutes; transfer to a blender. Cover and process until smooth; return to pan. Combine cornstarch and cold water until smooth. Gradually whisk into pan juices. Bring to a boil; cook and stir for 1-2 minutes or until thickened. Serve with meat and vegetables.

Yield: 8 servings.

jack-o'-lantern biscuits

Taste of Home Test Kitchen

These biscuits taste buttery and are simple to make. Cut them into jack-o'-lantern shapes for autumn and different shapes for other seasons.

1/4 cups all-purpose flour
3 teaspoons baking powder
1 teaspoon salt
3/4 cup cold butter
1 can (15-3/4 ounces) sweet potatoes, drained and mashed
1/2 cup half-and-half cream

1 In a large bowl, combine flour, baking powder and salt. Cut in butter until mixture resembles coarse crumbs. In a small bowl, combine sweet potatoes and cream until smooth; add to dry ingredients just until moistened.

2 Turn onto a lightly floured surface; knead 8-10 times. Pat or roll to 1/2-in. thickness. cut with a floured 2-in. pumpkin-shaped cookie cutter. Place 2 in. apart on lightly greased baking sheets.

3 Bake at 425° for 16-20 minutes or until edges are browned. Remove from pans to wire racks. Serve warm.

Yield: 13 biscuits.

southwest ghost town soup

Taste of Home Test Kitchen

This squash soup is nicely flavored for cool October days. The combination of chili powder, cumin and cayenne pepper gives it just enough kick. You can make different kinds of spooky Halloween images with the sour cream.

1 medium butternut squash (about 4 pounds)
1 medium onion, chopped
2 tablespoons butter
1 can (49-1/2 ounces) chicken broth
3 teaspoons chili powder
2 teaspoons ground cumin
1/2 teaspoon salt
1/2 teaspoon ground coriander
1/8 teaspoon cayenne pepper
Dash pepper
1/2 cup sour cream
1/4 cup heavy whipping cream
2 teaspoons lime juice

1 Cut squash in half lengthwise; discard seeds. Place the squash, cut side down, in a greased shallow baking pan. Bake, uncovered, at 350° for 1-1/2 hours or until tender. Cool slightly; scoop out pulp to measure 3 cups. Transfer to a large bowl.

2 In a small skillet, saute onion in butter until tender. Add to squash. Stir in chicken broth and seasonings. In a blender, process the squash mixture in batches until smooth. Transfer to the large saucepan; heat through.

3 In a small bowl, combine the sour cream, cream and lime juice. Top each serving with a dollop of sour cream mixture. Using a toothpick, swirl the dollop into the shape of a ghost.

Yield: 8 servings (2 quarts).

FUNNY BONE!
What is Dracula's favorite ice cream? VEIN-illa.

cheesy potatoes

Melissa Marzolf, Marysville, Michigan

For a comforting side dish that feeds a crowd, try these saucy slow-cooked potatoes. A simple topping of buttered croutons covers the creamy combination.

6	medium potatoes, peeled and cut into 1/4-inch strips
2	cups (8 ounces) shredded cheddar cheese
1	can (10-3/4 ounces) condensed cream of chicken soup, undiluted
1	small onion, chopped *or* 1 tablespoon dried minced onion
7	tablespoons butter, melted, *divided*
1	teaspoon *each* salt and pepper
1	cup (8 ounces) sour cream
2	cups seasoned stuffing cubes

1 Toss the potatoes and cheese; place in a 5-qt. slow cooker. Combine cream of chicken soup, onion, 4 tablespoons butter, salt and pepper; pour over potato mixture.

2 Cover and cook on low for 8-10 hours or until potatoes are tender. Stir in sour cream. Toss stuffing cubes and remaining butter; sprinkle over potatoes.

Yield: 10-12 servings.

1	pound bulk pork sausage
1	medium apple, peeled and chopped
1	medium onion, chopped
1/2	cup chopped celery
3	cups cooked long grain rice
1/2	cup raisins
1/3	cup minced fresh parsley
1	tablespoon brown sugar
1/2	teaspoon salt
1/4	teaspoon ground allspice
1/4	teaspoon ground cinnamon
1/8	teaspoon pepper

1 In a large skillet, cook sausage, apple, onion and celery over medium heat until the meat is no longer pink; drain. Stir in the remaining ingredients.

2 Transfer to a greased 2-qt. baking dish. Cover; bake at 350° for 25-30 minutes or until heated through.

Yield: 4-6 servings.

autumn sausage casserole

Diane Brunell, Washington, Massachusetts

Apple, raisins and spices give this tasty sausage-rice casserole a taste of cooler days. It would be a nice potluck dish, too—just double the recipe if needed.

FUNNY BONE!

What do you use to mend a jack-o'-lantern? A pumpkin patch.

chunky apple pumpkin bread

Lyletta Searle, Morgan, Utah

This moist quick bread combines both apples and pumpkin, making it a must in autumn. Every slice is chock-full of nuts and spices.

1-2/3	cups all-purpose flour
1-1/2	cups sugar
1	teaspoon baking soda
3/4	teaspoon salt
1/2	teaspoon ground cinnamon
1/2	teaspoon ground nutmeg
1/4	teaspoon baking powder
1/4	teaspoon ground cloves
1	cup canned pumpkin
1/2	cup water
2	eggs
1/3	cup canola oil
1	cup chopped peeled tart apples
3/4	cup chopped walnuts

1 In a large bowl, combine the flour, sugar, baking soda, salt, cinnamon, nutmeg, baking powder and cloves. In another large bowl, whisk the pumpkin, water, eggs and oil. Stir into dry ingredients just until moistened. Fold in apples and walnuts.

2 Pour into a greased 9-in. x 5-in. x 3-in. loaf pan. Bake at 325° for 1-1/2 to 1-3/4 hours or until a toothpick inserted near the center comes out clean. Cool for 10 minutes before removing from pan to a wire rack to cool.

Yield: 1 loaf (12 slices).

harvest soup

Janice Mitchell, Aurora, Colorado

Loaded with ground beef, squash, tomatoes and two kinds of potatoes, this hearty soup makes a great family meal on a busy night.

1	pound lean ground beef
3/4	cup chopped onion
2	garlic cloves, minced
3-1/2	cups water
2-1/4	cups chopped peeled sweet potatoes
1	cup chopped red potatoes
1	cup chopped peeled acorn squash
2	teaspoons beef bouillon granules
2	bay leaves
1/2	teaspoon *each* chili powder and pepper
1/8	teaspoon *each* ground allspice and ground cloves
1	can (14-1/2 ounces) diced tomatoes, undrained

1 In a large saucepan, cook the beef, onion and garlic over medium heat until the meat is no longer pink; drain well. Add the water, potatoes, squash, bouillon, bay leaves, chili powder, pepper, allspice and cloves. Bring to a boil. Reduce heat; cover and simmer for 15-20 minutes or until vegetable are tender.

2 Add the tomatoes. Cook and stir until heated through. Discard bay leaves.

Yield: 6 servings.

Harvesttime Traditions

Many areas across the country celebrate harvest festivals in early fall. Some harvesttime traditions include: making corn dollies, ringing churchbells, decorating horses with floral garlands and ribbons, and of course, huge community feasts featuring apples, pumpkins, squash, potatoes, corn, cabbage and cranberries in a variety of comforting dishes.

harvest vegetable tart

Ruth Lee, Troy, Ontario
You'll get oohs and aahs of approval when you serve this veggie tart. Its robust taste and aroma always get a warm reception.

1/2	cup all-purpose flour
1/4	cup *each* whole wheat flour and cornmeal
2	tablespoons grated Parmesan cheese
1/2	teaspoon salt
1/8	teaspoon cayenne pepper
1/4	cup cold butter, cubed
3	to 4 tablespoons cold water

FILLING:

1/2	cup thinly sliced green onions
2	garlic cloves, minced
1	tablespoon olive oil
5	slices peeled eggplant (3-1/2 inches x 1/4 inch)
2	tablespoons grated Parmesan cheese, *divided*
1	small tomato, cut into 1/4-inch slices
3	green pepper rings
3	sweet red pepper rings

1/2	cup frozen corn
2	eggs, lightly beaten
2/3	cup evaporated milk
3/4	teaspoon salt
1/4	teaspoon pepper

1 In a bowl, combine the first six ingredients. Cut in butter until crumbly. Gradually add water, tossing with a fork until dough forms a ball. Cover and refrigerate for at least 30 minutes.

2 Roll out pastry to fit a 9-in. tart pan with a removable bottom. Transfer pastry to pan; trim even with edge of pan. Line unpricked pastry shell with a double thickness of heavy-duty foil. Bake at 450° for 8 minutes. Remove foil; bake 5 minutes longer.

3 In a large nonstick skillet coated with cooking spray, cook onions and garlic in oil for 2 minutes. Add eggplant; cook for 4-5 minutes. Cook for 5 minutes. Spoon into crust. Sprinkle with 1 tablespoon Parmesan cheese. Top with tomato slices and pepper rings. Sprinkle with corn.

4 In a small bowl, whisk eggs, milk, salt and pepper; pour over veggies. Sprinkle with remaining cheese. Bake at 350° for 30-35 minutes.

Yield: 6 servings.

sweet potato stuffing

Kelly Pollock, London, Ontario

My mom slow-cooks this tasty dressing in addition to the traditional stuffing cooked inside the turkey.

1/2	cup *each* chopped celery and onion
1/4	cup butter, cubed
6	cups dry bread cubes
1	large sweet potato, cooked, peeled and finely chopped
1/2	cup chicken broth
1/4	cup chopped pecans
1/2	teaspoon *each* poultry seasoning and rubbed sage
1/2	teaspoon salt, optional
1/2	teaspoon pepper

1 In a large skillet, saute celery and onion in butter until tender. Stir in the remaining ingredients. Transfer to a greased 3-qt. slow cooker.

2 Cover and cook on low for 4 hours or until vegetables are tender.

Yield: 10 servings.

2-1/2	pounds medium sweet potatoes
1/3	cup packed brown sugar
1-1/2	teaspoons cornstarch
3/4	cup heavy whipping cream
2	teaspoons sauce from chipotle peppers in adobo sauce
3/4	teaspoon salt
1/4	teaspoon pepper
3	red chili peppers, optional

1 Place sweet potatoes in a large saucepan and cover with water. Bring to a boil. Reduce heat; cover. Cook for 20 minutes or until tender. Drain and cool slightly. Peel and cut into 1/4-in. slices. Arrange potato slices in overlapping rings in an ungreased 9-in. deep-dish pie plate.

2 In a small bowl, combine the brown sugar, cornstarch and cream until smooth; add the adobo sauce, salt and pepper. Pour evenly over potatoes.

3 Cut a mouth, eyes and nose from red peppers to resemble a jack-o'-lantern face; place over potatoes. Bake, uncovered, at 350° for 25-30 minutes or until hot and bubbly.

Yield: 6 servings.

Editor's Note: When cutting hot peppers, disposable gloves are recommended. Avoid touching your face.

silence of the yams

Taste of Home Test Kitchen

The adobo sauce gives just enough heat to make this a unique yam dish. The delicious side dish is the perfect color for a Halloween gathering.

FUNNY BONE!
Where do baby ghosts go during the day? Day-SCARE centers.

pretzel-topped sweet potatoes

Sue Mallory, Lancaster, Pennsylvania

Friends with whom I've shared this recipe say it's their favorite way to serve sweet potatoes. I like to make it for brunch as a colorful go-with dish. The mingled sweet, tart and salty tastes are an unusual treat.

2	cups chopped pretzel rods (about 13)
1	cup chopped pecans
1	cup fresh *or* frozen cranberries
1	cup packed brown sugar
1	cup butter, melted, *divided*
1	can (2-1/2 pounds) sweet potatoes, drained
1	can (5 ounces) evaporated milk
1/2	cup sugar
1	teaspoon vanilla extract

1 In a large bowl, combine the pretzels, pecans, cranberries, brown sugar and 1/2 cup butter; set aside.

2 In a large bowl, beat the sweet potatoes until smooth. Add milk, sugar, vanilla and remaining butter; beat until well blended.

3 Spoon into a greased shallow 2-qt. baking dish; sprinkle with pretzel mixture. Bake, uncovered, at 350° for 25-30 minutes or until the edges are bubbly.

Yield: 10-12 servings.

cabbage patch stew

Karen Ann Bland, Gove, Kansas

My family loves this hearty stew. I like to serve steaming helpings in old-fashioned soup plates with thick, crusty slices of homemade bread. For a quicker prep, substitute coleslaw mix for the chopped cabbage.

1	pound ground beef
1	cup chopped onion
2	celery ribs, chopped
11	cups coarsely chopped cabbage (about 2 pounds)
2	cans (14-1/2 ounces *each*) stewed tomatoes
1	can (15 ounces) pinto beans, rinsed and drained
1	can (10 ounces) diced tomatoes with green chilies
1/2	cup ketchup
1	to 1-1/2 teaspoons chili powder
1/2	teaspoon *each* dried oregano and pepper
1/4	teaspoon salt

Shredded cheddar cheese and sour cream, optional

1 In a large skillet, cook the beef over medium heat until meat is no longer pink. Stir in the onion and celery. Cook until crisp tender; drain.

2 Transfer to a 5-qt. slow cooker. Stir in the chopped cabbage, stewed tomatoes, beans, diced tomatoes, ketchup, chili powder, oregano, pepper and salt. Cover and cook on low for 6-8 hours or until cabbage is tender. Serve with cheese and sour cream if desired.

Yield: 8 servings.

FUNNY BONE!
What do monsters like to see at the theater? Romeo and GHOUL-iet.

Do You Believe?

According to a 2005 Gallup Poll, more than a third of Americans believe in haunted houses. There are many famous places in the United States where people have reported seeing ghosts, including the White House! Others are Alcatraz, the Gettysburg Battlefield, Disney's Magic Kingdom and the Queen Mary docked in Long Beach, California.

haunted potpie

Taste of Home Test Kitchen

Convenience items such as frozen hash browns, veggies and puff pastry make this potpie quick and easy to make. The rye bread crumbs add an interesting twist.

- 4 cups cubed cooked chicken
- 4 cups frozen Southern-style hash brown potatoes, thawed
- 1 package (16 ounces) frozen mixed vegetables, thawed and drained
- 1 can (10-3/4 ounces) condensed cream of chicken soup, undiluted
- 1 can (10-3/4 ounces) condensed cream of onion soup, undiluted
- 1 cup (8 ounces) sour cream
- 2/3 cup milk
- 2 tablespoons all-purpose flour
- 1/2 teaspoon *each* salt and pepper
- 1/4 teaspoon garlic powder
- 3 slices rye bread
- 1 sheet frozen puff pastry, thawed

1 In a large bowl, combine the first 11 ingredients. Transfer to a greased 13-in. x 9-in. x 2-in. baking dish. Place the bread in a food processor, cover and process to make crumbs; sprinkle over the chicken mixture. Bake at 350° for 40-45 minutes or until bubbly.

2 Meanwhile, on a lightly floured surface, unfold pastry sheet. Using a small floured ghost-shaped cookie cutter, cut out 12 ghosts. Place on an ungreased baking sheet. Remove potpie from oven; set aside and keep warm. Bake ghosts at 400° for 10 minutes or until puffy and golden brown. Place on top of potpie; serve immediately.

Yield: 12 servings.

Pumpkin Primer

According to the University of Illinois Extension, in early colonial times, pumpkins were used as an ingredient for the crust of pies, not the filling. The total U.S. pumpkin production in 2006 was valued at $101.3 million, with 90% of the crop grown within a 90-mile radius of Peoria, Illinois.

swirled pumpkin yeast bread

Shirley Runkle, St. Paris, Ohio
I call this my "hostess gift" pumpkin bread, but it's fantastic for any occasion at all. Swirls of cinnamon-sugar make every slice simply irresistible.

4-1/2 to 5	cups all-purpose flour
3	cups whole wheat flour
2	cups quick-cooking oats
2/3	cup packed brown sugar
2-1/2	teaspoons pumpkin pie spice
1-1/2	teaspoons salt
1	teaspoon sugar
2	packages (1/4 ounce *each*) active dry yeast
1-1/2	cups warm water (120° to 130°)
1	cup canned pumpkin
1/3	cup unsweetened applesauce
1/3	cup canola oil
2	eggs, lightly beaten
1/2	cup raisins

FILLING:

1/4	cup butter, softened
1/2	cup packed brown sugar
1	teaspoon ground cinnamon

1 In a large bowl, combine 2 cups all-purpose flour, whole wheat flour, oats, brown sugar, pumpkin pie spice, salt, sugar and yeast. Beat in the warm water, pumpkin, applesauce and oil just until moistened. Add eggs; beat until smooth. Stir in enough remaining all-purpose flour to form a firm dough. Add raisins.

2 Turn onto a lightly floured surface; knead until smooth and elastic, about 6-8 minutes. Place in a greased bowl, turning once to grease top. Cover; let rise in a warm place until doubled, about 1 hour.

3 Punch dough down. Turn onto a lightly floured surface; divide in half. Roll each portion into an 18-in. x 9-in. rectangle; brush with butter to within 1/2 in. of edges. Combine brown sugar and cinnamon; sprinkle over dough. Roll dough up jelly-roll style, starting with a short side; pinch seam to seal.

4 Place seam side down in two greased 9-in. x 5-in. x 3-in. loaf pans. Cover and let rise until doubled, about 30 minutes.

5 Bake at 350° for 55-65 minutes or until golden brown. Cool for 10 minutes before removing from pans to wire racks.

Yield: 2 loaves (16 slices each).

sweet potato chicken stew

Taste of Home Test Kitchen

Sweet potatoes, chicken and shredded cabbage are just a few of the ingredients that make this hearty stew a great one-bowl meal.

3	cups cubed peeled sweet potatoes
1/2	cup water
-1/2	pounds boneless skinless chicken breasts, cut into 1/2-inch cubes
2	tablespoons canola oil
3	cups shredded cabbage
3	cups chicken broth
1	can (15-1/2 ounces) black-eyed peas, rinsed and drained
1	can (14-1/2 ounces) diced tomatoes with onions, undrained
1	cup *each* sliced celery and tomato juice
1	teaspoon pepper
1/2	teaspoon salt

1 Place the sweet potatoes and water in a 2-qt. microwave-safe dish. Cover and microwave on high for 6 minutes or until tender; drain.

2 In a Dutch oven, saute the chicken in oil for 8-9 minutes or until juices run clear. Add the next eight ingredients and sweet potatoes. Bring to a boil. Reduce heat; cover and simmer for 20 minutes or until heated through.

Yield: 8 servings.

Editor's Note: This recipe was tested in a 1,100-watt microwave.

spicy two-bean chili

Lesley Pew, Lynn, Massachusetts

Chili fans will get a kick out of this untraditional recipe. Tomatoes with green chilies, lime juice and kidney and black beans give it an original twist.

2	pounds ground beef
3	large onions, chopped
6	garlic cloves, minced
2	cans (16 ounces *each*) kidney beans, rinsed and drained
2	cans (15 ounces *each*) black beans, rinsed and drained
2	cans (10 ounces *each*) diced tomatoes and green chilies, undrained
1	can (14-1/2 ounces) chicken broth
1/2	cup lime juice
6	tablespoons cornmeal
1/4	cup chili powder
4	teaspoons dried oregano
3	teaspoons ground cumin
2	teaspoons *each* salt and rubbed sage
1/2	teaspoon *each* white pepper, paprika and pepper

Hot cooked rice

Shredded cheddar cheese

1 In a Dutch oven, cook the ground beef, onions and garlic over medium heat until meat is no longer pink; drain. Transfer to a 5-qt. slow cooker. Stir in the beans, tomatoes, broth, lime juice, cornmeal and seasonings.

2 Cover and cook on low for 8 hours or until heated through. Serve chili with rice; sprinkle with shredded cheddar cheese.

Yield: 11 servings.

FUNNY BONE!
How do ghosts like their coffee? With scream and sugar.

chili potpies

Taste of Home Test Kitchen

Welcome your family in from the cold with these individual potpies. Our home economists created a simple corn bread crust that perfectly complements a filling of tangy chili.

1	medium onion, chopped
1	medium green pepper, chopped
2	teaspoons canola oil
2	cans (14-1/2 ounces *each*) diced tomatoes, drained
1	can (16 ounces) chili beans, undrained
1/4	cup tomato sauce
2	tablespoons chili powder
1	teaspoon brown sugar
1/2	teaspoon ground cumin
1/2	cup all-purpose flour
1/2	cup cornmeal
1/2	teaspoon baking powder
1/4	teaspoon salt
1	tablespoon butter, melted
3	to 4 tablespoons milk

1 In a large saucepan, saute onion and green pepper in oil until tender. Stir in the tomatoes, beans, tomato sauce, chili powder, brown sugar and cumin. Bring to a boil. Reduce heat to low heat, uncovered, while preparing crust.

2 In a small bowl, combine the flour, cornmeal, baking powder and salt. Stir in butter and enough milk to form a ball. On a lightly floured surface, roll dough into a 12-in. circle. Using an inverted 10-oz. baking dish as a guide, score four circles. Cut out circles. Cut a small circle in the center of each pastry (discard or reroll cutouts and use as decoration).

3 Coat four 10-oz. baking dishes with cooking spray. Fill with chili; top each with a dough circle. Tuck in edges of dough to seal. Bake at 375° for 13-17 minutes or until edges of crust are lightly browned.

Yield: 4 servings.

FUNNY BONE!
What kind of makeup do witches wear? Ma-SCARE-a.

50

apple-sweet potato bake

Taste of Home Test Kitchen

Apples and sweet potatoes are perfect partners in this slightly sweet casserole from our home economists. Every bite tastes like fall.

3	pounds sweet potatoes
4	medium tart apples, peeled
1/4	cup lemon juice
1/2	cup chopped pecans
1/2	cup butter, cubed
1/2	cup packed brown sugar
1/2	cup honey
2	tablespoons orange juice
1/2	teaspoon ground cinnamon
1/4	teaspoon ground ginger

1 Scrub sweet potatoes with a vegetable brush under cold water. Pierce skin in several places; place on a baking sheet. Bake at 400° for 35-45 minutes or until almost tender. Cool slightly; peel potatoes and cut into 1/4-in. slices.

2 Cut the apples into 1/4-in. slices; toss with lemon juice. In a greased 11-in. x 7-in. x 2-in. baking dish, alternately arrange sweet potato and apple slices. Sprinkle with pecans.

3 In a small saucepan, combine the butter, brown sugar, honey, orange juice, cinnamon and ginger. Bring to a boil, stirring constantly. Remove from the heat; pour over potatoes and apples. Bake, uncovered, at 400° for 25-30 minutes or until tender.

Yield: 8 servings.

gingerbread with chantilly cream

Pam Holloway, Marion, Louisiana

An old-fashioned family favorite, this treat has never lost its popularity. A blend of ginger, cinnamon and nutmeg make the bread extra flavorful...and my guests always comment on the cute dollop of whipped cream on top!

1/2	cup shortening
2	tablespoons sugar
1	tablespoon brown sugar
1	egg
1	cup hot water
1	cup molasses
2-1/4	cups all-purpose flour
1	teaspoon *each* baking soda, ground ginger and ground cinnamon
3/4	teaspoon salt
1/8	teaspoon ground nutmeg

CHANTILLY CREAM:

1	cup heavy whipping cream
1	teaspoon confectioners' sugar
1/4	teaspoon vanilla extract

1 In a large bowl, cream shortening and sugars until light and fluffy. Beat in egg; mix well. Beat in water and molasses. Combine flour, baking soda, ginger, cinnamon, salt and nutmeg; gradually add to creamed mixture.

2 Pour into a greased 9-in. square baking pan. Bake at 350° for 33-37 minutes or until a toothpick inserted near the center comes out clean.

3 In a small bowl, beat cream until it begins to thicken. Add confectioners' sugar and vanilla; beat until stiff peaks form. Serve gingerbread with warm gingerbread.

Yield: 9 servings.

herb 'n' spice turkey breast

Taste of Home Test Kitchen

This nicely seasoned turkey breast is so moist and tasty that you can make it all year-round.

- 3 tablespoons canola oil
- 1 tablespoon brown sugar
- 1 teaspoon salt

- 1/2 teaspoon *each* rubbed sage and dried thyme
- 1/2 teaspoon dried rosemary, crushed
- 1/4 teaspoon pepper
- 1/8 to 1/4 teapoon ground allspice
- 1 bone-in turkey breast (4-1/4 to 6 pounds)

1 In a small bowl, combine oil, brown sugar, salt, sage, thyme, rosemary, pepper and allspice. With fingers, carefully loosen the skin from both sides of turkey breast.

2 Spread half of the brown sugar mixture over meat on both sides of turkey. Secure skin to underside of breast with toothpicks. Spread the remaining brown sugar mixture over the skin.

3 Line the bottom of a large shallow roasting pan with foil. Place turkey breast side up on a rack in prepared pan. Bake, uncovered, at 325° for 2 to 2-1/2 hours or until a meat thermometer reads 170°. (Cover loosely with foil if turkey browns too quickly.) Cover and let stand for 15 minutes before carving.

Yield: 10-14 servings.

creamy turkey casserole

Mary Jo O'Brien, Hastings, Minnesota

This satisfying supper recipe puts turkey leftovers to terrific use. I will sometimes make turkey just so I have the extras for the casserole.

- 1 can (10-3/4 ounces) condensed cream of celery soup, undiluted
- 1 can (10-3/4 ounces) condensed cream of mushroom soup, undiluted
- 1 can (10-3/4 ounces) condensed cream of onion soup, undiluted
- 5 ounces process cheese (Velveeta), cubed
- 1/3 cup mayonnaise
- 4 cups cubed cooked turkey
- 1 package (16 ounces) frozen broccoli cuts, thawed
- 1-1/2 cups *each* cooked white rice
- 1-1/2 cups cooked wild rice
- 1 can (8 ounces) sliced water chestnuts, drained
- 1 jar (4 ounces) sliced mushrooms, drained
- 1-1/2 to 2 cups salad croutons

1 In a large bowl, combine the soups, cheese and mayonnaise. Stir in the turkey, broccoli, rice, water chestnuts and mushrooms.

2 Transfer to a greased 13-in. x 9-in. x 2-in. baking dish. Bake, uncovered, at 350° for 30 minutes; stir. Sprinkle with croutons. Bake 8-12 minutes longer or until bubbly.

Yield: 12 servings.

Editor's Note: Reduced-fat or fat-free mayonnaise is not recommended for this recipe.

gingered cherry pear cobbler

Taste of Home Test Kitchen

This is warm, sweet and filling—comfort food at its best! The fruity dessert is great for those crisp and cool autumn days.

4	cups chopped peeled fresh pears
1/2	cup dried cherries
1/4	cup packed brown sugar
2	tablespoons finely chopped candied *or* crystallized ginger
1	tablespoon all-purpose flour
3	tablespoons butter

TOPPING:

1/4	cup sugar
2	tablespoons chopped candied *or* crystallized ginger
1	cup all-purpose flour
1-1/2	teaspoons baking powder
1/8	teaspoon baking soda
1/4	teaspoon salt
5	tablespoons cold butter, cubed
1/2	cup buttermilk

1 In a large bowl, combine first five ingredients; transfer to a greased 2-qt. baking dish. Heat butter in a small saucepan over medium heat for 7 minutes or until golden brown; pour over pear mixture. Cover and bake at 350° for 20-25 minutes or until bubbly.

2 In a food processor, combine sugar and ginger; cover and process until finely chopped. Add flour, baking powder, baking soda and salt. Cover; process for 3 seconds or until blended. Add butter; process until mixture resembles coarse crumbs. Add buttermilk; pulse just until a soft dough forms. Drop by tablespoonfuls over warm pear mixture.

3 Bake, uncovered, for 35-40 minutes or until the topping is golden brown. Serve warm.

Yield: 8 servings.

FUNNY BONE!
Why did Dracula take cold medicine? To stop his coffin.

crafts &DECOR

Looking for new and BOO-rrific ways to spruce up your house this year? Look no further. You'll find creative pumpkin-carving ideas, squash centerpieces, treat holders, candle trims, scrapbook pages and more! You can even outfit your pet for the spooky day—see page 70 for details.

how to pick
A PUMPKIN

Thump a pumpkin—a ripe, hollow-sounding one will be easier to scoop out. Make sure it has no soft spots anywhere and has at least one smooth, unblemished face for carving. Put it back if there is major discoloration on any side, though. Having a strong, well-attached stem is a sign of healthiness. A medium-sized pumpkin is easier to work with than a huge or tiny one. But be flexible about the shape—a tall, skinny pumpkin may be just the thing for your design. Balance is important, too; a solid bottom that supports the pumpkin means less chance of rolling or being knocked over.

carving do's

Now that you purchased the perfect pumpkin, here's some advice on how to transform it into a jack-o'-lantern:

❑ For help removing the top and scooping out the seeds and pulp, see p. 65.

❑ Use a copier to enlarge one of the templates on the following pages, cut out the black shapes and trace it onto the pumpkin with a thin permanent marker.

❑ Carve along the outside of the lines you traced with a sturdy knife. Make sure your cuts are smooth and go all the way through to the center.

❑ Replace the top and you're done!

making pumpkin seeds

1 To make pumpkin seeds, remove the fibrous strings from the seeds and place the seeds in a colander.

2 Rinse them under cold water and drain.

3 Spread out on paper towels to dry.

4 Spread on a greased baking sheet.

5 Bake at 250° for 1 hour. Increase heat to 400°; bake 5 minutes longer.

6 Season with salt if desired.

FUNNY BONE!
How does a witch tell time? She looks at her witch-watch.

leaves

laughing JACK-O'-LANTERN

leaves

laughing JACK-O'-LANTERN

spider

surprised
JACK-O'-LANTERN

spider

surprised
JACK-O'-LANTERN

howling

cat on a FENCE

howling

cat on a FENCE

darth VADER

happy JACK

darth VADER

happy JACK

CRAFTS & DECOR

yes! you can drill your JACK-O'-LANTERN

Want an even more creative way to transform an ordinary pumpkin into a work of art? Use a drill to make holes in your pumpkin instead of carving it! You can use cookie cutters, one of our carving templates or come up with a new look all your own. This creative treatment will be the talk of the neighborhood come Halloween night!

Old newspapers

Smock or old T-shirt to wear

Sharp chef's knife, 6 to 8 inches long

Pumpkin-carving kit or thin-bladed serrated knives or saws

Large, strong tablespoon, serving spoon or ice-cream scoop

Sharp-tip marker (nonpermanent)

Electric screwdriver or drill with varying bit sizes

Bucket for seeds and pulp

1 Cut out lid with a chef's knife, sloping edges slightly inward.

2 Scoop out seeds and pulp until walls are about 1 inch thick.

3 Mark a dot design using a template or straight edge.

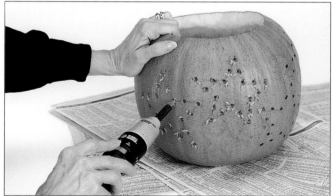

4 Drill dot holes with electric screw-driver— or cut out design with knife.

5 Place candle inside pumpkin and secure to bottom with hot wax.

FUNNY BONE!
What's the best place for a haunted house? On a dead-end street.

More Pumpkin Decorations

Pumpkins are abundant in the fall, so don't hesitate to try new and interesting ways to use them in your decor. Here are some ideas: Paint or carve letters into your pumpkins. You could use a grouping to spell out "BOO" or "WELCOME" to charm your guests. Use glitter to enhance the look of a carved or painted pumpkin. A little glue and a tube of glitter can make yours a truly glamorous jack-o'-lantern! Cut out the stems of smaller pumpkins, insert candles in the holes and use them in a tabletop centerpiece.

painting PUMPKINS

When it comes to decorating pumpkins—especially a lot of them—paint offers a fast, easy alternative to carving, and it gives you much more flexibility in creating striking and even wacky designs. Use water-based acrylic paint, available in small jars at craft or art supply stores, and apply it with artist's brushes. Pick strong colors that contrast with and stand out against the pumpkin's orange skin. Use a sharp-tip marker to draw fine details. And while you are at the craft store, also check out zany stick-on decorations like googly eyes.

Lots of fun without the mess!

winter SQUASH

Greatly varied in shape, size, and color, winter squash make a vibrant addition to your Halloween decor.

A simple arrangement of acorn, butternut, turban, and other hard-skinned winter squash creates a perfect table centerpiece or mantel decoration for Halloween—a grouping that practically says fall, especially if the squash are mixed with pumpkins and gourds. This also works well outdoors, especially near a front entry, where the squash can be loosely arranged or grouped in a wicker basket.

Clockwise from top left:
Crown Prince, Sweet Mama,
Carnival Squash, Jackpot Pumpkin

Making Squash

The cool part about using squash for decorating is that after a week or so, you can eat it! Here's how: 1. Slice in half lengthwise and scoop out the seeds. Discard seeds. 2. Place each half, flesh side down, on a lightly greased baking sheet. 3. Bake at 400° for 45-60 minutes or until a fork inserted through the skin moves in and out easily. 4. Cut flesh in to small pieces and serve, or go to www.tasteofhome.com for some great winter squash recipes!

Shopping Tips

Winter squash is available year-round. The peak season is October through November. Select squash that is heavy for its size. The shells should be hard with a deep color. Avoid any with soft spots or cracks.

winter squash varieties

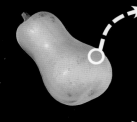

BUTTERNUT SQUASH *is medium-sized and shaped like a big peanut. It has smooth tan or yellow-orange skin. Its bright orange flesh is mildly sweet.*

CROOKNECK SQUASH *is small, skinny, and—true to its name—bends like the neck of a bird. It has yellow, bumpy skin. Its pale green flesh is tender.*

BUTTERCUP SQUASH *is small to medium in size, drum-shaped, with dark green skin marked with green and splotches. Its orange flesh has a sweet flavor and creamy texture.*

SPAGHETTI SQUASH *is medium-sized, oblong, with smooth yellow skin. After boiling or baking the squash whole, it is halved, and the flesh is pulled out with a fork into spaghetti-like strands that are slightly nutty-flavored.*

TURBAN SQUASH *has bright orange-red skin and a decorative turbanlike top knot. The shell is green, orange or white. It is a relative of the buttercup squash, with dry, mildly sweet flesh.*

ACORN SQUASH *is small- to medium-sized, acorn-shaped, with dark green, orange, green and orange, or white, deeply ridged skin. Its yellow flesh is sweet and moist. Acorn squash are best baked.*

Decor on the Cheap

Why spend lots of money if you don't have to? Make "curtains" for windows and doorways with large black garbage bags. Cut the bag into varied-length strips, leaving a 2-inch uncut band on one side. Tape the band-side up to the window or door frame with double-sided tape, and voila! Creepy curtains.

wrapped up halloween goodies

Not only do these fun little bundles make a great party favor, they can decorate your buffet or dessert table, too! You can fill them with whatever candy you like, and you can use a variety of different fabrics to make a hauntingly attractive display. Just make sure they don't get too close to any lit candles.

9-inch square of fabric with spiderweb motif

Halloween candies

6-inch-length of orange chenille

Pencil

1 Cut a 9-inch square of fabric that has a spider-web motif.

2 Place Halloween candies in center of fabric square. Bring corners and sides up to enclose candies.

3 Wrap a 6-inch-length of orange chenille stem around fabric to hold.

4 Wrap chenille ends around a pencil to coil. Remove pencil and arrange coils as desired.

wire candle trims

These candleholders will spark up your dinner table during the Halloween season, and you'll find that they're so easy to make, you just might modify the colors and foam shapes to make them for other holidays, too. Made with common craft materials, they're a snap to whip up for a party.

18-gauge silver craft wire

Orange taper candle

Art foam bat shapes

Black candleholders

1 Cut seven varying lengths of 18-gauge silver craft wire. (We used 13, 12, 11, 10, 9, 8 and 7-inch lengths.) Working with all pieces as one, twist ends together and wrap end around base of an orange taper candle. Fan out opposite ends of wire in an arc. Adhere black peel & stick purchased art foam bat shapes to ends of wires.

2 Place candles in black Halloween candleholders.

fuzzy pipe cleaner spider

These little creatures are so easy to make, kids as young as 4 years old can join the grownups in making them. Then they'll have a blast spreading the spiders around the house come Halloween for laughs and surprises. Another idea: make "spider kits" to hand out to trick-or-treaters instead of candy!

Two 12-inch fuzzy pipe cleaners

Miniature pompoms

Beads

Googly eyes

White glue

1 Form the spider's head by tightly coiling one end of a pipe cleaner three times. Then form the body by coiling the pipe cleaner around your finger. As you get toward the end, form the tail end by decreasing the size of the coils. Try to achieve a rounded, realistic shape, especially for the head. Hide the end of the pipe cleaner by folding it inside the body.

2 To make legs, cut two 3-1/2-inch and two 2-1/2-inch lengths from the second pipe cleaner.

Bend each piece into an M shape. Insert the longer legs between the coils in the center of the body. Insert one of the shorter ones between the coils just behind the head. Insert the other short one between the coils at the tail end of the body.

3 To create the eyes, apply the pompoms, beads or googly eyes using a small dot of glue on each.

how to make fabric ghosts

Making fabric ghosts of any size is really easy - and they add a great touch to Halloween decor. Hang them from the ceiling or just let them support themselves - the fabric stiffener will make the fabric strong enough to do this!

Fabric stiffener

Large pieces of solid *and/or* gauze-type fabric (size depends on how big you want the finished ghost to be)

Styrofoam ball (whatever size you like)

Rope or strip of cloth

Soda bottle or cardboard tube

Buttons or googly eyes

Glue

1 Just buy fabric stiffener at a craft store, pour it in a bowl and dip the fabric in it. When you pull the fabric out, put a Styrofoam ball in the center of the fabric and loosely tie a rope or strip of cloth around the "neck."

2 Place the ghost's head on some kind of prop to dry—it dries fairly quickly. For a small ghost, a soda bottle is perfect. For a larger one, you may have to rig up something like an old cardboard tube.

3 Once the ghost is dried, the fabric alone will support it. Glue buttons or googly eyes to face. To achieve the look shown in the photo, dip a gauzy piece of fabric in stiffener and drape over dry ghost. Make an entire family of ghosts of various sizes.

FUNNY BONE!
What do you call serious rocks? Grave stones.

Black Cats Revealed

Our human ancestors were very superstitious about darkness, and since cats are primarily nocturnal creatures, people grew suspicious of them. Since the color black is associated with the occult, black cats were considered especially dangerous. And cats sometimes bat their paws at unseen things, appearing as though they see ghosts. Thankfully, not everyone is afraid of black cats. The ancient Egyptians held them in the highest regard!

CAT JESTER COLLAR PATTERN

1 Trace 1—tracing paper

2 Cut 2 each—green and purple felt

3 Cut 4 (trimmed pattern)—orange felt

CUT SLITS FOR COLLAR

TOP

cat
JESTER COLLAR

You'll have the coolest cat in town when you make this cute collar for Halloween. It's a great costume for a pet—no hats or headbands to cause safety hazards. You can even modify the instructions to make it a little bigger to fit a dog, too!

Tracing paper

2	green felt pieces
2	purple felt pieces
4	orange felt pieces

Fabric glue

8 1/2-inch gold bells

Cat collar

1 Trace pattern onto tracing paper.

2 Cut two green felt pieces and two purple felt pieces following outline of pattern.

3 Trim shaded areas from pattern and using trimmed pattern, cut four orange felt pieces.

4 Lay out all the pieces alternating them as follows: one orange, one green, one orange, one purple, one orange, one green, one orange and one purple.

5 Apply a narrow bead of fabric glue along the shaded pattern areas of the green and purple pieces. With the top edges even, place the orange pieces on top of the glue, overlapping the shaded areas. Let dry.

6 Glue a 1/2-inch gold bell to each point of the collar.

7 Cut slits in each section of the collar where shown on pattern.

8 Slide cat's collar through the slits and place collar on cat.

FUNNY BONE!
What did the waitress ask Dracula? How do you like your stake?

halloween
SCRAPBOOKING

Scrapbooking has taken the country by storm, and for good reason! This fun hobby is creative, practical and very simple to do. Here are several homemade pages contributed by passionate scrapbookers. Use them as inspiration for your own work and savor those special moments captured on your camera.

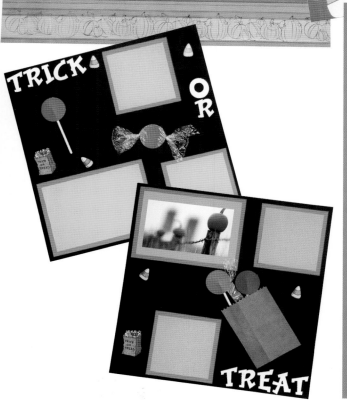

scrapbooking do's and don'ts

1 Avoid using books with adhesive pages. They will cause damage to your photos.

2 Be sure to use photo-safe tape and glue. There are many specialty brands now available at your local craft and stationery stores made just for scrapbooking.

3 Place photos on a couple of layers of paper to frame the image and add depth to your pages.

4 Watch out for items that have too much depth. Remember that it's a book which must be able to close easily.

5 Try new things! You'll find that your best work comes after a little experimentation.

6 Shop for good materials. You'll find large sections in craft stores devoted exclusively to scrapbooking enthusiasts. And why not? It's a fun way to preserve precious memories.

costumes &FACE PAINT

Quick and easy is the name of the game for the costumes and face paint developed by our Halloween experts here at Taste of Home.

halloween COSTUMES

Once you have an idea for a costume, you might want to check a party store for components that you won't have to make: a firefighter's hat, for example, or a glitzy tiara. Fabric and craft stores, particularly around Halloween, offer a wide assortment of costume materials - like faux fur, felt and fleece that won't ravel - and endless trimmings that can be sewn or glued on.

The first step in making a costume is to gather the various pieces together and check that you have everything you're going to need. Be sure that the basic garments you plan to embellish are clean and pressed.

Read the directions carefully. Check that your tools are ready: extra sticks for the hot glue gun, extra staples for the stapler, the correct color thread for your needles or sewing machine, and so on.

checklist

Here are nine items that are most often needed to make a costume:

- ❑ Base garments
- ❑ Cutting wheel and self-healing mat
- ❑ Fabrics
- ❑ Hot glue gun
- ❑ Needle and thread
- ❑ Patterns
- ❑ Scissors
- ❑ Sewing machine
- ❑ Staples

p. 76   p. 78   p. 82   p. 84

FUNNY BONE!
What is the favorite game of ghost children? Hide & Shriek.

turtle

A favorite animal for Halloween costumes, this slowpoke character is quick and easy to make using disposable turkey roasting pans from the grocery store.

1	square (12 inches) green stick-on felt
2	large oval aluminum roasting pans

Spray paint: yellow, orange and green

1	shoelace (72 inches)
1	green sweatshirt
1	pair green sweatpants
1	green cap

1 To make the tail, cut an 8-inch triangle out of green stick-on felt. Crease lengthwise, remove backing and fold tight.

2 To make the top shell, or carapace, punch two holes in top edge of one of the roasting pans. Paint the shell in a turtle pattern with green and yellow. Attach wide end of tail to bottom edge of the top shell, as shown in bottom photograph.

3 To make the bottom shell, or plastron, hold second pan to child's shoulder. Two inches down on each side, cut off 1 inch of the pan's hard edge all the way around. Fold cut edges in and crimp with pliers. Fold and crimp again to be sure there are no sharp edges. Punch two holes in top edge. Paint yellow with an orange center.

4 Dress the child in the green sweatshirt, sweatpants and cap. Thread the shoelace through holes in two shells and adjust over child's shoulders with bottom shell in front and top shell in back.

skunk

A 6-foot marabou feather boa (craft stores carry them) creates this skunk's stripes, while its head and tail are a soft faux fur. If you don't have baby-size black pants and a black shirt, try black tights and a black T-shirt.

- 1 scrap (12 x 15 inches) black faux fur
- 2 pipe cleaners
- 1 black shirt
- 1 white 6-foot marabou feather boa
- 1 black or white baby cap with ties
- 1 pair black pants

1 Cut fur into two pieces: one, 8 x 15 inches, will make the tail. The other, 4 x 15 inches, will make the hat (Step 3). Using the 8- x 15-inch piece of fur for the tail, put the right (furry) sides together and sew, glue or staple the long seam, leaving one end open. Invert the tail so the furry side is out and flatten with the seam underneath.

Insert the pipe cleaners on either side of the flattened tail and glue them in place. Attach the open end of the tail to shirt bottom using staples, glue or stitches. Use the pipe cleaners inside the tail to give it shape, such as curling upward.

2 Attach boa to the back of the black shirt, starting at the waist. Run it up to the left side of the neck, across the neck, and back down to the waist as shown in the photograph at far right, top. Then run it to the end of the tail. This creates two strips down the back and one down the tail.

3 To make the hat, take the 4- x 15-inch piece of fur and clip the corners of a 4-inch end to make a point. (Save the corners to become ears.) Place pointed piece of fur at top center of baby cap and attach across top of cap to nape. Attach boa on either side of cap fur to make two stripes on head. Attach corner pieces of fur to the sides of the cap below the boa stripes as ears (see photograph far right, bottom).

4 Dress the child in the cap, shirt and black pants.

FUNNY BONE!
Why are monsters good at playing hockey? They score lots of ghouls.

GHOULISH FOOD & FUN 77

angel

Whatever your child's temperament this Halloween, he or she is guaranteed to be a snow-white angel, complete with wings and a halo!

1	foam sheet (12 x 18 inches)
1	white sleeper
1	white 6-foot marabou feather boa
1	package of feathers
String or white shoelaces	
2	white pipe cleaners

1 Draw a pattern for an angel's wing, based on the shape above, around 10 inches tall and 8 inches wide. Cut your pattern out and use to cut two wings out of the foam sheet.

2 Along the straight edge of the wings, cut two holes at the top and the bottom. These will be used to attach the wings to the sleeper.

3 Next, decorate the wings. Use a hot glue gun to attach the feather boa onto the edge of the wings. Glue extra feathers to the wingtips. Attach the wings to the center back of the sleeper garment using string, white shoelaces or other soft materials.

4 To make the halo, form one pipe cleaner into a 4-inch circle. Glue a strip of boa around its edge. Attach the other pipe cleaner to the halo and make a 2-inch circle at its bottom, which you can sew, glue or tie to the hat.

5 Dress child in decorated jumpsuit and hat.

devil

No one will be too afraid of this cunning devil. You may already have enough red and black felt scraps to make the costume. You can substitute scraps of felt for the fiberfill.

1	piece (9 x 12 inches) black stick-on felt
1	red shirt
Fiberfill	
1	square (12 inches) black felt
1	red hat with ties
1	piece (2-1/2 x 18 inches) red felt
1	pair red pants

1 Draw a pattern for a 6- to 8-inch-tall pitchfork on a piece of paper. Cut it out and trace on the back of the black stick-on felt. Cut out, peel and stick on shirt.

2 Draw a pattern for a roughly 4-inch horn on a piece of paper and trace four of them onto the square of black felt. Cut the horns out, and sew or staple two together along the edge. Turn inside out and stuff with fiberfill. Do the same with the other two pieces, so you have two horns when complete. Attach to hat by sewing or stapling (if the latter, make sure staples don't protrude through to the hat's interior!).

3 To make tail, fold 2-1/2 x 18-inch piece of red felt lengthwise and sew, glue or staple along long edge. Turn inside out. Cut two triangular end pieces for the tail out of black felt and glue them together over the end of the tail. Attach tail to waist of pants.

4 Dress child in shirt, pants and hat.

FUNNY BONE!
What kind of music do ghosts prefer? Spirituals, of course.

jester

Here is a cheerful and easy costume to put together. Best of all, you can use most of the components later as part of your child's wardrobe.

12	baby socks in various colors and patterns
Fiberfill batting	
12	small bells
1	cap with ties
1	one-piece teal playsuit
1	pair polka-dot (or other fun, simple print) leggings

1 **To make the hat, stuff three socks with fiberfill and add a bell to each toe (see photographs). Stitch filled socks to top of hat, two in front and one in back (see photograph above right).**

2 **To make neck ruff, fill seven socks lightly with fiberfill. The photograph below right shows how the socks will look sewn to the neck of the playsuit. Add a bell to each toe.**

3 **Add a bell to each of the toes of the two remaining socks.**

4 **Dress the child in the cap, playsuit, leggings and socks with bells.**

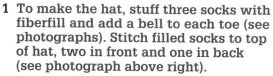

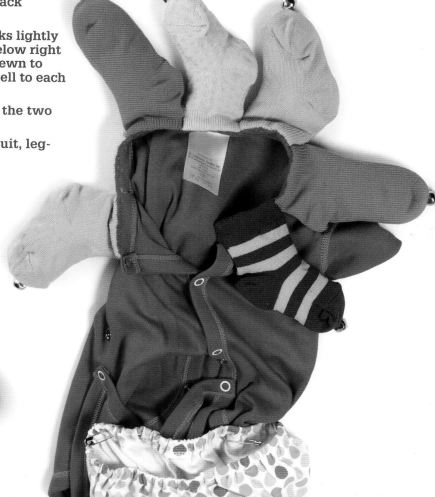

firefighter

Firefighters in recent years have become universal heroes, so many youngster—boys and girls—are likely to choose this costume. You can buy a firefighter's hat at a party store.

1	black plastic tablecloth (54 x 54 inches)
1	roll 3⁄4-inch black electrical tape
1	roll 3⁄4-inch yellow plastic tape
1	roll 3⁄4-inch yellow reflective tape
5	hook-and-loop self-stick buttons
1	black turtleneck or T-shirt
1	pair black pants
1	firefighter's hat

1 Fold tablecloth in half. On the left side, 10 inches down from the fold, cut in 17 inches, then straight down to bottom. (You will be removing two 17-inch square pieces of the plastic, which you can discard.) Repeat on right side. Staple cut edges together to create sleeves and side seams. Clip underarm corner. Invert the sleeves, turning the garment inside out. Fold seams inside garment to one side and tape flat with electrical tape.

2 Laying garment flat, mark the center of the folded top and cut a shallow neck that measures 3-1/2-inches to either side of the center mark. Starting at the center of the front, cut down the middle for a front opening. Fold in 1/2-inch of neck back and tape it down with electrical tape. Fold in 1 inch on each side of front opening and tape it in place with electrical tape. Tape around neck opening inside and outside. You can see these finishing touches in the photograph at right.

3 Fold up a 2-inch hem at the bottom and tape it inside with electrical tape. Fold up sleeve hems to fit child and tape in place.

4 Using yellow plastic tape, make stripes as shown on costume photograph: two on each sleeve, two on coat, one on each leg.

5 Make five tabs for buttons out of 3-1/2-inch pieces of electrical tape. Fasten each piece on the left side of coat opening with a 1-1/2-inch extension. Place a 2-inch piece of yellow reflective tape on the outside of each tab. Place hook-and-loop buttons under each tab and on opposite side of coat front.

6 Dress child in turtleneck, pants, jacket and hat.

FUNNY BONE!
What do you get when you drop a pumpkin? Squash.

FUNNY BONE!
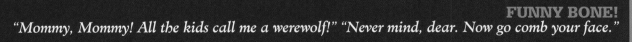
"Mommy, Mommy! All the kids call me a werewolf!" "Never mind, dear. Now go comb your face."

vampire

A classic costume for this season, the Dracula costume we have here is a cinch to whip up and is made of easy-to-obtain components.

1	piece (6 x 24 inches) stiff black felt
1	round (84-inch) black plastic tablecloth
1	round (84-inch) red plastic tablecloth
1	black headband
1	square (12 inches) black stick-on felt
1	long-sleeved white T-shirt
1	pair black pants
1	set of plastic fangs
1	tube fake blood

1 To make cape, first cut out collar from stiff black felt, based on photograph below. Fold black tablecloth in two, making a semicircle. Fold red tablecloth in two, making another semicircle. Put red semicircle on top of black semicircle and glue the two together at their folded edges.

2 Making one large central pleat and four smaller pleats in center of that glued seam (see photograph below), attach cape to headband with glue. Attach stiff collar to outside of headband using rectangles of black stick-on felt from the inside of the headband.

3 Dress youngster in white shirt and black pants, add cape, fangs, and a little fake blood at the corners of the mouth.

face PAINTING

Buy a face-painting kit that contains the colors you want and, if this is your first time, includes applicators and basic instructions to help you along (see checklist at right). Kits start at just $6 and are available at craft stores and, near Halloween, many drugstores and home stores.

Although most kits contain safe, washable paints, you might want to do an allergy test on your child before a full application. Dab some paint in the crook of the youngster's arm at the elbow. If no rash appears after 12 hours, you can proceed.

Sit your child in a chair high enough so that you can work on the face without bending over. Tie the hair away from the face. In addition to the manufacturer's applicators, soft sponges, like stipple sponges from an art store, are good for applying base paints. A wide, padded applicator draws the best fabric strips for a mummy. Thin paintbrushes or makeup sticks or crayons (available in some kits) are good for making lines. A powder puff is best for setting. You can use baby powder to set the paints and brush off the excess with a cosmetic brush.

At the end of the evening, removing the paint is simple: just start the cleanup process with commercial pre-moistened towelettes or a wet washrag with baby shampoo, and follow up with a good scrubbing with soap and water.

it's easier than you think!

There's no reason to limit the makeup to your subject's face. Adding color to the neck, ears, hands, and other exposed skin can enhance the overall look. You can even paint over a costume. In the photos below, adding black, orange, and yellow makeup to the gauze bandages gave our mummy an aged and ragged effect.

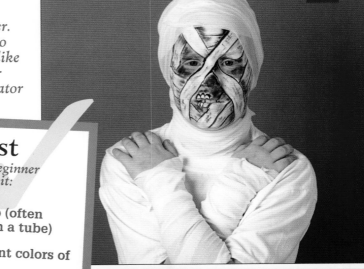

1.

2.

checklist

What's in a good beginner face-painting kit:

- ❑ Foundation makeup (often white, sometimes in a tube)
- ❑ Four or more different colors of makeup
- ❑ Black makeup pencil
- ❑ Paint sticks or crayons in various colors
- ❑ Application sponges
- ❑ Application brushes
- ❑ Step-by-step instructions with pictures

MOTLEY, THE MUMMY

A ghoulish reminder of the dead, this mummy is wrapped from head to foot and, thanks to face paint, across his face. Wide pad applicators make the white strips across the face, which are then outlined in black with a paintbrush. Since he is a very old mummy, his wrapping is a little dirty: paintbrushes accomplish this. When the child's mouth is closed, more teeth still show, outlined with a makeup stick and filled with a small padded applicator. A "dirtied" head wrap finishes off the mummy costume.

FUNNY BONE!
What is a mummy's favorite music? Ragtime.

GRUESELDA, THE GREEN-FACED WITCH

Starting with a green base, applied with a sponge, this fearsome coven member has black lines drawn by one paintbrush or makeup stick and highlighted in white by another. Her eyes are ringed with black lines (use a paintbrush or makeup stick), and her eyebrows are emphasized with black, white and green. Black makeup covers a tooth, making her look bedraggled - or eight years old.

FUNNY BONE!

Why should skeletons drink 10 glasses of milk per day? It's good for their bones.

88

BLACK BART, PIRATE OF THE HIGH SEAS

Shiver me timbers! This lad has been transformed into an outlaw sailor in just a few strokes of black face paint. The bushy brows, goatee and the overnight stubble can be made with a paintbrush or makeup stick. The shadows under the eyes were created with a sweep of the fingertip. The mustache is drawn with a small padded eye makeup applicator.

14 tricks for shooting GREAT PHOTOS

1   BE PREPARED.

Write a list of everything you will need to guarantee several hours of ongoing photography. Do you have backup batteries, a backup memory card for your digital camera or a system in place for quickly downloading a full memory card? Do you use flash cards? Will you need a tripod or a lens cloth? You might even want a backup camera. Just don't get caught short on gear when the best moments arrive.

2   OVERSHOOT.

One of the secrets of professional photography is that for each great photo there are dozens of so-so ones. While it used to cost a fortune to process an overflow of film photos, with digital photography there's no expense in shooting lots of shots. A good rule is for every image you want to capture, shoot at least four times.

3   GO FOR SPONTANEITY.

You'll want to take portraits of your loved ones in their costumes, but that's just a start. Shoot endless photos of the action: children carving pumpkins, making spooky decorations or grimacing at their costumed selves in the mirror. Keep your camera in your hand, purse or pocket, ready for instant action. Often the candid shots are the best.

4   SHOOT AT A FAST SETTING.

Set the ISO on your digital camera to 200 to 400, or if you use film, set it to ASA 400. You want a fast film so that you are not dependent on a flash for most of your pictures. Of course, as your light sources diminish, you might need to slow down your exposure to get the detail you want.

5   USE TWILIGHT FOR YOUR MOST IMPORTANT OUTDOOR SHOTS.

This is one of the best tricks of the trade. At twilight, you won't need a flash but the background will still appear dark. In particular, shoot jack-o'-lanterns around twilight without a flash. You'll get the candle's glow but it will still seem dark out.

6   USE A TRIPOD FOR POSED OR STATIC SHOTS.

Without one, you focus mostly on staying steady and preventing blurring. With a tripod, you focus more on lighting, the pose and the camera's framing. You particularly need a tripod or other steady surface when your photograph includes lit decorations. When shooting a light, even the slightest movement of the camera causes blurring.

7   EXPERIMENT.

A jack-o'-lantern on the front step is a pretty ordinary photo. But placing the pumpkin a few feet over in the bushes can completely change the shot. Look for unusual settings, surprise angles and interesting lighting to make your shots intriguing. In fact, a lit jack-o'-lantern in front of a lit fireplace can make for a fascinating image, thanks to the combination of backlighting and the light from inside a pumpkin.

8   SHOOT LOTS OF CLOSE-UPS.

The greatest sin of many amateur photographers is not getting close enough to their subject. You want to fill the frame with the person or object, not have them surrounded by bland or distracting background. So, for example, hone in on the parts of a child's costume that you think are the most original or most fun and then pull back just enough to capture the happy face, too. If you are shooting two children, get them as close together as possible and fill the frame with them.

9   ENCOURAGE YOUR SUBJECT.

Laugh, joke, prod, make faces—do whatever it takes to make your subjects come alive. In particular, if they are in costume, encourage them to act the part; ghouls should groan; vampires show their fangs; witches cackle and sneer.

10   USE LIGHT WELL.

Avoid using your flash when possible, and instead use flashlights, spotlights, and reflected room lights to create moody, interesting photos. The light source should be in front of your subjects, not behind them. Backlighting makes the front of your subjects hard to see. Be sure there are no mirrors or windows in the background to reflect the flash and ruin the photo. When a flash is necessary, be sure to stay within its range (about 6-12 feet, but you can check your camera guide). One trick to try: to diffuse the light from the flash, put one finger right in front of it as you take the shot.

11   USE EXTRA LIGHTS IN PUMPKINS.

To help the light within a carved jack-o'-lantern balance with the light you use to show off the outside of the pumpkin, use more than one light inside. Two or even three lights inside a jack-o'-lantern will give a better effect than just one. Battery-operated tea lights are a great, safe way to go for lighting.

12   TO PHOTOGRAPH YOUNGSTERS, SQUAT OR KNEEL DOWN.

The camera should be at the child's eye level so that the image is not distorted. Shooting down at kids (or worse, shooting up at adults) yields less than satisfactory images.

13   CREATE A SCARY EFFECT.

Get someone to hold a flashlight about 6 inches below the subject's chin as you take the picture; you will get spooky shadows and a truly ghoulish glow about the face.

14   MAKE GROUP SHOTS WORK.

If you want to photograph a group successfully, make them move as close together as possible—well beyond the socially acceptable level of closeness! Then get as close as you can and fill the frame completely with the people; no distracting background is necessary! Take several shots in rapid succession, chattering away the whole time so people focus on you and not each other.

Spirited Shindigs

CONTENTS | Spirited Shindigs

spooktacular party tips

YOUR Halloween party will be a hair-raising hit with these hints and tips. From trick-or-treating safety tips to games that will get your guests howling with laughter, these easy ideas guarantee chills and thrills for every ghost, witch or goblin who haunts your house on October 31.

HALLOWEEN PARTY PLANNER

Advanced planning is the key to any successful party. You won't be terrified to throw a Halloween bash with this spooktacular timeline!

SIX WEEKS BEFORE:

- Plan the kind of party you want to host. Will it be a ghoulish gala for grown-ups, a spine-tingling time for little tykes or a frightfully fun family affair? Will you have a theme (such as haunted house, mad scientist lab, etc.)?

- Plan your menu. Are you serving a full dinner or just some snacks and desserts? Select foods that tie into your theme.

- Create your guest list and send out invitations. Make sure the invitations indicate if it's a costume party.

FOUR WEEKS BEFORE:

- Choose costumes for your family.

- Start compiling a shopping list for food.

- Plan the party games and shop for supplies.

- Begin browsing party supply stores for decorations. Don't forget to create a spooky scene outside as well as in. The Internet is also a super source for finding unusual Halloween party decorations and supplies.

THREE WEEKS BEFORE:

- Call any guests who haven't responded.

- Set up your outdoor decorations. But don't carve the pumpkins just yet!

- Shop for non-perishable food items.

THE WEEK OF YOUR PARTY:

- Clean the house.

- Start preparing your foods.

- Set up the tables and indoor decorations.

- Carve your pumpkins.

- Prepare treat bags for your guests.

THE DAY OF YOUR PARTY:

- Spot-clean the house.

- Finish decorating.

- Prepare any last-minute foods.

- Check over party details.

- Put on your costume and help the rest of the family with theirs.

- Relax and have fun!

TRICK-OR-TREATING SAFETY TIPS

Here are some things to keep in mind when heading out to trick-or-treating:

- Masks can make it hard for young children to see and breathe. Consider face paint or make-up instead.

- Costumes that are too long pose a tripping hazard. Hem or pin them up if they're too long. Also, footwear should fit properly.

- Walk, don't run, from house to house. Stick to one side of the street instead of zigzagging back and forth. When you do cross, hold your child's hand and look both ways for cars.

- If trick-or-treating at night, add reflective tape to costumes. Or place glow sticks inside trick-or-treat bags. Older kids can carry flashlights.

- Only go to well-lit houses and go to the front door, not the garage or back door.

- Be careful of pumpkins with lit candles inside. Costumes can catch fire if they get too close.

- Grown-ups should inspect all candy before being eaten. If in doubt, throw it out.

- Travel in groups and never go into someone's house alone.

- Adults, be especially careful when driving around during trick-or-treating hours. Watch for kids darting out into the road. At home, be sure to make a clear pathway to your door. And make sure your outside is well lit.

GOODIE BAG TREAT IDEAS

No kid's Halloween party is complete without treat bags for each guest to take home. Make goodie bags (like those shown on page 171) or buy them at a party supply or discount department store.

Instead of filling treat bags with candy, consider these alternatives:

- **Balloons**
- **Crayons and markers**
- **Fast-food coupons**
- **Individual bags of pretzels, crackers or popcorn**
- **Juice boxes**
- **Key chains**
- **Pencils or pens and erasers**
- **Pennies**
- **Plastic spiders, worms or bugs**
- **Small coloring books**
- **Small toys, such as bubbles and yo-yos**
- **Stickers or tattoos**

SCARY INVITATIONS

Creative Halloween invitations hint at the ghostly good times guests will have when they attend your party. Consider these options:

- Write your invitations using a blood-red marker on a mask, rubber hand or other scary item.
- Write in invisible ink and include instructions for your guests to reveal the message.
- Record the details of your invite on a cassette tape or compact disc using a scary voice with Halloween music or spooky sounds in the background.
- Hand-deliver mini pumpkins with the party details written on the back and a face drawn on the front.
- Create a mini poster for a horror movie with your party details woven into the poster.

IF-YOU-DARE DECORATIONS

In a flash, your home can become happily haunted for Halloween. Here are some easy decorating ideas your guests will find frightfully delightful.

- Line your drive or walkway with paper-bag, carved-pumpkin or other Halloween-type luminaries.
- Hang fake spiders and webs from your front porch, bushes or trees.

- Turn your front yard into a horrifying cemetery by cutting tombstones out of cardboard. Paint them gray and write creepy or silly names on them like "Hal O. Ween," "Ima Nut" and "Scared E. Kat." Attach metal spikes to the back with duct tape and poke the tombstones into the ground around the yard.
- Inside, string more fake spiders and webs. Cover the furniture with white sheets to give your home the appearance of an abandoned house.
- Put scary decorations (fake severed head, skull, rubber hand, etc.) in unexpected places like inside the coat closet, bathroom, etc.
- Hang "ghosts" around. Blow up large white balloons and tie them off with long pieces of black string. Cut a tiny hole in the center of old sheets or purchased pieces of white fabric (about a yard for each ghost) and slip the string through the holes. Draw two black eyes and a scary mouth, then hang the ghosts with the black string from the ceiling and in trees outside.

More Ways to Set a Spooky Scene

- Rent videos or DVDs of some classic horror films and play them in the background during the party. Check out "Creature from the Black Lagoon," "Dracula," "Frankenstein," "The Invisible Man," "The Mummy" and "The Wolf Man."
- At the door where guests will enter your home, greet them with spooky sounds from a purchased cassette or compact disc.
- For an eerie glow, replace some of your regular light bulbs with green, black or orange bulbs, which can be found at hardware and party supply stores.

SPOOKY SMOKE

To create mysterious, mood-setting fog at your party like the creepy caudron at right, order dry ice from your local grocery store's seafood department or ice supplier two weeks before your party.

- Plan to pick up your dry ice as close as possible to the time you will need it. Bring an insulated container like an ice chest or Styrofoam cooler. Store the dry ice in the same type of container to slow sublimation (changing from a solid to a gas).
- Try to open and close the container as little as possible. Do not store dry ice in an air-tight container, because it could explode.
- DO NOT TOUCH dry ice with your fingers as severe burns can result. Keep dry ice out of the reach of children. Use tongs or thick gloves when handling it and use it in a well-ventilated area.
- To create fog, put chunks of dry ice in a water-tight container; cover with water. Warm water creates more fog, but the ice will disappear quickly. Cooler water will produce less dense fog, but the ice will last longer.
- If the amount of fog decreases during your party, add more dry ice and water.

spirited
snacks &
beverages

THREE-IN-ONE POPCORN CRUNCH

Carma Blosser, Livermore, Colorado

Folks with a sweet tooth will dig into these bite-size snacks. Candy corn is a colorful addition, so this mouth-watering mix is suitable for any autumn event.

4	quarts popped popcorn
2	cups dry roasted peanuts
1⅓	cups sugar
1⅓	cups packed brown sugar
1	cup dark corn syrup
½	cup water
½	cup butter
½	teaspoon salt
1½	cups candy corn

Place popcorn and peanuts in large buttered heat-proof containers or bowls; set aside. In a large heavy saucepan, combine the sugars, corn syrup, water, butter and salt. Cook over medium heat until a candy thermometer reads 285° (soft-crack stage), stirring occasionally.

Pour over popcorn mixture; stir gently to coat. Stir in candy corn. Drop into bite-size pieces onto waxed paper. Cool completely. Store in an airtight container.

YIELD: 6 quarts.

EDITOR'S NOTE: We recommend that you test your candy thermometer before each use by bringing water to a boil; the thermometer should read 212°. Adjust your recipe temperature up or down based on your test.

BONE SLICES

A savory seafood filling is featured in these creepy bone pieces from our home economists. For even more fun, stack slices on a platter to resemble a backbone.

½	cup mayonnaise
1	package (3 ounces) cream cheese, softened
2	tablespoons *each* finely chopped celery, green pepper and onion
1	tablespoon lemon juice
1	teaspoon ground mustard
1	teaspoon Worcestershire sauce
⅛	teaspoon lemon-pepper seasoning
⅛	to ¼ teaspoon hot pepper sauce
1½	cups cooked *or* canned crabmeat, drained, flaked and cartilage removed
4	flour tortillas (10 inches)

In a mixing bowl, beat mayonnaise and cream cheese until smooth. Add the celery, green pepper, onion, lemon juice, mustard, Worcestershire sauce, lemon-pepper and hot pepper sauce; mix well. Stir in the crab.

Spread about ½ cup filling over each tortilla. Roll up tightly; wrap in plastic wrap. Refrigerate for 2 hours or until chilled. Cut into ½-in. slices.

YIELD: about 6 dozen.

freaky fact

More than 2,000 years ago, the Celts celebrated the new year on November 1, which marked the end of the summer harvest (representing life), and the beginning of the dark, cold winter (representing death).

They believed ghosts and spirits roamed the Earth on October 31 to cause trouble and ruin crops. So the Celts built sacrificial bonfires and donned masks and costumes made of animal skins and heads to avoid being recognized as human.

BONE SLICES

GHOULISH FINGERS

Marilee Davieau, Allentown, Pennsylvania

We serve this fun finger food at our annual Halloween party alongside sandwich rolls and a variety of condiments.

3   packages (8 ounces *each*) assorted lunch meats
1   package (3 ounces) cream cheese, softened
12   grape tomatoes, halved lengthwise

Roll up each slice of lunch meat; spread a small amount of cream cheese at seam to secure roll. Insert a tomato half at one end of each roll to resemble a fingernail; secure the tomato in place with a small amount of cream cheese. Place seam side down on a platter. Cover and refrigerate until serving.

YIELD: 2 dozen.

ORANGE HALLOWEEN PUNCH

Edie DeSpain, Logan, Utah

This eye-catching orange punch is a Halloween tradition at my house. It's refreshing, frothy and quick to stir up—with only five ingredients.

1   can (46 ounces) pineapple juice, chilled
3   cups lemon-lime soda, chilled
3   cups orange drink
2   liters ginger ale, chilled
1/2 gallon orange sherbet

In a punch bowl, combine the juice, soda and orange drink. Stir in ginger ale. Top with scoops of sherbet. Serve immediately.

YIELD: about 6 quarts.

CREAMY ONION SPREAD

Janet Joecks, Menomonee Falls, Wisconsin

My daughter came across this recipe a few years ago, and I have adapted it to our tastes.

1   large sweet onion, finely chopped
1   garlic clove, minced
1   tablespoon olive oil
1/4 cup sliced green onions
3/4 teaspoon salt
1/2 teaspoon pepper
1/8 to 1/4 teaspoon cayenne pepper
3/4 cup sour cream
3/4 cup mayonnaise
1/2 cup whipped cream cheese
Additional sliced green onions
Breadsticks and sweet red and yellow pepper strips

In a skillet, saute onion and garlic in oil for 1 minute. Reduce heat to medium-low. Cover and cook for 8 minutes or until onion begins to turn golden brown. Add the green onions, salt, pepper and cayenne. Cook and stir for 2 minutes. Remove from the heat; cool to room temperature, about 15 minutes.

Meanwhile, in a small mixing bowl, combine the sour cream, mayonnaise and cream cheese until smooth. Stir in onion mixture. Garnish with additional green onions. Cover and refrigerate for at least 1 hour. Serve with breadsticks and peppers.

YIELD: about 2 cups.

with floured 2 1/2-in. Halloween-shaped cookie cutters. Place 1 in. apart on ungreased baking sheets. Bake at 425° for 4-6 minutes or until lightly browned. Remove to wire racks to cool.

Meanwhile, in a large skillet, saute apples, sugar and cinnamon in butter until apples are tender. Combine flour and cold water until smooth; stir into skillet. Bring to a boil; cook and stir for 2 minutes or until thickened. Spoon into a serving dish. Serve warm with cinnamon-sugar crisps.

YIELD: 3 cups dip (2 to 3 dozen crisps).

SUGAR SPICED ALMONDS

Sherri Jackson, Chillicothe, Ohio

These zippy almonds are spicy yet sweet. Once you start eating them, you can't stop!

1/4	cup sugar
2	tablespoons vegetable oil
1	teaspoon cayenne pepper
1/2	teaspoon garlic salt
1/2	teaspoon chili powder
1/4	teaspoon crushed red pepper flakes
2	cups unblanched whole almonds

In a bowl, combine the first six ingredients. Add almonds; toss to coat. Spread into a greased 15-in. x 10-in. x 1-in. baking pan. Bake at 250° for 30 minutes or until lightly browned, stirring occasionally. Cool. Store in an airtight container.

YIELD: 2 cups.

APPLE DIP WITH CRISPS

Joni Karcher, Geneva, Nebraska

My sister created this recipe for a family celebration, but it's great anytime. With the tempting taste of a home-baked pie, this finger food pairs warm spiced apples with cute cutout shapes from a prepared crust.

CINNAMON-SUGAR CRISPS:

	Pastry for double-crust pie (9 inches)
2	tablespoons sugar
1/2	teaspoon ground cinnamon

APPLE DIP:

6	medium tart apples, peeled and coarsely chopped
3/4	cup sugar
1	teaspoon ground cinnamon
1/4	cup butter
1/4	cup all-purpose flour
1	cup cold water

For cinnamon-sugar crisps, on a lightly floured surface, roll pastry to 1/8-in. thickness. Combine sugar and cinnamon; sprinkle over pastry. Cut

Meanwhile, in a bowl, combine the ketchup, lemon juice, peel, horseradish, Worcestershire sauce and pepper sauce. On a serving platter, arrange shrimp in groups of three to resemble dragon claws. Serve with sauce; garnish with lemon wedges if desired.

YIELD: 6 servings (1 1/4 cups sauce).

PEPPER POPPER FINGERS

Our creative home economists had a hand in making these Halloween-inspired jalapeno poppers. They're baked instead of fried, so making them is a real snap.

1	package (8 ounces) cream cheese, softened
1	cup (4 ounces) shredded sharp cheddar cheese
1	cup (4 ounces) shredded Monterey Jack cheese
6	bacon strips, cooked and crumbled
1/4	teaspoon garlic powder
1/4	teaspoon chili powder
12	medium jalapeno peppers, stems removed, halved lengthwise and seeded
1/2	cup dry bread crumbs
2	tablespoons ketchup
1/4	cup sliced almonds

In a large mixing bowl, combine the cheeses, bacon and seasonings. Spoon about 1 tablespoonful into each pepper half. Dip tops of stuffed peppers into bread crumbs.

Place a small amount of ketchup at the end of each popper; top with a sliced almond to resemble a fingernail. Place in a greased 15-in. x 10-in. x 1-in. baking pan. Bake, uncovered, at 300° for 25-30 minutes or until golden brown.

YIELD: 2 dozen.

EDITOR'S NOTE: When cutting or seeding hot peppers, use rubber or plastic gloves to protect your hands. Avoid touching your face.

DRAGON CLAWS WITH BLOOD SAUCE

Stand back and watch guests gobble up this cold appetizer from our Test Kitchen!

10	cups water
1	teaspoon salt
1	pound uncooked medium shrimp, peeled and deveined
1	cup ketchup
2	tablespoons lemon juice
2	teaspoons grated lemon peel
4	teaspoons prepared horseradish
1/4	teaspoon Worcestershire sauce
1/8	to 1/4 teaspoon hot pepper sauce

Lemon wedges, optional

In a large saucepan, combine water and salt; bring to a boil. Add shrimp. Reduce heat; simmer, uncovered, for 2-3 minutes or until shrimp turn pink, stirring occasionally. Drain. Cool in ice water; drain. Refrigerate until serving.

HALLOWEEN PARTY MIX

Jeanette Urbom, Overland Park, Kansas

This colorful mix has a light coating that also makes it perfect for gatherings.

1   package (11 ounces) pretzels
1   package (10 1/2 ounces) miniature peanut butter filled butter-flavored crackers
1   cup dry roasted peanuts
1   cup sugar
1/2 cup butter
1/2 cup light corn syrup
2   tablespoons vanilla extract
1   teaspoon baking soda
1   package (10 ounces) M&M's
1   package (18 1/2 ounces) candy corn

In a large bowl, combine the pretzels, crackers and peanuts. In a large saucepan, combine sugar, butter and corn syrup. Bring to a boil over medium heat; boil for 5 minutes.

Remove from the heat; stir in vanilla and baking soda (mixture will foam). Pour over pretzel mixture and stir until coated. Pour into a greased 15-in. x 10-in. x 1-in. baking pan. Bake at 250° for 45 minutes, stirring every 10-15 minutes. Break apart while warm. Toss with M&M's and candy corn. Cool completely. Store in airtight containers.

YIELD: 16 cups.

LICORICE CARAMELS

Donna Higbee, Riverton, Utah

Fans of black licorice won't be able to stop eating these gooey caramels.

1   teaspoon plus 1 cup butter, *divided*
2   cups sugar
1 1/2 cups light corn syrup
1   can (14 ounces) sweetened condensed milk
1/2 teaspoon salt
2   teaspoons anise extract
1/4 teaspoon black food coloring

Line an 8-in. square baking pan with heavy-duty foil; butter foil with the 1 teaspoon butter. Set aside. In a heavy saucepan, combine the sugar, corn syrup, sweetened condensed milk, salt and remaining butter; bring to a boil over medium heat. Cook and stir until a candy thermometer reads 244° (firm-ball stage).

Remove from the heat; stir in extract and food coloring (keep face away from mixture as odor is very strong). Pour into prepared pan (do not scrape saucepan). Cool completely before cutting. Lift foil and candy out of pan; remove foil. Cut into 1-in. squares; wrap each in waxed paper.

YIELD: about 5 dozen.

EDITOR'S NOTE: We recommend that you test your candy thermometer before each use by bringing water to a boil; the thermometer should read 212°. Adjust your recipe temperature up or down based on your test.

CANDY CORN SNACK MIX

Denise Neal, Yorba Linda, California

It's no trick—this Halloween party treat requires only three ingredients and 5 minutes to prepare.

1   cup *each* candy corn, milk chocolate M&M's and salted peanuts

In a serving bowl, combine all ingredients. Store in an airtight container.

YIELD: 3 cups.

GINGERSNAP DIP

Tessie Hughes, Marion, Virginia

This easy-to-fix dip is a fun way to dress up a package of gingersnaps. It's great for fall gatherings and makes a sweet snack for the holidays.

1   package (8 ounces) cream cheese, softened
1   cup confectioners' sugar
2   teaspoons pumpkin pie spice
1   carton (8 ounces) frozen whipped topping, thawed
1   package (16 ounces) gingersnaps

In a small mixing bowl, combine the cream cheese, confectioners' sugar and pumpkin pie spice. Beat in whipped topping until blended. Refrigerate until serving. Serve with gingersnaps.

YIELD: 3 cups.

CREAMY CHIPPED BEEF FONDUE

Beth Fox, Lawrence, Kansas

My mother often served fondue at parties, and I've since followed in that tradition. It's nice to offer a hearty appetizer that requires very little work.

$1^1/3$ to $1^1/2$ cups milk
2   packages (8 ounces *each*) cream cheese, softened
1   package ($2^1/2$ ounces) thinly sliced dried beef, chopped
$1/4$ cup chopped green onions
2   teaspoons ground mustard
1   loaf (1 pound) French bread, cubed

In a saucepan, heat milk and cream cheese over medium heat; stir until smooth. Stir in beef, onions and mustard; heat through. Transfer to a fondue pot or slow cooker; keep warm. Serve with bread cubes.

YIELD: about 4 cups.

PECAN CEREAL CLUSTERS

Debbie Zorn, Vidalia, Georgia

Featuring crunchy cereal, colorful candies, pecans and loads of peanut butter flavor, these chocolaty bites offer plenty of make-ahead convenience. They're a cinch to whip up when you're in a hurry.

$3/4$ cup peanut butter
1   cup (6 ounces) semisweet chocolate chips
3   cups Cheerios
1   package (14 ounces) milk chocolate M&M's
$3/4$ cup pecan halves

Line three 15-in. x 10-in. x 1-in. baking pans with waxed paper. In a large heavy saucepan over low heat, cook and stir the peanut butter and chocolate chips until chips are melted. Remove from the heat; stir in Cheerios, M&M's and pecans until evenly coated. Drop by rounded tablespoonfuls onto prepared pans. Refrigerate for 4 hours or until firm.

YIELD: about 5 dozen.

EDITOR'S NOTE: Reduced-fat or generic brands of peanut butter are not recommended for this recipe.

CAULDRON DIP

This witch's cauldron holds a Halloween snack that's frightfully fun. Our Test Kitchen formed a pot by toasting a slice of rye bread, then filled it with a creamy dip that's perfect with the pretzel "logs" and sweet pepper "flames" placed underneath.

1   cup (8 ounces) sour cream
1   tablespoon dried parsley flakes
1   teaspoon sugar
1/2   teaspoon onion powder
1/4   teaspoon garlic salt
1/4   teaspoon pepper
1   slice soft dark rye bread
1   *each* medium sweet red, yellow and orange pepper, julienned
10   pretzel rods, broken in half

In a small bowl, combine sour cream, parsley, sugar, onion powder, garlic salt and pepper. Cover and refrigerate.

Flatten bread with a rolling pin. Press over an inverted greased 10-oz. custard cup. Top with another 10-oz. custard cup. Place on an ungreased baking sheet. Bake at 350° for 7 minutes. Carefully remove top dish. Bake 3-5 minutes longer or until bread is lightly toasted. Immediately remove the bread from dish. Cool.

Fill bread bowl with dip. Arrange peppers and pretzels under and around bowl.

YIELD: 1 cup.

HOT APPLE CIDER

Sue Gronholz, Beaver Dam, Wisconsin

A hot beverage like this is savored here when chilly weather returns after summer. The clove-studded orange slices are so attractive.

1   medium navel orange, cut into 1/2-inch slices
50   to 60 whole cloves
6   cups apple cider *or* juice
1   cinnamon stick (4 inches)
2 1/4   cups unsweetened pineapple juice
1/4   cup honey
3   tablespoons lemon juice
1   teaspoon grated lemon peel
1/4   teaspoon ground nutmeg
Additional cinnamon sticks, optional

Cut orange slices in half. Using a wooden toothpick, poke holes in the peel of each orange slice at 1/2-in. intervals. Insert a clove into each hole; set aside.

In a large saucepan, bring apple juice and cinnamon stick to a boil. Reduce heat; cover and simmer for 5 minutes. Stir in the pineapple juice, honey, lemon juice and peel and nutmeg; return to a boil. Reduce heat; cover and simmer for 5 minutes. Discard cinnamon stick. Garnish with orange slices. Serve warm with additional cinnamon sticks for stirrers if desired.

YIELD: 8-10 servings.

spirited snacks & beverages

MARSHMALLOW WITCHES

Get ready for an assembly line because these no-bake marshmallow witches from our Test Kitchen are easy to prepare, and kids will love helping. They're perfect for gatherings because a dozen can be put together in just 30 minutes.

¹⁄₂	cup vanilla frosting, *divided*
36	miniature semisweet chocolate chips
12	large marshmallows
1	drop *each* green, red and yellow food coloring
¹⁄₄	cup flaked coconut
12	chocolate wafers
12	miniature peanut butter cups
12	milk chocolate kisses

For the face of each witch, place a dab of frosting on the bottom of three chocolate chips; press two for eyes and one for nose onto each marshmallow.

For hair, combine green food coloring and a drop of water in a small resealable plastic bag; add coconut and shake well. Spread a small amount of frosting on sides of marshmallows; press coconut hair into frosting. Place 3 tablespoons of frosting in a small heavy-duty resealable plastic bag; tint orange with red and yellow food coloring. Set aside.

For hats, spread some of the remaining frosting in the center of chocolate wafers; press peanut butter cups upside down into frosting. Lightly spread bottoms of chocolate kisses with frosting; place on peanut butter cups.

Cut a small hole in the corner of plastic bag; insert a small star tip. Fill the bag with reserved orange frosting and pipe stars around the base of each peanut butter cup. Secure a hat to each witch with a dab of frosting.

YIELD: 1 dozen.

spooky tip

Whip up an extra batch of Marshmallow Witches, put them in plastic wrap and tie with curly orange or black ribbon for festive party favors.

TO PREPARE HOT COCOA: Dissolve $1/3$ cup cocoa mix in 1 cup boiling water. Float a Peeps ghost in each cup of hot cocoa.

YIELD: 1 serving per batch.

PUMPKIN SEED CHEESE BALL

Save some of your home-roasted pumpkin seeds to coat this creamy green onion spread from our home economists.

1	package (8 ounces) cream cheese, softened
1	cup (4 ounces) shredded part-skim mozzarella cheese
$1/2$	cup chopped green onions
1	teaspoon Italian seasoning
$1/2$	teaspoon dried parsley flakes
$1/8$	teaspoon cayenne pepper
$1/4$	cup roasted pumpkin seeds
$1/4$	cup unsalted sunflower kernels

Assorted crackers *or* fresh vegetables

In a small mixing bowl, combine the first six ingredients. Cover and refrigerate for 30 minutes or until easy to handle. Meanwhile, on a plate, combine pumpkin seeds and sunflower kernels; set aside.

Shape cream cheese mixture into a ball; gently roll in pumpkin seed mixture (lightly press seeds into cream cheese mixture if necessary). Wrap in plastic wrap. Refrigerate for at least 2 hours or until firm. Serve with crackers or vegetables.

YIELD: 1 cheese ball ($1\,3/4$ cups).

GHOSTLY HOT COCOA

Ruby Gibson, Newton, North Carolina

Chocolate pudding mix is the convenient start to this clever cocoa mix. Kids of all ages get a kick out of the marshmallow ghost floating on top.

$6\,2/3$	cups nonfat dry milk powder
1	cup instant chocolate drink mix
1	package (5 ounces) cook-and-serve chocolate pudding mix
$1/2$	cup confectioners' sugar
$1/2$	cup powdered nondairy creamer
$1/2$	cup baking cocoa

ADDITIONAL INGREDIENTS:

30	cups boiling water
30	Peeps ghost candy

In a very large bowl, combine the first six ingredients. Store in an airtight container in a cool dry place for up to 3 months.

YIELD: 30 batches (7 cups total).

freaky fact

Halloween is the second-most commercially successful holiday, with Christmas being the first.

spirited snacks & beverages

GOBLINS WITH PUMPKIN DIP

Christy Johnson, Columbus, Ohio

Scare up some fun at your Halloween bash with these ghostly good chips and pleasing pumpkin dip.

GOBLINS:

1/2 cup sugar
1 to 2 teaspoons ground cinnamon
20 flour tortillas (10 inches)

PUMPKIN DIP:

1 package (8 ounces) cream cheese, softened
2 cups confectioners' sugar
1 can (15 ounces) solid-pack pumpkin
3 teaspoons pumpkin pie spice
1 teaspoon vanilla extract
1/2 teaspoon ground ginger

In a bowl, combine sugar and cinnamon; set aside. Cut tortillas with a ghost-shaped 3¹/₂-in. cookie cutter; place on baking sheets coated with non-stick cooking spray. Spritz goblins with nonstick cooking spray; sprinkle with reserved cinnamon-sugar. Bake at 350° for 6-8 minutes or until edges are lightly browned. Remove to wire racks.

In a small mixing bowl, beat cream cheese and confectioners' sugar. Gradually add the pumpkin, pie spice, vanilla and ginger; beat until smooth. Serve warm or chilled with goblins. Refrigerate leftover dip.

YIELD: About 40 goblins and 3¹/₂ cups dip.

SPOOKY SNACKS

Andrea Chapman, Helena, Oklahoma

These clever crawlers come together in a snap!

1/2 cup plus 1 tablespoon peanut butter
48 butter-flavored crackers
1/2 cup chow mein noodles
1/4 cup raisins

Spread 1 teaspoon of peanut butter on the tops of 24 crackers. Place three noodles on each side of each cracker for legs; top with the remaining crackers. Spread a small amount of peanut butter on each raisin; place two on each cracker for eyes.

YIELD: 2 dozen.

MUSHROOM PARTY PUFFS

Patricia Kile, Greentown, Pennsylvania

Full of cheese and seasonings, these puffs are satisfying by themselves.

36 medium fresh mushrooms
3 tablespoons butter
1 cup mayonnaise
1 cup (4 ounces) finely shredded Swiss cheese
1/4 cup Dijon mustard
1/4 cup minced fresh parsley
1/2 teaspoon onion powder
2 egg whites

Remove and discard mushroom stems. In a skillet, saute mushroom caps in butter. In a bowl, combine mayonnaise, cheese, mustard, parsley and onion powder. Beat egg whites until stiff; fold into mayonnaise mixture. Spoon into mushroom caps. Place in an ungreased 15-in. x 10-in. x 1-in. baking pan. Bake at 450° for 8-10 minutes or until golden.

YIELD: 12-15 servings.

EDITOR'S NOTE: Reduced-fat or fat-free mayonnaise may not be substituted for regular mayonnaise in this recipe.

SERPENT TONGUE POTATOES

Sue Murphy, Greenwood, Michigan

Seasoned with chili powder and cayenne pepper, these paper-thin chips are surefire crowd-pleasers.

4   medium unpeeled baking potatoes
4   teaspoons salt, *divided*
4   cups ice water
1   tablespoon chili powder
1   teaspoon garlic salt
1   teaspoon dried parsley flakes
1/4   to 1/2 teaspoon cayenne pepper
Oil for deep-fat frying

Using a vegetable peeler or metal cheese slicer, cut potatoes into very thin lengthwise strips. Place in a large bowl; add 3 teaspoons salt and ice water. Soak for 30 minutes; drain. Place potatoes on paper towels and pat dry. In a small bowl, combine the chili powder, garlic salt, parsley, cayenne and remaining salt; set aside.

In an electric skillet or deep-fat fryer, heat oil to 375°. Cook potatoes in oil in batches for 2-3 minutes or until deep golden brown, stirring frequently. Remove with a slotted spoon; drain on paper towels. Immediately sprinkle with reserved seasoning mixture. Store in an airtight container.

YIELD: 10 cups.

SPOOKY CITRUS PUNCH

Irene Kusler, Eureka, South Dakota

There's no doubt this refreshing beverage will quench your thirst. Food coloring makes it fun for Halloween.

1   can (12 ounces) frozen limeade concentrate, thawed
3/4   cup lemonade concentrate
2   cups water
1/4   cup sugar, optional
2   liters ginger ale, chilled
Food coloring of your choice, optional
Ice cubes

In a large punch bowl, combine the limeade and lemonade concentrates. Stir in water and sugar if desired. Stir in the ginger ale and food coloring if desired. Serve immediately over ice.

YIELD: about 3 quarts.

SPIDERWEB DIP WITH BAT TORTILLA CHIPS

Sonia Candler, Edmonton, Alberta

Every year, our daughter and her friends anticipate our annual Halloween party. Among the menu items is this taco dip with bat-shaped tortilla chips.

20   chipotle chili and pepper tortillas *or* flour tortillas (8 inches)
3/4   teaspoon garlic salt
3/4   teaspoon ground coriander
3/4   teaspoon paprika
1/4   teaspoon plus 1/8 teaspoon pepper

DIP:

1   package (8 ounces) cream cheese, softened
3/4   cup salsa
1/2   cup prepared guacamole
1   to 2 tablespoons sour cream

Cut tortillas into bat shapes with a 3 3/4-in. cookie cutter. Place tortillas on baking sheets coated with nonstick cooking spray. Spritz tortillas with nonstick cooking spray. Combine the garlic salt, coriander, paprika and pepper; sprinkle over tortillas. Bake at 350° for 5-8 minutes or until edges just begin to brown.

In a small mixing bowl, combine cream cheese and salsa. Spread into a 9-in. pie plate. Carefully spread guacamole to within 1 in. of edges. Place sour cream in a small resealable plastic bag; cut a small hole in a corner of bag. Pipe thin concentric circles an inch apart over guacamole. Beginning with the center circle, gently pull a knife through circles toward center edge. Wipe knife clean. Repeat to complete spiderweb pattern. Serve with tortilla bats.

YIELD: about 7 dozen chips and 1 1/2 cups dip.

spirited snacks & beverages

SERPENT TONGUE POTATOES

CINNAMON CARAMEL APPLES

Our Test Kitchen staff used cinnamon and chocolate to give a fun and tasty twist to traditional caramel apples. Rolled in nuts, coconut or colorful candies, they'll delight kids of all ages.

2 packages (14 ounces *each*) caramels
3 tablespoons milk chocolate chips
3 tablespoons water
1 teaspoon ground cinnamon
3/4 teaspoon vanilla extract
8 Popsicle sticks
8 large tart apples
Chocolate-covered toffee bits, finely chopped salted peanuts and cashews, flaked coconut, M&M miniature baking bits *and/or* chocolate sprinkles

In a microwave-safe bowl, combine the caramels, chocolate chips, water, cinnamon and vanilla. Microwave, uncovered, on high for 1 1/2 minutes; stir. Microwave 30-60 seconds longer or until caramels are melted. Insert Popsicle sticks into the apples; dip into caramel mixture, turning to coat. Roll in or press on desired toppings. Place on waxed paper; let stand until set.

YIELD: 8 servings.

EDITOR'S NOTE: This recipe was tested in a 1,100-watt microwave.

PUMPKIN SEED TRAIL MIX

Our home economists combine a bounty of fall goodies to create this hearty, colorful snack mix.

1 cup seeds from freshly cut pumpkin, washed and dried
2 tablespoons canola oil
1/4 teaspoon salt
1 cup roasted salted almonds
1 cup salted cashew halves
1 cup Reese's pieces
2/3 cup *each* raisins, golden raisins and dried cranberries

In a large skillet, saute seeds in oil for 5 minutes or until lightly browned. Using a slotted spoon, transfer seeds to an ungreased 15-in. x 10-in. x 1-in. baking pan; spread into a single layer. Sprinkle with salt. Bake at 325° for 15-20 minutes or until crisp. Remove to paper towels to cool completely.

In a large bowl, combine the almonds, cashews, Reese's pieces, raisins, golden raisins and dried cranberries. Add pumpkin seeds; toss to combine. Store in an airtight container.

YIELD: 6 cups.

SLOW COOKER CHEESE DIP

Marion Bartone, Conneaut, Ohio

I brought this slightly spicy cheese dip to a gathering with friends, where it was a huge hit.

1 pound ground beef
1/2 pound bulk hot pork sausage
2 pounds process American cheese, cubed
2 cans (10 ounces *each*) diced tomatoes and green chilies
Tortilla chips

In a skillet, cook beef and sausage over medium heat until no longer pink; drain. Transfer to a 5-qt. slow cooker. Add cheese and tomatoes; mix well. Cover and cook on low for 4 hours or until the cheese is melted, stirring occasionally. Serve with tortilla chips.

YIELD: 3 quarts.

spirited snacks & beverages

GOBLIN EYEBALLS

Our home economists had great vision when creating these devilish deviled eggs. Guests at your Halloween party will be "goblin" them up!

12   eggs
Red food coloring
3/4   cup mayonnaise
1   tablespoon prepared mustard
Salt and pepper to taste
12   large stuffed olives, halved widthwise

Place eggs in a single layer in a large saucepan; add enough cold water to cover eggs by 1 in. Bring to a boil over high heat. Reduce heat; cover and simmer for 15 minutes. Drain; let stand until cool enough to handle. Gently crack eggs (do not peel).

Fill a large bowl with hot water; add food coloring to tint water a dark red. Add eggs, making sure they are completely covered by water; let stand for 30 minutes. Remove eggs from water; peel (eggs should have a veined appearance).

Cut eggs in half widthwise; place yolks in a bowl. Set whites aside. Mash yolks with a fork; stir in the mayonnaise, mustard, salt and pepper. To make eggs stand better on serving plate, slice a small piece from the bottom of egg white halves. Stuff with yolk mixture. Place an olive half in the center of each to resemble an eyeball. Refrigerate until serving.

YIELD: 2 dozen.

freaky fact

It's thought that the tradition of bobbing for apples originated from the Roman harvest festival that honors Pamona, the goddess of fruit trees.

HERBED CHEESE SPREAD

Laurel Leslie, Sonora, California

Flavored with several herbs, this appetizer certainly lives up to its name. It's one of the best cream cheese spreads I've tried.

1   package (8 ounces) cream cheese, softened
1/4   cup butter, softened
1   tablespoon minced fresh parsley
2   teaspoons minced chives
2   teaspoons minced fresh chervil *or* 1/2 teaspoon dried chervil
1   to 2 garlic cloves, minced
3/4   teaspoon minced fresh tarragon *or* 1/4 teaspoon dried tarragon
1/4   teaspoon lemon-pepper seasoning
Assorted crackers

In a mixing bowl, beat cream cheese and butter until smooth. Add the parsley, chives, chervil, garlic, tarragon and lemon-pepper; mix well. Transfer to a serving dish. Cover and refrigerate for 4 hours or overnight. Remove from the refrigerator 15 minutes before serving. Serve with crackers.

YIELD: 1 1/2 cups.

haunting
halloween
buffets

CRANBERRY APPETIZER MEATBALLS

Jim Ulberg, Elk Rapids, Michigan

A tangy non-traditional sauce nicely coats these meatballs for a memorable fall party snack.

2	eggs, beaten
1	cup dry bread crumbs
1/3	cup minced fresh parsley
1/3	cup ketchup
2	tablespoons finely chopped onion
2	tablespoons soy sauce
2	garlic cloves, minced
1/2	teaspoon salt
1/4	teaspoon pepper
2	pounds ground beef

CRANBERRY SAUCE:

1	can (16 ounces) whole-berry cranberry sauce
1	bottle (12 ounces) chili sauce
1	tablespoon brown sugar
1	tablespoon prepared mustard
1	tablespoon lemon juice
2	garlic cloves, minced

In a large bowl, combine the eggs, bread crumbs, parsley, ketchup, onion, soy sauce, garlic, salt and pepper. Crumble beef over mixture and mix well. Shape into 1-in. balls.

Place meatballs on a rack in a shallow baking pan. Bake, uncovered, at 400° for 15 minutes or until no longer pink. Transfer with a slotted spoon to a slow cooker or chafing dish.

Combine sauce ingredients in a saucepan; simmer for 10 minutes, stirring occasionally. Pour over meatballs. Serve warm.

YIELD: about 7 dozen.

JACK-O'-LANTERN SANDWICHES

Be prepared for happy faces when you make these eye-catching jack-o'-lanterns from our Test Kitchen cooks. They loaded the sandwiches with flavorful fillings, then easily formed fun pumpkin shapes using cookie cutters.

1/2	cup mayonnaise
2	teaspoons Italian salad dressing mix
16	slices whole wheat *or* white bread
8	slices American cheese
1	pound shaved deli chicken *or* turkey
8	lettuce leaves

In a bowl, combine the mayonnaise and salad dressing mix; spread on each slice of bread. Top half of the slices with cheese, chicken and lettuce. Top with remaining bread. Cut sandwiches with a 4-in. pumpkin-shaped cutter. Remove top slice; cut out eyes and nose with a small triangle cutter. Use cutout pieces for mouth.

YIELD: 8 servings.

GUMBO JOES

Shirley Wranosky, Eagle River, Wisconsin

The guys in our family like to spoon the zesty beef filling over both halves of the roll and eat it with a fork. Now that I no longer work outside of the home, I find myself in the kitchen reading recipes, cooking and baking.

1 1/2	pounds ground beef
1	large onion, chopped
1/4	cup chopped green pepper
1	can (10 3/4 ounces) condensed chicken gumbo soup, undiluted
1/2	cup ketchup
1/4	cup packed brown sugar
3	tablespoons cider vinegar
1	tablespoon prepared horseradish
1	bay leaf
1	teaspoon salt
1/4	teaspoon pepper
12	sandwich rolls, split

In a large skillet, cook beef, onion and green pepper over medium heat until meat is no longer pink; drain. Stir in soup, ketchup, brown sugar, vinegar, horseradish, bay leaf, salt and pepper. Cover and simmer for 30 minutes. Discard bay leaf. Spoon onto rolls.

YIELD: 12 servings.

spooky tip

Gumbo Joes are great to serve at parties. Prepare the filling the day before and chill. Reheat and place in a slow cooker to keep warm.

Complete the meal with baked beans, potato chips, pickles and a festive Halloween dessert.

CRANBERRY CHEESE SPREAD

Nancy Johnson, Laverne, Oklahoma

Here's a creamy sweet-tart spread that's ideal for a holiday buffet.

1	package (8 ounces) cream cheese, softened
1/2	cup sour cream
2	tablespoons honey
1/4	teaspoon ground cinnamon
1	can (16 ounces) whole-berry cranberry sauce
1/3	cup slivered almonds, toasted

Assorted crackers

In a small mixing bowl, beat the cream cheese, sour cream, honey and cinnamon until smooth. Spread onto a serving dish or plate. In a bowl, stir cranberry sauce until it reaches spreading consistency; spread over cream cheese mixture. Sprinkle with almonds. Cover and refrigerate for 2-3 hours. Serve with crackers.

YIELD: 12-14 servings.

LIKE 'EM HOT WINGS

Myra Innes, Auburn, Kansas

These spicy chicken wings are wonderfully seasoned. They're an easy crowd-pleasing snack.

12	whole chicken wings (about 2 1/2 pounds)
1	bottle (2 ounces) hot pepper sauce (about 1/4 cup)
1	to 2 garlic cloves, minced
1 1/2	teaspoons dried rosemary, crushed
1	teaspoon dried thyme
1/4	teaspoon salt
1/4	teaspoon pepper

Celery and carrot sticks and blue cheese salad dressing, optional

Cut chicken wings into three sections; discard wing tips. In a large resealable plastic bag, combine the hot pepper sauce, garlic and seasonings. Add wings; toss to evenly coat. Transfer to a well-greased 13-in. x 9-in. x 2-in. baking dish. Bake, uncovered, at 425° for 30-40 minutes or until chicken juices run clear, turning every 10 minutes. Serve with celery, carrots and blue cheese dressing if desired.

YIELD: 4-6 servings.

EDITOR'S NOTE: 2 pounds of uncooked chicken wing sections may be substituted for the whole chicken wings. Omit the first step of the recipe.

MINI MEXICAN QUICHES

Linda Hendrix, Moundville, Missouri

This fun finger food is great for a party or whenever you want to munch a yummy treat.

1/2	cup butter, softened
1	package (3 ounces) cream cheese, softened
1	cup all-purpose flour
1	cup (4 ounces) shredded Monterey Jack cheese
1	can (4 ounces) chopped green chilies, drained
2	eggs
1/2	cup heavy whipping cream
1/4	teaspoon salt
1/8	teaspoon pepper

In a small mixing bowl, cream butter and cream cheese. Add flour; beat until well blended. Shape into 24 balls; cover and refrigerate for 1 hour. Press balls onto the bottom and up the sides of greased miniature muffin cups. Sprinkle a rounded teaspoonful of cheese and 1/2 teaspoon of chilies into each shell.

In a bowl, beat eggs, cream, salt and pepper. Spoon into shells. Bake at 350° for 30-35 minutes or until golden brown. Let stand for 5 minutes before serving. Refrigerate leftovers.

YIELD: 2 dozen.

ITALIAN SAUSAGE SANDWICHES

Mike Yaeger, Brookings, South Dakota

When my wife and I have friends over, we love to serve these sandwiches. This is a convenient recipe, since it can be prepared the day before and reheated.

20	Italian sausages
4	large green peppers, thinly sliced
1/2	cup chopped onion
1	can (12 ounces) tomato paste
1	can (15 ounces) tomato sauce
1	cup water
1	tablespoon sugar
4	garlic cloves, minced
2	teaspoons dried basil
1	teaspoon dried oregano
1	teaspoon salt
20	sandwich buns

Shredded part-skim mozzarella cheese, optional

In a large Dutch oven, brown sausages a few at a time; discard all but 2 tablespoons drippings. Saute peppers and onion in drippings until crisp-tender; drain. Return sausages to pan along with tomato paste, tomato sauce, water, sugar, garlic, basil, oregano and salt; bring to a boil. Reduce heat; cover and simmer for 30 minutes. Serve on buns. Top with cheese if desired.

YIELD: 20 servings.

GINGER SQUASH SOUP

Laurel Leslie, Sonora, California

Everyone likes the lovely golden color and creamy consistency of this soup. A touch of ginger sparks the mild squash flavor.

3	cups chicken broth
2	packages (10 ounces *each*) frozen cooked winter squash, thawed
1	cup unsweetened applesauce
3	tablespoons sugar
1	teaspoon ground ginger
1/2	teaspoon salt
1/2	cup heavy whipping cream, whipped

In a large saucepan, simmer broth and squash. Add the applesauce, sugar, ginger and salt. Bring to a boil. Reduce heat to low; stir in cream. Cook for 30 minutes or until soup reaches desired consistency, stirring occasionally.

YIELD: 6 servings.

DINNER IN A PUMPKIN

SuAnn Bird, Lindon, Utah

Scoop out hearty helpings of meat, rice and cooked pumpkin in this fun fall entree.

4	medium pie pumpkins (2$\frac{1}{2}$ pounds *each*)
1$\frac{1}{4}$	pounds ground beef
$\frac{1}{2}$	cup chopped onion
$\frac{1}{2}$	cup chopped celery
$\frac{1}{4}$	cup chopped green pepper
1	can (10$\frac{3}{4}$ ounces) condensed cream of chicken soup, undiluted
1	can (4 ounces) mushroom stems and pieces, drained
$\frac{1}{4}$	cup soy sauce
2	tablespoons brown sugar
2	cups hot cooked rice
2	tablespoons canola oil

Wash each pumpkin; cut a 4-in. circle around stem. Remove top and set aside; discard seeds and loose fibers from inside. Place pumpkins in a shallow sturdy baking pan; set aside.

In a large skillet, cook the beef, onion, celery and green pepper over medium heat until meat is no longer pink and vegetables are tender; drain. Stir in the soup, mushrooms, soy sauce and brown sugar. Cook for 3-4 minutes or until heated through. Fold in rice; spoon into pumpkins and replace tops. Brush outside of pumpkins with oil.

Bake at 350° for 50-60 minutes or just until pumpkin is tender (do not overbake). Place on individual serving plates.

YIELD: 4 servings.

SPOOKY MONSTER SANDWICHES

Why serve chicken salad on ordinary rolls when you can make these spooky sandwiches from our Test Kitchen?

2	cups cubed cooked chicken breast
$\frac{1}{2}$	cup dried cranberries, optional
$\frac{1}{2}$	cup mayonnaise
$\frac{1}{4}$	cup finely chopped onion
$\frac{1}{4}$	cup chopped celery
$\frac{1}{4}$	teaspoon salt
$\frac{1}{4}$	teaspoon pepper
12	dinner rolls, split and toasted
1	jar (15 ounces) process cheese sauce
24	pimiento-stuffed olives
12	pimiento strips
6	whole baby dill pickles, cut in half lengthwise

In a bowl, combine the chicken, cranberries if desired, mayonnaise, onion, celery, salt and pepper. Fill rolls with chicken mixture. Heat cheese sauce to soften; drizzle or pipe over top of each sandwich to resemble hair. For each monster sandwich, attach olives for eyes, pimiento strips for noses and pickles for fangs.

YIELD: 1 dozen.

spooky tip

You can make Spooky Monster Sandwiches with a variety of fillings, including tuna salad and sloppy joes, and a variety of cheeses and lunch meats. Get creative to suit your family's taste...and enlist the kids to help with assembling!

Thaw bread dough according to package directions; let rise until doubled.

Meanwhile, in a large skillet over medium heat, cook the sausage until no longer pink; drain and transfer to a large bowl. Add the spinach, cheeses, oregano and garlic powder; set side. Roll each loaf of bread into a 14-in. x 12-in. rectangle. Spread sausage mixture lengthwise down the center of each rectangle. Gently press the filling down; dot with butter.

Bring edges of dough to the center over filling; pinch to seal. Place each loaf seam side down on a greased baking sheet. Tuck ends under and form into a snake shape. Place an egg yolk in each of two small bowls. Tint one orange with red and yellow food coloring and the other with green food coloring if desired. Brush stripes on snake. Bake at 350° for 25-30 minutes or until golden brown.

Cut out small holes in olives; gently press into bread for eyes. Cut a slit in each loaf; insert a red pepper strip for tongues.

YIELD: 2 loaves.

SAUSAGE-STUFFED SLITHERY SNAKES

This cheese-, spinach- and sausage-filled bread from our Test Kitchen is a sssserious party pleaser! It ties in well with any Halloween theme.

2   loaves (1 pound *each*) frozen bread dough, thawed
1   pound bulk Italian sausage
1   package (10 ounces) frozen chopped spinach, thawed and squeezed dry
4   cups (1 pound) shredded part-skim mozzarella cheese
1/4   cup grated Parmesan cheese
1   teaspoon dried oregano
1/2   teaspoon garlic powder
2   tablespoons butter
2   egg yolks
4   drops *each* red, yellow and green food coloring, optional
4   pitted ripe olives
2   roasted sweet red pepper strips

BARBECUED FRANKS

Dorothy Anderson, Ottawa, Kansas

Guests won't be able to resist "goblin" up these special sausages at your Halloween party!

2   teaspoons cornstarch
2   tablespoons cold water
1   jar (18 ounces) peach preserves
1   cup barbecue sauce
2   packages (1 pound *each*) miniature hot dogs *or* smoked sausages

In a large saucepan, combine the cornstarch and water until smooth. Stir in the preserves and barbecue sauce. Bring to a boil; cook and stir for 2 minutes or until thickened. Stir in hot dogs until coated. Cover and cook for 5 minutes or until heated through.

YIELD: 20 servings.

CAJUN PORK SANDWICHES

Mae Kruse, Monee, Illinois

This recipe's specially seasoned rub gives tender juicy pork a slightly spicy flavor. You'll watch in delight as these delicious, open-faced sandwiches disappear from your buffet table!

2 pork tenderloins (1 pound *each*), trimmed
2 teaspoons canola oil
3 tablespoons paprika
2 teaspoons dried oregano
2 teaspoons dried thyme
1¹/₂ teaspoons garlic powder
¹/₂ teaspoon pepper
¹/₂ teaspoon salt, optional
¹/₂ teaspoon ground cumin
¹/₄ teaspoon ground nutmeg
¹/₄ teaspoon cayenne pepper
36 French bread slices *or* mini buns
Butter *or* mayonnaise
Lettuce leaves
Thin slivers of green and sweet red pepper

Place tenderloins in a greased 13-in. x 9-in. x 2-in. baking pan. Rub each with 1 teaspoon oil. In a bowl, combine paprika, oregano, thyme, garlic powder, pepper, salt if desired, cumin, nutmeg and cayenne; pat over tenderloins. Cover and refrigerate overnight.

Bake at 425° for 25-30 minutes or until a meat thermometer reads 160°-170°. Let stand for 10 minutes; thinly slice. Spread bread or buns with butter or mayonnaise; top with lettuce, pork and green and red pepper.

YIELD: 3 dozen.

SLIMY STEWED WORMS

Shelley Way, Cheyenne, Wyoming

I top spaghetti "worms" with a hearty meat sauce for a mouth-watering main dish that's guaranteed to please all of your party guests.

1 pound ground beef
1 can (28 ounces) crushed tomatoes
2 cups water
1 can (14¹/₂ ounces) beef broth
1 can (6 ounces) tomato paste
1¹/₂ cups chopped onion
¹/₄ cup minced fresh parsley
2 garlic cloves, minced
³/₄ teaspoon dried basil
¹/₂ teaspoon onion salt
¹/₂ teaspoon dried oregano
¹/₂ teaspoon sugar
¹/₄ teaspoon pepper
¹/₄ teaspoon dried thyme
8 ounces uncooked spaghetti
¹/₄ cup grated Parmesan cheese

In a Dutch oven or soup kettle, cook beef over medium heat until no longer pink; drain. Add the next 13 ingredients; bring to a boil. Reduce heat; cover and simmer for 15 minutes. Add spaghetti; cover and simmer for 15-20 minutes or until spaghetti is tender, stirring occasionally. Stir in Parmesan cheese.

YIELD: 8-10 servings.

on an ungreased baking sheet. Bake at 400° for 8-10 minutes or until crisp.

Meanwhile, in a large saucepan, cook beef and onion over medium heat until meat is no longer pink; drain. Stir in the water, vegetables, beans, tomatoes, sugar and remaining taco seasoning. Cover and simmer for 10 minutes or until heated through, stirring occasionally.

Discard toothpicks from cones. To assemble hats, place cones on circles; pipe a band of cheese around base of cones. Ladle soup into bowls and top with hats.

YIELD: 8 servings (2 quarts).

BAKED MACARONI 'N' CHEESE

Karen Ochs, Erie, Pennsylvania

Folks love the cheesy goodness so much, I'm asked to bring this dish to many gatherings. It's comfort food at its finest.

WITCH'S HAT SOUP

Get into the Halloween spirit with this cute soup created by our Test Kitchen. With a mix of vegetables, beans and seasonings, it's a thick broth with a kick of spice that heats up October 31 menus.

4	flour tortillas (8 inches)
1	envelope taco seasoning, *divided*
1	pound ground beef
1/3	cup chopped onion
2	cups water
2	cups frozen mixed vegetables
1	can (15 1/2 ounces) chili beans, undrained
1	can (15 ounces) black beans, rinsed and drained
1	can (14 1/2 ounces) diced tomatoes with mild green chilies, undrained
1/2	teaspoon sugar

Canned pasteurized cheddar cheese snack

Spritz the tortillas with nonstick cooking spray; sprinkle with 1/2 teaspoon taco seasoning. With a 2 1/2-in. round cookie cutter, cut out four circles from each tortilla (discard scraps). Cut a slit into the center of eight circles; shape each into a cone and secure with toothpicks. Place circles and cones

1	package (16 ounces) elbow macaroni
2	pounds process American cheese, cubed
8	ounces Swiss cheese, cubed
1	medium green pepper, chopped
1	medium onion, chopped
1	jar (2 ounces) diced pimientos, drained
4	eggs
4	cups milk
1	teaspoon salt
1/2	teaspoon pepper
1/4	teaspoon paprika

Cook macaroni according to package directions. Drain and rinse in cold water. Add cheese, green pepper, onion and pimientos. Combine eggs, milk, salt and pepper; pour over macaroni mixture and mix well.

Pour into two greased 13-in. x 9-in. x 2-in. baking dishes. Sprinkle with paprika. Bake, uncovered, at 350° for 30-35 minutes or until bubbly and browned.

YIELD: 18 servings (3/4 cup each).

SOUTHWESTERN PIZZA

Caroline Grooms, Dickinson, North Dakota

Seasoned ground beef, corn and black beans deliciously top off a cornmeal crust in this hearty appetizer pizza.

1 1/4 cups all-purpose flour
3/4 cup cornmeal
1/4 cup sugar
2 teaspoons baking powder
1 teaspoon cayenne pepper
1 teaspoon chili powder
1/2 teaspoon salt
1 cup milk
1/4 cup canola oil
1 egg
3/4 cup *each* shredded cheddar and Monterey Jack cheese

TOPPING:
1 1/2 pounds ground beef
2/3 cup water
2 envelopes taco seasoning, *divided*
2 cups (16 ounces) sour cream
1 3/4 cups (10 ounces) *each* shredded cheddar and Monterey Jack cheese, *divided*
1 can (15 1/4 ounces) whole kernel corn, drained

1 can (15 ounces) black beans, rinsed and drained
1 cup salsa

In a large bowl, combine the flour, cornmeal, sugar, baking powder, cayenne, chili powder and salt. Combine the milk, oil and egg; stir into dry ingredients just until moistened. Stir in the cheeses. Spread into a greased 15-in. x 10-in. x 1-in. baking pan. Bake at 400° for 10-12 minutes or until a toothpick comes out clean.

In a large skillet, cook beef over medium heat until no longer pink; drain. Stir in water and one envelope of taco seasoning. Bring to a boil. Reduce heat; simmer, uncovered, for 5 minutes. Set aside.

In a small bowl, combine the sour cream and remaining taco seasoning; mix well. Spread over crust. Sprinkle with the beef mixture and half of the cheeses. Combine the corn, beans and salsa; spoon over cheese. Sprinkle with remaining cheese. Broil 5-10 minutes or until cheese is melted.

YIELD: 12-15 servings.

TRULY TEXAN CHILI

Betty Brown, San Antonio, Texas

I am a native Texan, and this is the best chili recipe I've ever tasted. It's meaty and spicy. I'd make this whenever I was homesick during the years we spent away from Texas due to my husband's military career.

3   pounds ground beef
2   to 3 garlic cloves, minced
3   tablespoons chili powder (or to taste)
1   tablespoon ground cumin
1/4   cup all-purpose flour
1   tablespoon dried oregano
2   cans (14 1/2 ounces *each*) beef broth
1   teaspoon salt
1/4   teaspoon pepper
1   can (15 ounces) pinto beans, rinsed and drained, optional

Optional garnishes: shredded cheddar cheese, tortilla chips, sour cream *and/or* lime wedges

In a large kettle or heavy saucepan, cook beef over medium heat until no longer pink; drain. Reduce heat; stir in garlic. Combine chili powder, cumin, flour and oregano; sprinkle over meat, stirring until evenly coated. Add broth, salt and pepper; bring to a boil, stirring occasionally.

Reduce heat; cover and simmer for 1 1/4 to 2 hours, stirring occasionally. (Chili can be transferred to a slow cooker for simmering if desired.) Cool. Cover and refrigerate overnight.

Reheat in a heavy saucepan, double boiler or slow cooker over low heat. If desired, add beans and heat through. Garnish individual bowls, if desired, with cheese, tortilla chips, sour cream and/or lime wedges.

YIELD: 4-6 servings (5 cups).

ITALIAN BEEF HOAGIES

Lori Piatt, Danville, Illinois

You'll need just five ingredients to feed a crowd these tender tangy sandwiches. On weekends, I start the roast the night before, so I can shred it in the morning.

1   boneless sirloin tip roast (about 4 pounds), halved
2   envelopes Italian salad dressing mix
2   cups water
1   jar (16 ounces) mild pepper rings, undrained
18   hoagie buns, split

Place roast in a 5-qt. slow cooker. Combine the salad dressing mix and water; pour over roast. Cover and cook on low for 8 hours or until meat is tender. Remove meat; shred with a fork and return to slow cooker. Add pepper rings; heat through. Spoon 1/2 cup meat mixture onto each bun.

YIELD: 18 servings.

In a large skillet, cook beef over medium heat until no longer pink; drain. Stir in the tomatoes, tomato paste, parsley and garlic; remove from the heat. In a large bowl, combine the eggs, cheeses, salt and pepper. Layer three noodles in a greased 13-in. x 9-in. x 2-in. baking dish. Top with half of the cottage cheese mixture, 1 cup mozzarella cheese and half of the meat sauce. Repeat layers.

Cover and bake at 375° for 30 minutes. Uncover; bake 25-30 minutes longer or until edges are bubbly. Let stand for 10 minutes before cutting.

YIELD: 12-15 servings.

POTLUCK LASAGNA

Colleen Wolfisberg, Everson, Washington

This is a variation on a lasagna dish a co-worker made for a company potluck. When I was expecting our third son, I often prepared meals and froze them. It was so nice to have a substantial entree like this one on hand to bake.

1	pound ground beef
1	can (14 1/2 ounces) Italian stewed tomatoes, cut up
1	can (6 ounces) tomato paste
1	tablespoon minced fresh parsley
1/2	teaspoon minced garlic
2	eggs
1 1/2	cups small-curd cottage cheese
1 1/2	cups ricotta cheese
1	cup grated Parmesan cheese
1	teaspoon salt
1	teaspoon pepper
6	lasagna noodles, cooked and drained
2	cups (8 ounces) shredded part-skim mozzarella cheese

PUMPKIN CHILI

Betty Butler, Greencastle, Indiana

This unique chili freezes well...but it still doesn't last around our farmhouse very long, especially when my five children and 13 grandchildren are around! They often are—we are a very close-knit family.

3	pounds ground beef
1	medium onion, chopped
1	cup canned pumpkin
1	teaspoon salt
1	teaspoon pepper
2	teaspoons pumpkin pie spice
2	cans (10 3/4 ounces *each*) condensed tomato soup, undiluted
2	cans (16 ounces *each*) chili sauce
1	teaspoon sugar
1	teaspoon chili powder

In a large Dutch oven or soup kettle, cook beef and onion over medium heat until meat is no longer pink; drain. Add remaining ingredients; stir to mix well. Add water if desired to reduce thickness. Bring to a boil; reduce heat and simmer 1 hour.

YIELD: 10-12 servings (11 cups).

SPOOKY JOES

Darla Webster, Meriden, Iowa

Where we live, trick-or-treating is difficult. So I plan at-home Halloween parties for my son and his friends. These sloppy joes are a highlight!

2	pounds ground beef
2	cans (10³/₄ ounces *each*) condensed tomato soup, undiluted
1	teaspoon onion salt
2	cups (8 ounces) shredded cheddar cheese
8	hamburger buns, split
8	slices cheddar cheese

In a large skillet, cook beef over medium heat until no longer pink; drain. Stir in the soup and onion salt; heat through. Stir in shredded cheddar cheese until melted. Spoon about 1/4 cup onto the bottom of each bun. Cut cheese slices with 2¹/₂-in. Halloween cookie cutters; place over beef mixture. Serve with bun tops on the side.

YIELD: 8 servings.

FINGERS OF FRIGHT

Kids' eyes usually widen at the sight of these chewy digits made with circus peanut candies.

5	red, black *and/or* green jelly beans
10	circus peanut candies

Cut jelly beans in half lengthwise. Press each half into the end of a circus peanut.

YIELD: 10 servings.

SPIDER CUPCAKES

These sweet treats are creepy—and easy! Make a chocolate cupcake into a spider by adding a half-marshmallow "body" under the frosting, licorice legs and mini M&M eyes. Add chocolate sprinkles for a "hairy" effect.

1	package (18¹/₄ ounces) chocolate cake mix
2	cups sugar
1/2	cup baking cocoa
1/2	cup butter, cubed
1/2	cup milk
2	teaspoons vanilla extract
12	large marshmallows
Chocolate sprinkles	
48	M&M's miniature baking bits
192	pieces black licorice (3 inches)

Prepare cake batter according to package directions. Fill 24 greased or paper-lined muffin cups. Bake at 350° for 21-26 minutes or until a toothpick comes out clean. Cool for 5 minutes before removing from pans to wire racks to cool completely.

For frosting, combine the sugar, cocoa, butter and milk in a small saucepan. Bring to a boil over medium heat, stirring constantly. Remove from the heat; stir in vanilla. Cool to 110°. Beat with a wooden spoon until thickened and mixture begins to lose its gloss, about 8 minutes.

Cut marshmallows in half widthwise; place a half on each cupcake. Frost the marshmallows and tops of cupcakes. Dip cupcakes in chocolate sprinkles. Place a dab of frosting on each baking bit and press on cupcakes for eyes.

For spider legs, use a metal or wooden skewer to poke four holes on opposite sides of cupcakes; insert a piece of licorice into each hole.

YIELD: 2 dozen.

GREAT PUMPKIN BROWNIE

To make this eye-catching treat, simply bake brownie batter in a pizza pan and decorate as desired or follow my easy instructions.

1	package fudge brownie mix (13-inch x 9-inch pan size)
1	can (16 ounces) vanilla frosting
Orange paste food coloring	
16	green milk chocolate M&M's
22	yellow milk chocolate M&M's
13	orange milk chocolate M&M's
8	dark brown milk chocolate M&M's
20	pieces candy corn

Prepare brownie batter according to package directions for fudge-like brownies. Spread on a greased 12-in. pizza pan to within 1 in. of edges.

Bake at 350° for 20-25 minutes or until a toothpick inserted near the center comes out clean. Cool on a wire rack.

Tint frosting orange; frost entire top of brownie. For stem, arrange green M&M's in a square pattern at top of pumpkin. For each eye, arrange 11 yellow M&M's in a triangle. For nose, arrange orange M&M's in a triangle. For mouth, place brown M&M's in a horizontal line; surround with candy corn, tips pointing out. Cut into squares to serve.

YIELD: 16-20 servings.

HALLOWEEN CARAMEL APPLES

When making this treat, be sure to start with the apples at room temperature so the caramel won't slip off like it tends to on chilled apples.

1	package (11½ ounces) milk chocolate chips
2	tablespoons shortening
2	packages (14 ounces *each*) caramels
¼	cup water
8	large tart apples, room temperature
8	Popsicle sticks
3	to 4 Butterfinger candy bars (2.1 ounces *each*), coarsely crushed

In a microwave-safe bowl, melt chocolate chips and shortening; set aside. In another microwave-safe bowl, microwave the caramels and water, uncovered, on high for 1 minute; stir. Heat 30-45 seconds longer or until caramels are melted.

Line a baking sheet with waxed paper and grease the paper; set aside. Wash and thoroughly dry apples. Insert a Popsicle stick into each; dip into caramel mixture, turning to coat.

Place on prepared pan. Drizzle with melted chocolate. Sprinkle with crushed candy bars. Refrigerate until set. Remove from refrigerator 5 minutes before serving; cut into wedges.

YIELD: 8 servings.

EDITOR'S NOTE: This recipe was tested in a 1,100-watt microwave.

HALLOWEEN
CARAMEL APPLES
SPIDER CUPCAKES
SPOOKY JOES
GREAT PUMPKIN
BROWNIE

bewitching
breads &
salads

CRUNCHY APPLE SALAD

Julie Pearsall, Union Springs, New York

This old-fashioned salad is part of my favorite meal that Mom used to make. Crunchy apples, celery and walnuts blend well with the creamy mayonnaise.

4	large red apples, diced
1	cup chopped celery
1	cup raisins
1	cup chopped walnuts
1/2	cup mayonnaise

In a large bowl, combine the apples, celery, raisins and walnuts. Blend in mayonnaise. Cover and refrigerate until serving.

YIELD: 16 servings.

AUTUMN SALAD WITH ORANGE VINAIGRETTE

A light orange dressing nicely accents sweet dried cranberries and crunchy almonds in this salad from our Test Kitchen. If you prefer, you can use your favorite salad greens in place of the ready-to-serve package.

3	tablespoons olive oil
1	tablespoon sugar
1	tablespoon red wine vinegar
2	teaspoons orange juice concentrate
1/8	teaspoon salt

Pinch coarsely ground pepper

4	cups ready-to-serve salad greens
1/2	cup sliced almonds, toasted
1/4	cup dried cranberries
1/4	cup thinly sliced red onion

In a jar with a tight-fitting lid, combine the first six ingredients; shake well. In a large bowl, combine the salad greens, almonds, cranberries and onion. Add vinaigrette; toss to coat.

YIELD: 4 servings.

SPICED SWEET POTATO BISCUITS

Flo Burtnett, Gage, Oklahoma

A pumpkin cookie cutter can be used for sweet treats and for savory biscuits as well. These biscuits are a fun addition to any meal in fall.

1 1/2	cups all-purpose flour
2	teaspoons baking powder
1/2	teaspoon salt
1/4	teaspoon ground cinnamon
1/8	teaspoon ground nutmeg
1/3	cup cold butter
1	cup cold mashed sweet potatoes (prepared without milk *or* butter)
1/3	cup milk
1	egg, lightly beaten
1/2	teaspoon sugar

In a bowl, combine the first five ingredients. Cut in butter until crumbly. Combine sweet potato and milk; stir into crumb mixture just until moistened. Turn onto a floured surface; knead 10-15 times. Roll out to 1/2-in. thickness; cut with a floured 2 1/2-in. pumpkin-shaped cookie cutter or biscuit cutter.

Place 2 in. apart on a greased baking sheet. Brush with egg; sprinkle with sugar. Bake at 425° for 10-12 minutes or until golden brown. Serve warm.

YIELD: 1 dozen.

bewitching breads & salads

SPICED SWEET POTATO BISCUITS

133

PUMPKIN SPICE BREAD

Delora Lucas, Belle, West Virginia

This recipe is at least 40 years old. It makes a very moist bread that tastes like pumpkin pie without the crust.

3   cups sugar
1   cup canola oil
4   eggs, lightly beaten
1   can (16 ounces) solid-pack pumpkin
3½   cups all-purpose flour
1   teaspoon baking soda
1   teaspoon salt
1   teaspoon ground cinnamon
1   teaspoon ground nutmeg
½   teaspoon baking powder
½   teaspoon ground cloves
½   teaspoon ground allspice
½   cup water

In a large bowl, combine sugar, oil and eggs. Add pumpkin and mix well. Combine dry ingredients; add to the pumpkin mixture alternately with water. Pour into two greased 9-in. x 5-in. x 3-in. loaf pans.

Bake at 350° for 60-65 minutes or until a toothpick inserted near the center comes out clean. Cool in pans 10 minutes before removing to a wire rack; cool completely.

YIELD: 2 loaves.

PARSLEY TORTELLINI TOSS

Jacqueline Graves, Lawrenceville, Georgia

Tortellini, cheese, ham, turkey and a harvest of veggies make this pasta toss satisfying enough for a main meal.

1   package (16 ounces) frozen cheese tortellini
1½   cups cubed provolone cheese
1½   cups cubed part-skim mozzarella cheese
1   cup cubed fully cooked ham
1   cup cubed cooked turkey
1   cup frozen peas, thawed
2   medium carrots, shredded
½   medium sweet red pepper, diced
½   medium green pepper, diced
1   cup minced fresh parsley
½   cup olive oil
3   tablespoons red wine vinegar
2   tablespoons grated Parmesan cheese
2   garlic cloves, minced

Cook tortellini according to package directions; rinse in cold water and drain. Place in a large bowl; add the next eight ingredients. In a jar with a tight-fitting lid, combine the remaining ingredients and shake well. Pour over salad and toss to coat. Cover and refrigerate until serving.

YIELD: 12-15 servings.

bewitching breads & salads

CRANBERRY SWEET POTATO MUFFINS

Diane Musil, Lyons, Illinois

Bold autumn flavors of sweet potatoes, cranberries and cinnamon give seasonal appeal to these golden muffins.

1½   cups all-purpose flour
½   cup sugar
2   teaspoons baking powder
¾   teaspoon salt
½   teaspoon ground cinnamon
½   teaspoon ground nutmeg
1   egg
½   cup milk
½   cup cold mashed sweet potatoes (without added butter *or* milk)
¼   cup butter, melted
1   cup chopped fresh *or* frozen cranberries
     Cinnamon-sugar

In a bowl, combine flour, sugar, baking powder, salt, cinnamon and nutmeg. In a small bowl, combine egg, milk, sweet potatoes and butter; stir into dry ingredients just until moistened. Stir in cranberries.

Fill greased or paper-lined muffin cups half full. Sprinkle with cinnamon-sugar. Bake at 375° for 18-22 minutes or until a toothpick comes out clean. Cool in pan 10 minutes before removing to a wire rack.

YIELD: 1 dozen.

CHEESY ONION BREAD

Kay Daly, Raleigh, North Carolina

It's impossible to stop nibbling on warm pieces of this cheesy onion bread. The sliced loaf fans out for a fun presentation.

1   unsliced large round loaf bread (about 1½ pounds)
1   pound sliced Monterey Jack cheese
½   cup chopped green onions
⅓   cup butter, melted
2   to 3 teaspoons poppy seeds

Cut the bread lengthwise and widthwise in a curvy pattern without cutting through the bottom crust. Insert cheese between cuts. Combine onions, butter and poppy seeds; drizzle over the bread. Wrap in foil; place on a baking sheet. Bake at 350° for 15 minutes. Unwrap; bake 10 minutes longer or until the cheese is melted.

YIELD: 8 servings.

WALNUT PEAR SALAD

Marian Platt, Sequim, Washington

This nutty salad is absolutely beautiful with mixed greens. Pears and apricot nectar add fruity sweetness.

⅓   cup apricot nectar
2   tablespoons olive oil
2   tablespoons red wine vinegar
1   teaspoon minced fresh mint *or* ¼ teaspoon dried mint
⅛   teaspoon salt
⅛   teaspoon ground mustard
3   medium pears, peeled, halved and sliced
12   cups mixed salad greens
¾   cup chopped walnuts, toasted

In a jar with a tight-fitting lid, combine the first six ingredients; shake well. Combine the pears and dressing in a large serving bowl. Cover and refrigerate until chilled. Just before serving, add greens to pear mixture; toss to coat. Sprinkle with walnuts.

YIELD: 6 servings.

SUNFLOWER CORN MUFFINS

Nadine Brimeyer, Denver, Iowa

These golden mini muffins with a rich corn taste capture the flavor of fall.

1 cup (8 ounces) sour cream
1 can (8 ounces) whole kernel corn, drained
1 can (8 ounces) cream-style corn
1/2 cup shredded cheddar cheese
1/4 cup sliced green onions
1/4 cup butter, melted
1 egg, beaten
1 package (8 1/2 ounces) corn bread/muffin mix
3 tablespoons sunflower kernels

In a bowl, combine the first seven ingredients; stir in corn bread mix just until moistened. Spoon into greased miniature muffin cups. Sprinkle with sunflower kernels. Bake at 375° for 30-35 minutes or until a toothpick comes out clean. Cool for 2 minutes before removing from pans to a wire rack. Serve warm.

YIELD: 3 1/2 dozen mini muffins.

CRANBERRY ORANGE BREAD

Marsha Ransom, South Haven, Michigan

I found this recipe in a children's storybook. Now it's a family favorite.

1/4 cup butter, softened
1 cup sugar
1 egg
1 teaspoon grated orange peel
2 cups all-purpose flour
1 teaspoon baking powder
1 teaspoon salt
1/2 teaspoon baking soda
3/4 cup orange juice
1 cup chopped fresh or frozen cranberries
1 cup golden raisins

In a large mixing bowl, cream butter and sugar. Beat in egg and orange peel. Combine the dry ingredients; add to creamed mixture alternately with juice. Fold in cranberries and raisins. Pour into a greased 9-in. x 5-in. x 3-in. loaf pan.

Bake at 350° for 60-65 minutes or until a toothpick inserted near the center comes out clean. Cool for 10 minutes; remove from pan to a wire rack to cool completely.

YIELD: 1 loaf (16 slices).

SLIMY RED GOOP SALAD

Judy Nix, Toccoa, Georgia

This frightfully fun salad features cola, which adds to the bright, sparkling taste.

1 can (15 ounces) mandarin oranges
1/2 cup water
2 packages (3 ounces each) cherry gelatin
1 can (21 ounces) cherry pie filling
3/4 cup cola

Drain mandarin oranges, reserving juice; set fruit aside. In a large saucepan, bring mandarin orange juice and water to a boil; remove from the heat. Stir in gelatin until dissolved. Stir in pie filling and cola.

Pour into a 1 1/2-qt. serving bowl. Refrigerate for 50 minutes or until slightly thickened. Fold in reserved oranges. Refrigerate 3 hours longer or until firm.

YIELD: 8 servings.

bewitching breads & salads

SLIMY RED GOOP SALAD

137

PARMESAN ROLLS

Marietta Slater, Augusta, Kansas

My family just can't seem to get enough of these fun, cheesy rolls. They have a delightful texture from the cornmeal and are a great switch from traditional dinner rolls. I like to serve them with spaghetti, lasagna and stew.

2	packages (1/4 ounce *each*) active dry yeast
1/2	cup warm water (110° to 115°)
1	cup warm milk (110° to 115°)
1/2	cup grated Parmesan cheese
1/3	cup butter, melted
3	tablespoons sugar
1	teaspoon salt
1	cup cornmeal
2	eggs
4 1/2	to 5 cups all-purpose flour

TOPPING:

1/4	cup butter, melted
1/4	cup grated Parmesan cheese

In a large mixing bowl, dissolve yeast in water. Add milk, Parmesan cheese, butter, sugar, salt, cornmeal and eggs; mix well. Add 3 cups of flour and beat until smooth. Add enough remaining flour to form a soft dough. Turn onto a floured surface; knead until smooth and elastic, about 6-8 minutes. Place in a greased bowl, turning once to grease top. Cover and let rise in a warm place until doubled, about 1 hour.

Punch dough down. Shape into 24 ovals; dip each into melted butter and Parmesan cheese. Place on greased baking sheets. Cover and let rise until doubled, about 30 minutes. Bake at 375° for 20-25 minutes or until golden brown. Remove from pans to cool on wire racks.

YIELD: 2 dozen.

COCONUT PUMPKIN LOAVES

Anne Smithson, Cary, North Carolina

A friend made this moist bread for us years ago. Because it makes three loaves, I can give one loaf to a neighbor, enjoy one with my family and freeze one for later.

5	eggs
2	cups canned pumpkin
2	cups sugar
1 1/4	cups canola oil
3	cups all-purpose flour
2	packages (3.4 ounces *each*) instant coconut pudding mix
3	teaspoons ground cinnamon
2	teaspoons baking soda
1	teaspoon ground nutmeg
3/4	cup chopped pecans

In a large mixing bowl, beat the eggs and pumpkin until smooth. Add sugar and oil; mix well. Combine the flour, pudding mixes, cinnamon, baking soda and nutmeg; add to the pumpkin mixture. Stir in nuts.

Transfer to three greased and floured 8-in. x 4-in. x 2-in. loaf pans. Bake at 350° for 60-65 minutes or until a toothpick inserted near the center comes out clean. Cool for 10 minutes before removing from pans to wire racks to cool completely.

YIELD: 3 loaves.

bewitching breads & salads

FROSTY CRANBERRY
SALAD CUPS

FROSTY CRANBERRY SALAD CUPS

Bernadine Bolte, St. Louis, Missouri

Instead of traditional cranberry sauce, consider these individual fruit salads. They're a make-ahead treat terrific for autumn potlucks.

1   can (16 ounces) jellied cranberry sauce
1   can (8 ounces) crushed pineapple, drained
1   cup (8 ounces) sour cream
1/4   cup confectioners' sugar
3/4   cup miniature marshmallows
Red food coloring, optional

In a bowl, combine the first five ingredients; add red food coloring if desired. Fill foil- or paper-lined muffin cups two-thirds full. Cover and freeze until firm, about 3 hours.

YIELD: 16 servings.

EASY BANANA BREAD

Sharon Ward, King Ferry, New York

I taught my four children to bake using guaranteed-to-be-good recipes like this.

1/3   cup shortening
1/2   cup sugar
2   eggs
1 3/4   cups all-purpose flour
1   teaspoon baking powder
1/2   teaspoon baking soda
1/2   teaspoon salt
1   cup mashed ripe bananas (2 medium)

In a mixing bowl, cream shortening and sugar. Add eggs; mix well. Combine flour, baking powder, baking soda and salt; add to creamed mixture alternately with bananas, beating well after each addition. Pour into a greased 8-in. x 4-in. x 2-in. loaf pan.

Bake at 350° for 50-55 minutes or until a toothpick inserted near the center comes out clean. Let stand for 10 minutes before removing from pan; cool on a wire rack.

YIELD: 1 loaf.

cookie
& bar
boo-nanza

TRIPLE-CHOCOLATE BROWNIE COOKIES

Linda Robinson, New Braunfels, Texas

Our family of chocolate lovers gets triply excited when these cookies come out of the oven. They have the texture and taste of fudge brownies.

- 3/4 cup butter, cubed
- 4 squares (1 ounce *each*) unsweetened chocolate
- 2 cups sugar
- 4 eggs
- 1 1/2 cups all-purpose flour
- 1/2 cup baking cocoa
- 2 teaspoons baking powder
- 1/2 teaspoon salt
- 2 cups (12 ounces) semisweet chocolate chips, *divided*
- 2 teaspoons shortening

In a small saucepan over low heat, melt butter and unsweetened chocolate; cool. Transfer to a large mixing bowl; add sugar and eggs. Beat until smooth. Combine the flour, cocoa, baking powder and salt; gradually add to chocolate mixture. Stir in 1 1/2 cups chocolate chips. Cover and refrigerate for 2 hours or until easy to handle.

Drop by tablespoonfuls 2 in. apart onto greased baking sheets. Bake at 350° for 7-9 minutes or until edges are set and tops are slightly cracked. Cool for 2 minutes before removing from pans to wire racks to cool completely.

In a microwave-safe bowl, heat the shortening and remaining chocolate chips on high for 1 minute or until chips are melted; stir until smooth. Drizzle over cookies. Let stand for 30 minutes or until chocolate is set. Store in an airtight container.

YIELD: 6 dozen.

MELTED WITCH PUDDLES

In honor of the doomed wicked witch in "The Wizard of Oz," our home economists had fun fashioning these simply delicious snacks.

- 1 teaspoon water
- 4 drops yellow food coloring
- 1 1/2 cups flaked coconut
- 2 cups (12 ounces) semisweet chocolate chips
- 6 tablespoons shortening, *divided*
- 36 cream-filled chocolate sandwich cookies
- 36 Bugles
- 4 cups vanilla *or* white chips
- 36 pretzel sticks

In a large resealable plastic bag, combine water and food coloring; add coconut. Seal bag and shake to tint coconut; set aside. In a microwave, melt chocolate chips and 2 tablespoons shortening; stir until smooth.

For witch's hats, place about 1/3 cup chocolate mixture in a resealable plastic bag; cut a small hole in a corner of bag. Pipe a small amount of chocolate on a cookie. Dip a Bugle in some of the remaining chocolate; allow excess to drip off. Position over chocolate on cookie, forming a witch's hat. Set on waxed paper to dry. Repeat with remaining chocolate, Bugles and cookies.

For brooms, melt vanilla chips and the remaining shortening; stir until smooth. Place mixture in a large heavy-duty resealable plastic bag; cut a small hole in a corner of bag. Pipe mixture into the shape of a puddle onto waxed paper-lined baking sheets. Immediately place a witch's hat on the puddle. Place a pretzel stick alongside the hat; sprinkle reserved tinted coconut at the end of the pretzel stick. Repeat with remaining puddles, hats and brooms. Chill for 15 minutes or until set. Store in an airtight container.

YIELD: 3 dozen.

MELTED WITCH PUDDLES

143

Bake at 350° for 20-25 minutes or until a toothpick inserted near the center comes out clean. Cool on a wire rack.

For glaze, in a small bowl, combine confectioners' sugar, cocoa, vanilla and enough water to achieve desired consistency. Spread over brownies. Decorate with candy sprinkles if desired. Cut into bars.

YIELD: 1 dozen.

HAZELNUT CRUNCHERS

Ruth Sayles, Pendleton, Oregon

I often make ice cream sandwiches using these yummy cookies. They're also scrumptious all by themselves!

- 1/2 cup butter, softened
- 1/2 cup packed dark brown sugar
- 1/3 cup sugar
- 1 egg
- 1/2 teaspoon vanilla extract
- 1 cup plus 2 tablespoons all-purpose flour
- 1/2 teaspoon baking soda
- **Pinch salt**
- 1 cup vanilla *or* white chips
- 1 cup chopped hazelnuts *or* filberts, toasted

In a large mixing bowl, cream butter and sugars. Add egg and vanilla; mix well. Combine dry ingredients; add to creamed mixture and mix well. Stir in chips and nuts.

Shape into 1 1/2-in. balls; place on greased baking sheets. Flatten to 1/2-in. thickness with a glass dipped in sugar. Bake at 350° for 10-12 minutes or until lightly browned. Remove to a wire rack to cool.

YIELD: about 2 dozen.

CHOCOLATE-GLAZED BROWNIES

Deb Anderson, Joplin, Missouri

These moist and fudgy brownies are ideal for taking to bake sales and family gatherings. For holidays, I like to dress them up with colorful candy sprinkles.

- 1/3 cup butter, softened
- 1 cup sugar
- 3 egg whites
- 1 teaspoon vanilla extract
- 2/3 cup all-purpose flour
- 1/2 cup baking cocoa
- 1/2 teaspoon baking powder
- 1/4 teaspoon salt

CHOCOLATE GLAZE:

- 2/3 cup confectioners' sugar
- 2 tablespoons baking cocoa
- 1/4 teaspoon vanilla extract
- 3 to 4 teaspoons hot water
- **Halloween candy sprinkles, optional**

In a mixing bowl, cream butter and sugar. Add egg whites; beat well. Beat in vanilla. Combine the flour, cocoa, baking powder and salt; gradually add to creamed mixture. Spread into an 8-in. square baking pan coated with nonstick cooking spray.

freaky fact

Orange and black are Halloween colors because orange represents the colorful fall harvest and black represents the darkness of winter.

144

cookie & bar boo-nanza

CINNAMON CRACKLE COOKIES

Vicki Lair, Apple Valley, Minnesota

This recipe is the compilation of many years of baking. I make these cookies year-round for our family. They freeze well.

1/2	cup butter, softened
1/2	cup shortening
1	cup sugar
1/2	cup packed brown sugar
1	egg
1	teaspoon vanilla extract
1/2	teaspoon almond extract
2 1/2	cups all-purpose flour
1	tablespoon ground cinnamon
2	teaspoons baking soda
2	teaspoons cream of tartar
2	teaspoons ground nutmeg
2	teaspoons grated orange peel
1	teaspoon grated lemon peel
1/2	teaspoon salt

Additional sugar

In a mixing bowl, cream butter, shortening and sugars. Add egg and extracts; mix well. Combine the next eight ingredients; gradually add to the creamed mixture.

Shape into 1-in. balls; roll in sugar. Place 2 in. apart on ungreased baking sheets. Bake at 350° for 10-15 minutes or until lightly browned.

YIELD: about 6 dozen.

EASY OWL COOKIES

"Who" wouldn't love these adorable cookies? Our Test Kitchen cooks use a roll-out refrigerated cookie dough, chocolate-chip eyes and a candy-corn nose, making these a cinch to assemble. If you don't have chocolate chips on hand, use M&M's instead for a kid-friendly fall treat.

1	tube (18 ounces) refrigerated peanut butter cookie dough
1/2	cup all-purpose flour
18	yellow candy coating disks
18	semisweet chocolate chips
9	pieces candy corn

In a large mixing bowl, beat cookie dough and flour until combined. Set aside 4 1/2 teaspoons of dough for the ears. Drop dough by 1/4 cupfuls into nine mounds 2 in. apart on ungreased baking sheets. Coat the bottom of a glass with nonstick cooking spray; flatten dough with glass to 1/8-in. thickness.

Position two candy coating disks on each cookie for eyes. Place a chocolate chip on each disk. Use 1/4 teaspoon of reserved dough to shape each ear; position on top of head.

Bake at 350° for 8-10 minutes or until golden brown. Immediately position a piece of candy corn on each cookie for beak. Cool for 2 minutes before removing from pans to wire racks.

YIELD: 9 cookies.

spirited shindigs

CANDY-TOPPED BARS
Renee Anderson, Franklin, Tennessee

These yummy, colorful bars have a nutty short-bread crust and a sweet cream cheese filling.

1	cup all-purpose flour
1/3	cup packed brown sugar
1/2	cup cold butter
1/2	cup chopped pecans
1	package (8 ounces) cream cheese, softened
1/4	cup sugar
1	egg
2	tablespoons milk
1	tablespoon lemon juice
1/2	teaspoon vanilla extract
1/2	to 1 cup M&M miniature baking bits

In a large bowl, combine flour and brown sugar. Cut in butter until mixture resembles coarse crumbs. Stir in pecans. Set aside 1/2 cup for topping. Press remaining crumb mixture into a greased 9-in. square pan. Bake at 350° for 12-15 minutes or until edges are lightly browned.

In a mixing bowl, beat cream cheese and sugar. Add egg, milk, lemon juice and vanilla; mix well. Pour over warm crust. Sprinkle with reserved crumb mixture. Bake for 25-30 minutes or until set. Immediately sprinkle with baking bits. Cool on a wire rack. Cut into bars. Refrigerate leftovers.

YIELD: 16 servings.

PB&J BARS
Mitzi Sentiff, Alexandria, Virginia

Big and little kids alike will love these four-in-gredient bars that offer a cookie crust, a layer of jam and a crunchy peanut butter and granola topping.

1	package (18 ounces) refrigerated sugar cookie dough, *divided*
2/3	cup strawberry jam
3/4	cup granola cereal without raisins
3/4	cup peanut butter chips

Line a 9-in. square baking pan with foil and grease the foil. Press two-thirds of the cookie dough into prepared pan. Spread jam over dough to within 1/4 in. of edges. In a mixing bowl, beat the granola, peanut butter chips and remaining dough until blended. Crumble over jam.

Bake at 375° for 25-30 minutes or until golden brown. Cool on a wire rack. Using foil, lift out of pan. Cut into bars and remove from foil.

YIELD: 9-12 servings.

SWEET SANDWICH COOKIES
Pat Schar, Zelienople, Pennsylvania

This caramel cookie is a past winner of our family's holiday bake-off. The tender brown sugar cookie melts together with the rich browned butter filling for a yummy flavor combination.

1	cup butter, softened
3/4	cup packed brown sugar
1	egg yolk
2	cups all-purpose flour
1/4	teaspoon salt

BROWNED BUTTER FILLING:

2	tablespoons butter
1 1/4	cups confectioners' sugar
1/2	teaspoon vanilla extract
4	to 5 teaspoons milk

In a small mixing bowl, cream butter and brown sugar. Beat in egg yolk. Combine flour and salt; gradually add to creamed mixture. Cover and re-frigerate for 20 minutes.

Shape into 1-in. balls. Place 1 1/2 in. apart on un-greased baking sheets; flatten with a fork, forming a crisscross pattern. Bake at 325° for 8-10 minutes or until golden brown. Remove to wire racks to cool.

For filling, heat butter in a saucepan over medium heat until golden brown. Remove from the heat; stir in confectioners' sugar, vanilla and enough milk to achieve spreading consistency. Spread on the bottom of half of the cookies; top with remaining cookies.

YIELD: about 1 1/2 dozen.

cookie & bar boo-nanza

JACK-O'-LANTERN BROWNIES

Flo Burtnett, Gage, Oklahoma

Hosting a Halloween party? Use a cookie cutter to easily cut these homemade chocolate brownies into pumpkin shapes, then give them personality with orange, black and green frosting. Our grandchildren think these are great.

1½ cups sugar
¾ cup butter, melted
1½ teaspoons vanilla extract
3 eggs
¾ cup all-purpose flour
½ cup baking cocoa
½ teaspoon baking powder
¼ teaspoon salt
1 can (16 ounces) vanilla frosting
Orange paste food coloring
Green and black decorating gel
Candy corn and M&M's, optional

In a large mixing bowl, combine the sugar, butter and vanilla. Beat in the eggs until well blended. Combine the flour, cocoa, baking powder and salt; gradually add to sugar mixture. Line a greased 13-in. x 9-in. x 2-in. baking pan with waxed paper; grease the paper. Spread batter evenly in pan. Bake at 350° for 18-22 minutes or until brownies begin to pull away from sides of pan. Cool on a wire rack.

Run a knife around edge of pan. Invert brownies onto a work surface and remove waxed paper. Cut brownies with a 3-in. pumpkin cookie cutter, leaving at least ⅛ in. between each shape. (Discard scraps or save for another use.) Tint frosting with orange food coloring; frost brownies. Use green gel to create the pumpkin stems and black gel and candy corn and M&M's if desired to decorate the faces.

YIELD: about 1 dozen.

PRETZEL PUMPKIN GRAHAMS

This sweet-and-salty snack from our Test Kitchen is easy enough for kids to make. Miniature pretzels make great pumpkin shapes.

12	whole chocolate graham crackers
1/2	pound white candy coating, chopped
24	miniature pretzels

Orange colored sugar *or* sprinkles

6	green gumdrops, cut into four lengthwise slices

Cut graham crackers in half, making squares. In a microwave, melt white candy coating; stir until smooth. Dip one pretzel in candy coating; let excess drip off.

Place on a graham cracker square. If desired, fill pretzel holes with candy coating. Decorate with orange sugar or sprinkles. For stem, dip the back of one gumdrop piece into candy coating; place above the pumpkin. Repeat. Let stand until set, about 30 minutes.

YIELD: 2 dozen.

GRANOLA BLONDIES

Janet Farley, Snellville, Georgia

A mix of good-for-you ingredients makes these chewy blond brownies impossible to pass up. The granola adds crunch while dried fruit lends pleasing sweetness. I serve them to just about anybody who walks in our front door.

1	egg
1	egg white
1 1/4	cups packed brown sugar
1/4	cup canola oil
1	cup all-purpose flour
1	teaspoon baking powder
1/2	teaspoon salt
2	cups granola with raisins
1	cup dried cranberries *or* cherries

In a mixing bowl, combine the egg, egg white, brown sugar and oil; mix well. Combine the flour, baking powder and salt; stir into sugar mixture just until blended. Stir in granola and cranberries (batter will be thick).

Spread into a 9-in. square baking pan coated with nonstick cooking spray. Bake at 350° for 25-30 minutes or until golden and set. Cool on a wire rack. Cut into bars.

YIELD: 1 dozen.

freaky fact

The Irish placed candles in hollowed-out turnips to keep away spirits. Over time, people began using pumpkins instead.

cookie & bar boo-nanza

PRETZEL PUMPKIN GRAHAMS

149

GERMAN CHOCOLATE BARS

Jennifer Sharp, Murfreesboro, Tennessee

My mom gave me this recipe at Christmas when I wanted to make something different and yummy for gifts. The chewy bars can be cut into larger pieces, but they're very rich.

1	package (18$\frac{1}{4}$ ounces) German chocolate cake mix
$\frac{2}{3}$	cup cold butter
1	cup (6 ounces) semisweet chocolate chips
1	can (15 ounces) coconut-pecan frosting
$\frac{1}{4}$	cup milk

Place cake mix in a bowl; cut in butter until crumbly. Press 2$\frac{1}{2}$ cups into a greased 13-in. x 9-in. x 2-in. baking pan. Bake at 350° for 10 minutes; immediately sprinkle with chocolate chips. Drop frosting by tablespoonfuls over the chips. Stir milk into the remaining crumb mixture; drop by teaspoonfuls over top.

Bake 25-30 minutes longer or until bubbly around the edges and top is cracked. Cool on a wire rack. Refrigerate for 4 hours before cutting.

YIELD: 4 dozen.

BUTTERSCOTCH PEANUT BARS

Margery Richmond, Fort Collins, Colorado

With lots of peanuts and butterscotch flavor plus a rich, buttery crust, these easy-to-make bars are so good.

$\frac{1}{2}$	cup butter, softened
$\frac{3}{4}$	cup packed brown sugar
1$\frac{1}{2}$	cups all-purpose flour
$\frac{1}{2}$	teaspoon salt
3	cups salted peanuts

TOPPING:

1	package (10 to 11 ounces) butterscotch chips
$\frac{1}{2}$	cup light corn syrup
2	tablespoons butter
1	tablespoon water

Line a 15-in. x 10-in. x 1-in. baking pan with aluminum foil. Coat the foil with nonstick cooking spray; set aside. In a small mixing bowl, cream butter and brown sugar. Add flour and salt; mix well. Press into prepared pan. Bake at 350° for 6 minutes. Sprinkle with peanuts.

In a large saucepan, combine topping ingredients. Cook and stir over medium heat until chips and butter are melted. Spread over hot crust. Bake for 12-15 minutes or until topping is bubbly. Cool on a wire rack. Cut into bars.

YIELD: 4 dozen.

freaky fact

According to Hallmark, about 90% of American families (roughly 50 million people) participate in Halloween events each year.

cookie & bar boo-nanza

CHOCOLATE CHUNK COOKIES

Elaine Anderson, New Galilee, Pennsylvania

It's such a pleasure to serve delicious cookies like these to neighbors and family. I enjoy baking cookies and my four young daughters are eager to help with mixing, measuring and stirring!

6	squares (1 ounce *each*) white baking chocolate, *divided*
1	cup butter, softened
1/2	cup sugar
1/2	cup packed brown sugar
2	eggs
2	teaspoons vanilla extract
2 1/2	cups all-purpose flour
1	teaspoon baking soda
1/4	teaspoon salt
1	package (11 1/2 ounces) semisweet chocolate chunks *or* 2 cups semisweet chocolate chips

Melt three squares of white chocolate; cool. In a large mixing bowl, cream butter and sugars. Add eggs, one at a time, beating well after each addition. Beat in melted chocolate and vanilla. Combine the flour, baking soda and salt; gradually add to the creamed mixture. Stir in semisweet chocolate chunks.

Drop by tablespoonfuls onto ungreased baking sheets. Bake at 375° for 10-12 minutes or until golden brown. Cool for 1 minute before removing to wire racks. Melt remaining white chocolate; drizzle over cookies.

YIELD: 3 dozen.

SHORTBREAD CUTOUTS

Jean Henderson, Montgomery, Texas

I found this recipe in a magazine over 30 years ago and have made the cutouts year-round ever since. Four ingredients make them an oh-so-simple recipe to whip up.

1	cup butter, softened
1/2	cup sugar
2 1/2	cups all-purpose flour

Colored sugar, optional

In a mixing bowl, cream butter and sugar; gradually add flour. Divide dough in half.

On a lightly floured surface, roll out each portion of dough to 1/4-in. thickness. Cut with 2-in. to 3-in. cookie cutters dipped in flour. Place 1 in. apart on ungreased baking sheets. Sprinkle with colored sugar if desired.

Bake at 300° for 20-25 minutes or until lightly browned. Remove to wire racks to cool.

YIELD: about 2 dozen.

CUTOUT PUMPKIN SANDWICH COOKIES

Schelby Thompson, Winter Haven, Florida

Apricot preserves peek out of these buttery, tender sugar cookies. Make them throughout the year with a variety of cookie cutter shapes.

1   cup butter, softened
1¼   cups sugar, *divided*
2   eggs, *separated*
2½   cups all-purpose flour
¼   teaspoon salt
Confectioners' sugar
½   cup ground almonds
¾   cup apricot preserves

In a large mixing bowl, cream butter and ¾ cup sugar. Add egg yolks, one at a time, beating well after each addition. Combine flour and salt; gradually add to creamed mixture. Shape dough into a ball; chill for 1 hour or until firm.

On a surface dusted with confectioners' sugar, roll dough to ⅛-in. thickness; cut with a 3-in. pumpkin-shaped cookie cutter. Cut a 1½-in. pumpkin from the center of half the cookies and remove (set aside small pumpkin cut-outs to bake separately).

Place on greased baking sheets. Beat egg whites until frothy. Combine almonds and remaining sugar. Brush each cookie with egg whites; sprinkle with almond mixture. Bake at 350° for 6-8 minutes or until lightly browned. Remove immediately to wire racks to cool completely.

Spread 1½ teaspoons of apricot preserves over the plain side of solid cookies. Place cookies with centers cut out, almond side up, on top of the preserves, making a sandwich.

YIELD: 2 dozen.

HOLIDAY PEANUT BARS

Peg Woitel, Fairbanks, Alaska

Oats, peanut butter and M&M's give these bars mass appeal. When I have free time, I often bake a pan and pop it in the freezer to take to a future potluck or bake sale.

2   cups quick-cooking oats
1½   cups all-purpose flour
¾   cup packed brown sugar
1½   teaspoons baking soda
½   teaspoon salt
¾   cup butter, melted
1   package (14 ounces) peanut M&M's
1   can (14 ounces) sweetened condensed milk
½   cup chunky peanut butter
1   tablespoon vanilla extract

In a mixing bowl, combine the oats, flour, brown sugar, baking soda and salt. Add butter; mix until crumbly. Set aside 1 cup. Press the remaining crumb mixture into a greased 13-in. x 9-in. x 2-in. baking pan. Bake at 350° for 9-11 minutes or until edges are lightly browned (bars will puff up slightly).

Meanwhile, set aside 1 cup M&M's; chop remaining M&M's. In a mixing bowl, combine the milk, peanut butter and vanilla; mix well. Stir in chopped M&M's. Pour over crust; carefully spread evenly. Sprinkle with reserved M&M's; gently press into peanut butter mixture. Sprinkle with reserved crumb mixture. Bake 18-22 minutes longer or until edges are lightly browned. Cool on a wire rack before cutting.

YIELD: 3 dozen.

spooky tip

Plastic spiders are an easy way to add a bit of creepiness to your Halloween party. Buy them in bulk and place them on the tabletop as well as on serving platters. You can also hang the spiders from the ceiling with fish line.

CUTOUT PUMPKIN SANDWICH COOKIES

ghostly
good
desserts

COCONUT CHOCOLATE CAKE

Rene Schwebach, Dumont, Minnesota

I tuck a coconut filling into this moist chocolate cake. It's easy to assemble with convenience products, including a boxed cake mix, instant pudding mix and prepared frosting.

4	eggs
3/4	cup canola oil
3/4	cup water
1	teaspoon vanilla extract
1	package (18 1/4 ounces) chocolate cake mix
1	package (3.9 ounces) instant chocolate pudding mix

FILLING:

2	cups flaked coconut
1/3	cup sweetened condensed milk
1/4	teaspoon almond extract
1	can (16 ounces) chocolate frosting

In a mixing bowl, beat the eggs, oil, water and vanilla. Add the cake and pudding mixes; beat for 5 minutes. Pour 3 cups into a greased and floured 10-in. fluted tube pan. Combine the coconut, milk and extract; mix well. Drop by spoonfuls onto batter. Cover with remaining batter.

Bake at 350° for 50-60 minutes or until a toothpick inserted near the center comes out clean. Cool for 10 minutes before removing from pan to a wire rack to cool completely. Frost cake with chocolate frosting.

YIELD: 12-15 servings.

PEANUT BUTTER TARTS

These tiny tarts will surely become a big part of your recipe collection because they chill while you're enjoying the rest of the meal. Children especially like having their own "little pie" to help decorate.

1	cup peanut butter chips
1	tablespoon canola oil
1	package (3.9 ounces) instant chocolate pudding mix
1 3/4	cups cold milk
1	package (6 count) individual graham cracker tart shells

Whipped topping

Halloween candy, sprinkles *and/or* cake decorations

In the top of a double boiler over simmering water, melt chips with oil, stirring until smooth. Remove top pan from water and cool for 5 minutes.

Meanwhile, in a bowl, whisk pudding and milk until thick. Fold in peanut butter mixture. Spoon into tart shells. Chill for 15 minutes. Top with a dollop of whipped topping and decorate as desired.

YIELD: 6 servings.

spooky tip

To keep the punch cold during your Halloween party, try this "handy" trick!

Fill several rubber gloves with water and freeze until ready to use. Run warm water over the gloves and peel away from the ice. Float the frozen hands in the punch.

ghostly good desserts

SWEET POTATO CUSTARD PIE

Kathy Roberts, New Hebron, Mississippi

I love to bake and experiment with ingredients. I came up with a hit when I developed this deliciously different pie.

2	small sweet potatoes, peeled and chopped
3/4	cup marshmallow creme
1/2	cup butter, cubed
1	can (5 ounces) evaporated milk
3	eggs
1	teaspoon vanilla extract
1/4	teaspoon almond extract
3/4	cup sugar
1/4	cup packed brown sugar
1	tablespoon all-purpose flour
1/8	teaspoon ground cinnamon
1/8	teaspoon ground nutmeg
1	unbaked pastry shell (9 inches)
1/2	cup whipped topping

Place sweet potatoes in a large saucepan and cover with water. Bring to a boil. Reduce heat; cover and simmer for 10 minutes or until tender. Drain potatoes and place in large mixing bowl; mash. Add marshmallow creme and butter; beat until smooth. Add the milk, eggs and extracts; mix well.

Combine the sugars, flour, cinnamon and nutmeg; gradually beat into potato mixture until well blended. Pour into pastry shell.

Bake at 350° for 45-50 minutes or until a knife inserted near the center comes out clean. Cool on a wire rack. Serve with whipped topping. Refrigerate leftovers.

YIELD: 8 servings.

CARAMEL BREAD PUDDING

Tammie Peebles, Naples, Florida

My mom gave me the recipe for this easy-to-make pudding. It's a great way to use up day-old bread.

6	slices day-old bread, cut into 1/2 -inch cubes
1	cup hot water
1	cup packed brown sugar
4	eggs, lightly beaten
2	cups warm milk
1/2	cup sugar
1/2	teaspoon vanilla extract
1/2	teaspoon ground cinnamon
1/8	teaspoon salt

Place bread in a greased 2-qt. baking dish. Combine the water and brown sugar; pour over bread. Combine the remaining ingredients; pour over bread. Bake at 350° for 50-60 minutes or until a knife inserted near the center comes out clean. Serve warm or cold.

YIELD: 6-8 servings.

BANANA POUND CAKE

Nancy Zimmerman
Cape May Court House, New Jersey

I adapted a basic pound cake recipe from my great-aunt for this treat. It makes a moist cake that pops out of the pan perfectly.

3	teaspoons plus 3 cups sugar, *divided*
1	cup butter, softened
6	eggs
1	cup mashed ripe banana (about 2 medium)
1½	teaspoons vanilla extract
½	teaspoon lemon extract
3	cups all-purpose flour
¼	teaspoon baking soda
1	cup (8 ounces) sour cream

GLAZE:

1½	cups confectioners' sugar
½	teaspoon vanilla extract
3	to 4 teaspoons milk

Grease a 10-in. fluted tube pan. Sprinkle with 3 teaspoons sugar; set aside. In a large mixing bowl, cream butter and remaining sugar until light and fluffy, about 5 minutes. Add eggs, one at a time, beating well after each addition.

Stir in bananas and extracts. Combine flour and baking soda; add to the creamed mixture alternately with sour cream, beating just until combined.

Pour into prepared pan (pan will be full). Bake at 325° for 75-85 minutes or until a toothpick inserted near the center comes out clean. Cool for 10 minutes before removing from pan to a wire rack to cool completely.

In a small bowl, whisk glaze ingredients until smooth; drizzle over cake. Store in refrigerator.

YIELD: 12-15 servings.

APPLE CRANBERRY COBBLER

Regina Stock, Topeka, Kansas

My family enjoys the sweetness of the apples as well as the tartness of the cranberries in this old-fashioned treat. It's a great dessert to make during the peak of apple season.

5	cups sliced peeled tart apples
1¼	cups sugar
1	cup fresh *or* frozen cranberries
3	tablespoons quick-cooking tapioca
½	teaspoon ground cinnamon
1	cup water
2	tablespoons butter

TOPPING:

¾	cup all-purpose flour
2	tablespoons sugar
1	teaspoon baking powder
⅛	teaspoon salt
¼	cup cold butter
¼	cup milk

In a large saucepan, combine the apples, sugar, cranberries, tapioca, cinnamon and water. Let stand for 5 minutes, stirring occasionally. Cook and stir over medium heat until mixture comes to a full boil. Cook and stir 3 minutes longer. Pour into a greased 2-qt. baking dish. Dot with butter.

For topping, combine the flour, sugar, baking powder and salt in a bowl. Cut in butter until crumbly. Stir in milk to form a soft dough. Drop dough by tablespoonfuls over hot apple mixture. Bake, uncovered, at 375° for 30-35 minutes or until topping is golden brown and a toothpick inserted into topping comes out clean.

YIELD: 8 servings.

ghostly good desserts

HALLOWEEN POKE CAKE

This cute cake, created by our Test Kitchen, will make your favorite trick-or-treaters smile with delight when you serve it on Halloween. The moist marble cake features a buttery frosting and fun candy pumpkins on top.

1   package (18¼ ounces) fudge marble cake mix
2   packages (3 ounces *each*) orange gelatin
1   cup boiling water
½   cup cold water
½   cup butter, softened
3½ cups confectioners' sugar
⅓   cup baking cocoa
¼   cup milk
1   teaspoon vanilla extract
12 to 15 candy pumpkins *or* candy corn

Prepare and bake cake according to package directions, using a greased 13-in. x 9-in. x 2-in. baking pan. Cool on a wire rack for 1 hour.

In a small bowl, dissolve gelatin in boiling water; stir in cold water. With a meat fork or wooden skewer, poke holes in cake about 2 in. apart. Slowly pour gelatin over cake. Refrigerate for 2-3 hours.

For frosting, in a small mixing bowl, cream butter until fluffy. Beat in the confectioners' sugar, cocoa, milk and vanilla until smooth. Spread over cake; top with candy pumpkins or candy corn. Cover and refrigerate until serving.

YIELD: 12-15 servings.

SPIDERWEB PUMPKIN CHEESECAKE

Bev Kotowich, Winnepeg, Manitoba

This spiced cheesecake makes an appearance on my Halloween table every year. Folks get a kick out of the candy web and chocolate spiders.

1³/₄ cups chocolate wafer crumbs (about 28 wafers)

¹/₄ cup butter, melted

FILLING:

3 packages (8 ounces *each*) cream cheese, softened

³/₄ cup sugar

¹/₂ cup packed brown sugar

3 eggs

1 can (15 ounces) solid-pack pumpkin

2 tablespoons cornstarch

3 teaspoons vanilla extract

1¹/₂ teaspoons pumpkin pie spice

TOPPING:

2 cups (16 ounces) sour cream

3 tablespoons sugar

2 teaspoons vanilla extract

SPIDERWEB GARNISH:

1 cup sugar

¹/₈ teaspoon cream of tartar

¹/₃ cup water

4 squares (1 ounce *each*) semisweet chocolate, melted

Combine wafer crumbs and butter; press onto the bottom and 1 in. up the sides of a greased 10-in. springform pan. Set aside. In a mixing bowl, beat cream cheese and sugars until smooth. Add eggs; beat on low speed just until combined. Whisk in pumpkin, cornstarch, vanilla and pumpkin pie spice just until blended. Pour into crust. Place on a baking sheet. Bake at 350° for 60-65 minutes or until center is almost set. Cool on a wire rack for 10 minutes.

Combine topping ingredients; spread over filling. Bake at 350° for 6 minutes. Cool on a wire rack for 10 minutes. Carefully run a knife around the edge of pan to loosen; cool 1 hour longer. Refrigerate overnight. Remove sides of pan; set aside.

For spiderwebs, draw six 3-in. x 2-in. half circles on two sheets of parchment paper on top; tape both securely to work surface. In a saucepan, bring the sugar, cream of tartar and water to a boil over medium heat. Boil, without stirring, until mixture turns a light amber color and candy thermometer reads 350°. Immediately remove from the heat and stir. Cool, stirring occasionally, for 10-15 minutes or until hot sugar mixture falls off a metal spoon in a fine thread.

Using a spoon or meat fork, carefully drizzle syrup over half-circle outlines and inside the outlines to form spiderwebs; reheat syrup if needed. Cool completely. Place melted chocolate in a resealable plastic bag; cut a small hole in a corner of bag. Pipe 1-in. spiders onto parchment or foil; cool completely. With remaining melted chocolate, pipe two or three dots on each web; attach spiders.

Remove sides of springform pan. Cut cheesecake; place a web on top of each slice and remaining spiders on the side. Refrigerate leftovers.

YIELD: 12 servings.

EDITOR'S NOTE: We recommend that you test your candy thermometer before each use by bringing water to a boil; the thermometer should read 212°. Adjust your recipe temperature up or down based on your test.

ghostly good desserts

ORANGE SPICE CAKE

Connie Simon, Reed City, Michigan

I like to serve slices of this gingerbread-like cake with whipped topping, but it's just as delicious plain.

1²/₃   cups all-purpose flour
¹/₃   cup sugar
1¹/₂   teaspoons baking soda
1   teaspoon ground ginger
1   teaspoon ground cinnamon
¹/₂   teaspoon ground cloves
¹/₂   cup orange juice
¹/₂   cup molasses
¹/₃   cup canola oil
1   egg
¹/₂   cup orange marmalade
Whipped topping, optional

In a bowl, combine the flour, sugar, baking soda, ginger, cinnamon and cloves. Combine the orange juice, molasses, oil and egg; add to dry ingredients and stir just until combined. Pour into a greased 9-in. square baking pan.

Bake at 350° for 16-20 minutes or until a toothpick inserted near the center comes out clean. Spoon marmalade over warm cake. Cool on a wire rack. Serve with whipped topping if desired.

YIELD: 9 servings.

MOUSSE-FILLED WITCHES' HATS

Our Test Kitchen staff had a "spooktacular" time coming up with these rich snacks, featuring sugar cones filled with a creamy homemade mousse.

1³/₄   cups heavy whipping cream, *divided*
1   cup milk chocolate chips
4   squares (1 ounce *each*) semisweet chocolate, chopped
¹/₂   teaspoon shortening
1   package (4³/₄ ounces) chocolate ice cream sugar cones
Halloween sprinkles
12   thin chocolate wafers (2¹/₄-inch diameter)

In a small saucepan, bring ¹/₂ cup cream to a boil; remove from heat. Stir in chocolate chips until smooth. Transfer to a bowl; cool to room temperature, stirring occasionally. In a small mixing bowl, beat remaining cream until stiff peaks form; fold into chocolate mixture. Cover; chill.

In a microwave-safe bowl, melt semisweet chocolate and shortening; stir until smooth. Dip pointed tips of ice cream cones a third of the way into melted chocolate; roll in sprinkles. Refrigerate until set. Just before serving, spoon mousse into cones. Top each with a chocolate wafer. Invert onto a serving platter.

YIELD: 1 dozen.

spirited shindigs

SPIDERWEB CHEESECAKE

Jan White, Plainview, Nebraska

The trick to this tempting treat is pulling a tooth-pick through rings of melted chocolate to create the web effect. This no-bake cream cheese pie goes together quickly and tastes delicious.

1	envelope unflavored gelatin
1/4	cup cold water
2	packages (8 ounces *each*) cream cheese, softened
1/2	cup sugar
1/2	cup heavy whipping cream
1	teaspoon vanilla extract
1	chocolate crumb crust (8 *or* 9 inches)
2	tablespoons semisweet chocolate chips
1	tablespoon butter

In a small saucepan, sprinkle gelatin over water; let stand for 1 minute. Heat gelatin; stir until dissolved. Remove from the heat; cool slightly. In a mixing bowl, beat the cream cheese and sugar until smooth. Gradually beat in cream, vanilla and gelatin mixture until smooth. Pour into crust.

In a microwave, melt chocolate chips and butter; stir until smooth. Transfer to a heavy-duty resealable bag; cut a small hole in a corner of bag. Pipe a circle of chocolate in center of cheesecake. Pipe evenly spaced thin concentric circles about 1/2 in. apart over filling. Beginning with the center circle, gently pull a toothpick through circles toward outer edge. Wipe toothpick clean. Repeat to complete web pattern. Cover and refrigerate for at least 2 hours before cutting.

YIELD: 6-8 servings.

CARAMEL FLAN

Anelle Mack, Midland, Texas

Sometimes I like to top this Mexican dessert with whipped cream and toasted slivered almonds.

1/2	cup sugar
1 2/3	cups sweetened condensed milk
1	cup milk
3	eggs
3	egg yolks
1	teaspoon vanilla extract

In a large skillet over medium heat, cook sugar until melted, about 12 minutes. Do not stir. When sugar is melted, reduce heat to low and continue to cook, stirring occasionally, until syrup is golden brown, about 2 minutes. Quickly pour into an ungreased 2-qt. round souffle dish, tilting to coat the bottom; let stand for 10 minutes.

In a blender, combine the condensed milk, milk, eggs, yolks and vanilla. Cover and process for 15 seconds or until well blended. Slowly pour over syrup.

Place the souffle dish in a larger baking pan. Add 1 in. of boiling water to baking pan. Bake at 350° for 55-60 minutes or until center is just set (mixture will jiggle). Remove souffle dish from larger pan. Place on a wire rack; cool for 1 hour. Cover and refrigerate overnight.

To unmold, run a knife around edge and invert flan onto a large rimmed serving platter. Cut into wedges or spoon onto dessert plates; spoon sauce over each serving.

YIELD: 8-10 servings.

freaky fact

When people fled Ireland's potato famine during the 1840s and came to the United States, they brought with them their Halloween customs.

ghostly good desserts

SPIDERWEB CHEESECAKE

163

In a bowl, whisk milk and pudding mixes for 2 minutes or until slightly thickened. Let stand for 2 minutes or until soft set. Stir in pumpkin and spices; mix well.

In a trifle bowl or 3½-qt. glass serving bowl, layer a fourth of the cake crumbs, half of the pumpkin mixture, a fourth of the cake crumbs and half of the whipped topping. Repeat layers. Garnish with reserved cake crumbs. Serve immediately or refrigerate.

YIELD: 18 servings.

EDITOR'S NOTE: This recipe was tested with Betty Crocker gingerbread cake mix.

CANDY CORN CUPCAKES

Renee Schwebach, Dumont, Minnesota

These moist, tender white cupcakes are perfect for Halloween. But for fast yet fabulous results any time of year, simply choose candy decorations appropriate to the season.

½	cup shortening
1½	cups sugar
1	teaspoon vanilla extract
2	cups all-purpose flour
3½	teaspoons baking powder
1	teaspoon salt
1	cup milk
4	egg whites

Frosting of your choice
Candy corn *or* other decorations

In a mixing bowl, cream shortening and sugar. Beat in vanilla. Combine flour, baking powder and salt; add to the creamed mixture alternately with milk. Beat in the egg whites. Fill greased or paper-lined muffin cups half full.

Bake at 350° for 18-22 minutes or until a toothpick comes out clean. Cool for 10 minutes before removing from pans to wire racks. Frost cooled cupcakes; decorate as desired.

YIELD: 2 dozen.

PUMPKIN TRIFLE

Lyla Lehenbauer, New London, Missouri

This impressive trifle looks so elegant with alternating layers of gingerbread cake and a blend of pumpkin and butterscotch pudding. Try making it ahead of time for a fuss-free dessert when you're planning to entertain guests.

1	package (14½ ounces) gingerbread cake mix
1¼	cups water
1	egg
4	cups cold milk
4	packages (1 ounce *each*) instant butterscotch pudding mix
1	can (15 ounces) solid-pack pumpkin
1	teaspoon ground cinnamon
¼	teaspoon *each* ground ginger, nutmeg and allspice
1	carton (12 ounces) frozen whipped topping, thawed

In a mixing bowl, combine the cake mix, water and egg; mix well. Pour into an ungreased 8-in. square baking pan. Bake at 350° for 35-40 minutes or until a toothpick inserted near the center comes out clean. Cool for 10 minutes before removing from pan to a wire rack. When completely cooled, crumble the cake. Set aside ¼ cup crumbs for garnish.

ghostly good desserts

SWEET JACK-O'-LANTERNS

Hannah Bjerkseth, Three Hills, Alberta

There's no trick to making these Halloween-flavored cupcakes. By using a convenient cake mix, you can turn them out in a jiffy. Simplify them even more with canned frosting.

1   package (18¼ ounces) yellow cake mix *or* cake mix of your choice

3¾   cups confectioners' sugar

3   tablespoons butter, softened

⅔   to ¾ cup milk

1   to 1½ teaspoons orange paste food coloring

4   green gumdrops

12   black jujubes

Prepare and bake cake according to package directions for cupcakes. Fill 24 greased muffin cups two-thirds full. Bake at 350° for 15-18 minutes or until a toothpick comes out clean. Cool for 5 minutes before removing from the pans to wire racks to cool completely.

For frosting, in a small bowl, combine confectioners' sugar, butter and enough milk to achieve spreading consistency. Stir in food coloring. Cut a thin slice off the top of each cupcake. Spread frosting on 12 cupcakes. Invert remaining cupcakes and place on top; frost top and sides.

For stems, cut each gumdrop into three lengthwise wedges; place one piece on top of each cupcake. Cut jujubes into thin slices; use a bottom slice for each mouth. From remaining slices, cut one large triangle and two smaller ones. Position two small triangles and a large triangle on each cupcake for eyes and nose.

YIELD: 1 dozen.

and salt; add to chocolate mixture. Stir in walnuts. Pour into a greased 9-in. pie plate. Bake at 350° for 28-30 minutes or until a toothpick inserted near the center comes out clean. Cool on a wire rack.

For fudge sauce, heat chocolate chips, milk, sugar and butter in a microwave or double boiler until chocolate and butter are melted; stir until smooth. Drizzle some over pie. Cut into wedges; serve with ice cream and additional sauce.

YIELD: 6-8 servings.

BROWNIE PIE A LA MODE

Beverly Thornton, Cortlandt Manor, New York

This is a quick dessert recipe for when you need something good and chocolaty. Cutting them into wedges and topping them with fudge sauce dresses them up.

$1/2$	cup sugar
2	tablespoons butter
2	tablespoons water
$1^1/2$	cups semisweet chocolate chips
2	eggs
1	teaspoon vanilla extract
$2/3$	cup all-purpose flour
$1/4$	teaspoon baking soda
$1/4$	teaspoon salt
$3/4$	cup chopped walnuts

FUDGE SAUCE:

1	cup (6 ounces) semisweet chocolate chips
$1/2$	cup evaporated milk
$1/4$	cup sugar
1	tablespoon butter

Vanilla ice cream

In a small saucepan over medium heat, bring sugar, butter and water to a boil. Remove from the heat; stir in chocolate chips until melted. In a mixing bowl, beat eggs and vanilla. Add chocolate mixture; mix well. Combine flour, baking soda

PUMPKIN CHIFFON PIE

Linda Gartner, Feasterville, Pennsylvania

This delicious pie is so light and fluffy that folks will have room for a slice no matter how full they are! Guests are always delighted with the delicate flavor.

1	envelope unflavored gelatin
$1/2$	cup cold water
$3/4$	cup milk
1	cup packed brown sugar
1	cup canned pumpkin
$1/2$	teaspoon ground ginger
$1/2$	teaspoon ground cinnamon
$1/4$	teaspoon salt
$1^1/2$	cups whipped topping
1	graham cracker crust (9 inches)

In a small bowl, sprinkle the gelatin over cold water; let stand for 1 minute. In a saucepan, heat the milk over medium heat until bubbles form around sides of saucepan. Add gelatin mixture; stir until dissolved. Stir in the brown sugar until dissolved. Remove from the heat. Add the pumpkin, ginger, cinnamon and salt; mix well. Refrigerate until thickened, about $1^1/2$ hours.

Fold whipped topping into pumpkin mixture. Pour into crust. Refrigerate for at least 4 hours or until firm. Refrigerate leftovers.

YIELD: 6-8 servings.

ghostly good desserts

BUTTERSCOTCH PECAN DESSERT

Becky Harrison, Albion, Illinois

Light and creamy, this terrific treat never lasts long when I serve it. The fluffy cream cheese layer topped with cool butterscotch pudding is a lip-smacking combination.

1/2	cup cold butter
1	cup all-purpose flour
3/4	cup chopped pecans, *divided*
1	package (8 ounces) cream cheese, softened
1	cup confectioners' sugar
1	carton (8 ounces) frozen whipped topping, thawed, *divided*
31/2	cups milk
2	packages (3.4 or 3.5 ounces *each*) instant butterscotch *or* vanilla pudding mix

In a bowl, cut the butter into the flour until crumbly; stir in 1/2 cup pecans. Press into an ungreased 13-in. x 9-in. x 2-in. baking pan. Bake at 350° for 20 minutes or until lightly browned. Cool.

In a mixing bowl, beat the cream cheese and sugar until fluffy. Fold in 1 cup whipped topping; spread over crust. Combine the milk and pudding mix until smooth; pour over cream cheese layer. Refrigerate for 15-20 minutes or until set. Top with the remaining whipped topping and pecans. Refrigerate for 1-2 hours.

YIELD: 16-20 servings.

SWEET POTATO LAYER CAKE

Christy Shepard, Marion, North Carolina

This cake is a hit with everyone who eats a piece. The coconut-pecan frosting is especially good!

11/2	cups canola oil
2	cups sugar
4	eggs, *separated*
11/2	cups finely shredded uncooked sweet potato (about 1 medium)
1/4	cup hot water
1	teaspoon vanilla extract
21/2	cups cake flour
3	teaspoons baking powder
1	teaspoon ground cinnamon
1	teaspoon ground nutmeg
1/4	teaspoon salt
1	cup chopped pecans

FROSTING:

1/2	cup butter
11/3	cups sugar
2	cans (5 ounces *each*) evaporated milk
4	egg yolks, beaten
22/3	cups flaked coconut
1	cup chopped pecans
2	teaspoons vanilla extract

In a mixing bowl, beat oil and sugar. Add egg yolks, one at a time, beating well after each addition. Add sweet potato, water and vanilla; mix well. In a small mixing bowl, beat egg whites until stiff; fold into sweet potato mixture. Combine flour, baking powder, cinnamon, nutmeg and salt; add to potato mixture. Stir in pecans. Pour into three greased 9-in. round cake pans. Bake at 350° for 22-27 minutes or until a toothpick inserted near the center comes out clean. Cool for 10 minutes; remove to wire racks.

For frosting, melt the butter in a saucepan; whisk in sugar, milk and egg yolks until smooth. Cook and stir over medium heat for 10-12 minutes or until thickened and bubbly. Remove from the heat; stir in the coconut, pecans and vanilla. Cool slightly. Place one cake layer on a serving plate; spread with a third of the frosting. Repeat layers.

YIELD: 10-12 servings.

spirited shindigs

APPLE-RAISIN BUNDT CAKE

Maryellen Hays, Wolcottville, Indiana

This moist, old-fashioned dessert has a pleasant blend of spices and is loaded with nuts and raisins.

- $3/4$ cup butter, softened
- $1^1/2$ cups sugar
- 1 cup plus 2 tablespoons strawberry jam
- $3^1/3$ cups all-purpose flour
- $1^1/2$ teaspoons baking soda
- $1^1/2$ teaspoons ground nutmeg
- $3/4$ teaspoon *each* ground allspice, cloves and cinnamon
- $1^1/2$ cups buttermilk
- $1^3/4$ cups raisins
- $3/4$ cup chopped walnuts
- $3/4$ cup chopped peeled apple

GLAZE:

- 1 cup confectioners' sugar
- 4 teaspoons milk

In a large mixing bowl, cream the butter and sugar. Stir in the jam. Combine the flour, baking soda and spices; beat into creamed mixture alternately with buttermilk. Add the raisins, walnuts and apple; mix well. Pour into a greased and floured 10-in. fluted tube pan.

Bake at 350° for 1 hour or until a toothpick inserted near the center comes out clean. Cool for 10 minutes before removing from pan to a wire rack to cool completely. Combine glaze ingredients; drizzle over cake.

YIELD: 12-16 servings.

PUMPKIN-FACE ICE CREAM SANDWICHES

Pattie Ann Forssberg, Logan, Kansas

These friendly faces will elicit smiles from friends and family. You can use homemade or purchased sugar cookies.

- 3 tablespoons butter, softened
- $1^1/2$ cups confectioners' sugar
- $1/2$ teaspoon vanilla extract
- 1 to 2 tablespoons milk
- Red and yellow food coloring
- 48 round sugar cookies
- 72 raisins
- Red and green decorating icing
- 1 quart vanilla ice cream, softened

In a small mixing bowl, combine the butter, confectioners' sugar, vanilla and enough milk to achieve spreading consistency. Tint orange with red and yellow food coloring. Frost the tops of 24 sugar cookies. Make pumpkin faces, using raisins for eyes and nose. Add a smile with red icing and stem with green icing. Let dry completely.

Spoon ice cream onto bottom of plain cookies; top with frosted cookies. Place in individual plastic bags; seal. Freeze until serving.

YIELD: 2 dozen.

PUMPKIN ICE CREAM

Linda Young, Longmont, Colorado

This delicious ice cream really captures the flavor of fall. Enjoy it alone or with gingersnaps.

- 1 cup canned pumpkin
- $1/4$ teaspoon pumpkin pie spice
- 1 quart vanilla ice cream, softened
- Gingersnaps, optional

In a large bowl, combine the pumpkin and pie spice until well blended. Stir in ice cream. Freeze until serving. Garnish with gingersnaps if desired.

YIELD: 4-6 servings.

ghostly good desserts

frightfully fun crafts

JUST as important as the festive foods at Halloween are the devilishly fun decorations that go along with it! The creepy crafts, creative costumes and scarecrow styling ideas on the following pages will help you set an unforgettable All Hallows' Eve atmosphere.

GIFT BAGS

To hold trick-or-treat candy or party favors, these bags will be a hit on Halloween.

1. Purchase inexpensive gift bags in Halloween colors, such as orange, black, purple and green.

2. Use craft foam cutouts, chenille stems, cheese cloth and wiggle eyes to create decorative trims on the bags.

PINT JAR LUMINARIES

Shine a little light on a mantle or tabletop with these cute candle holders.

1. Paint the outside of a pint-size glass canning jar orange, purple or black.

2. Cut Halloween motifs from fabric.

3. Glue motifs around jar.

4. Place a votive pot and votive candle into jar with jar rim supporting votive holder.

5. Wrap a narrow torn fabric strip or strands of raffia around top of jar. Tie ends in a small bow or an overhand knot.

MARBLE/SPIDERWEB PUMPKIN

For a delightfully different way to carve a pumpkin, try this special method, which uses clear glass marbles to create a decorative web.

1. Cut an opening in the bottom of a pumpkin and remove the seeds.

2. Draw a spiderweb and spider on a piece of tracing paper.

3. Hold the pattern on the pumpkin with a couple of push pins. Use another push pin to pierce the pattern and transfer the design onto the pumpkin. Gently carve away the outside of the pumpkin following the pin holes to create the solid lines. Use a small drill to drill holes where desired. Insert clear marbles into the drilled holes. Carve away the shell of the pumpkin to create the spider's body and press marbles into the carved-out area.

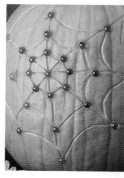

4. Place a string of white mini lights in the bottom of the pumpkin.

5. Add leaves around the bottom of the pumpkin.

GLUE-STICK SPIDERWEBS

Making these spiderwebs is child's play by using everyday glue sticks!

1. Use a black marker to draw a spiderweb on a piece of paper for pattern.

2. Place parchment paper over pattern.

3. Using a glue gun and glue sticks, apply glue over spiderweb pattern. If desired, sprinkle spiderweb with iridescent glitter before glue dries.

4. Hang from ceiling with monofilament thread in front of a dark velvet curtain.

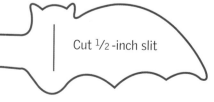

BAT NAPKIN RING (for one)

1. Trace pattern below onto tracing paper.

2. Cut shape from black felt.

3. Cut slit where shown on pattern.

4. Glue a 1/2-inch black pom-pom to bat for body, being careful not to glue slit closed.

5. Glue two yellow seed beads to bat's head for eyes.

6. With right side out, slip opposite end of wing through slit.

7. Insert napkin into napkin ring.

HALLOWEEN PHOTO ALBUM

Forever capture Halloween memories in this dressed-up mini-photo album.

1. Use a small piece of household sponge and orange and gold acrylic craft paint to sponge-paint the outside of a purchased mini-photo album.

2. Adhere Halloween motif fabric right side up to double-stick adhesive.

3. Cut out desired designs.

4. Remove backing from double-stick adhesive and attach fabric right side up on front of photo album.

5. Adhere "Trick or Treat" craft foam lettering to spine of photo album.

BAT NAPKIN RING PATTERN
Trace 1—tracing paper
Cut 1—black felt
Cut slit
Enlarge pattern 50%

Cut 1/2 -inch slit

frightfully fun crafts

BLACK VOTIVE CAULDRON

These "terror-ific" candle holders are sure to shed just the right spooky light on your Halloween party snack table!

1. Paint a jelly jar black.

2. Spray a clear votive holder with crystal spray or sponge paint with white paint.

3. Place a small amount of polyester fiberfill inside black jar and stretch it out to cover outside of jar as shown.

4. Place votive holder in opening of jar.

5. Add plastic spiders where desired.

POM-POM CATS

Kids of all ages will have fun making these funny black cats.

1. Glue two 1½-inch black pom-poms together for the head and body of cat. Glue four ½-inch black pom-poms to cat's body for legs.

2. Cut two small triangles of black felt and two smaller triangles of pink felt. Glue a pink felt piece to one side of each black felt piece for ears. Glue ear pieces to top of cat's head.

3. Glue two wiggle eyes to cat's head.

4. Cut three 1½-inch-long pieces of nylon fishing line for whiskers. Glue center of the whiskers together and add a 3mm pink pom-pom as shown in photo. Glue whiskers and nose to front of cat's head.

5. Glue a ½-inch-long piece of green chenille stem to a 1-inch orange pom-pom for the stem of the pumpkin. Glue the pumpkin to the front of the cat.

GHOSTLY TABLETOP

Nella Parker, Hershey, Michigan

To create a spooky atmosphere and set the mood for a Halloween party, I transformed my table into a ghost.

1. Place a pumpkin in the middle of the table and spread a white sheet evenly over the pumpkin and tabletop.

2. Using white string, gather the fabric at the base of the pumpkin to resemble a ghost.

3. To make the face, cut out eyes and mouth from black felt and glue them on. If you wish, cut out felt bats, spiders, etc. to scatter on the table.

PERKY PUMPKIN CENTERPIECE

Lisa Habig, Beallsville, Ohio

Pumpkin tier decorations are easy to make and receive many compliments.

1. Find three pumpkins, each slightly smaller than the other, to stack.

2. Scoop out the insides of the two bottom pumpkins and throw away their lids.

3. Insert dried flowers or leaves between each tier and place the small whole pumpkin on top as the finishing touch.

4. This centerpiece doesn't keep well in a warm house, so make it the day of your party or place it on the porch or by a gate.

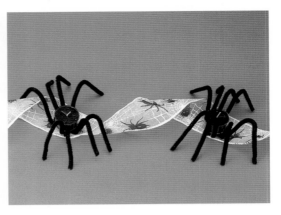

FRANKENSTEIN
TREAT HOLDER

Loretta Mateik, Petaluma, California

Quick to make, these clay pot candy holders are sure to bring a smile.

1. Paint the outside of a 2 1/2 -inch-diameter clay pot black.

2. Paint a green rectangle on one side of clay pot for face as shown in photo.

3. Paint two 1/2 -inch wooden balls and a 1/4 -inch furniture plug green for ears and nose.

4. With a nearly dry brush and red paint, add cheeks to face. Use black fine-line marker to add eyes and remaining details.

5. Glue ears and nose to face.

6. Use a liner brush to add white highlights to nose and eyes and to add stripes around the top of the clay pot.

7. Drill holes in sides of pot. Thread buttons onto craft wire for handle. Insert wire through holes and twist to secure.

8. Place a plastic portion cup inside pot. Fill pot with candy.

SPIDERS ON
SPIDER RIBBON

This table decoration will be a "run-away" hit at your Halloween gathering.

1. Place a length of wire-edge spider-motif ribbon down the length of a table.

2. Twist four black chenille stems together at the center. Shape each end to make eight spider legs.

3. Place the spiders along the ribbon and add a black tea light candle to the center of each spider.

POPCORN BALL GHOSTS

These ghoulish guys can serve as decorations and then go home with guests as favors.

1. Prepare or purchase popcorn balls or Rice Krispies Treats. Insert a wooden skewer into each popcorn ball or mold each Rice Krispies Treat around a skewer.

2. Wrap ball with plastic wrap.

3. Center a white cloth napkin over wrapped ball and fasten with a white chenille stem.

4. Cut out small circles for eyes and small ovals for mouths from black construction paper. Glue eyes and mouths to one side of each ball as shown in photo.

5. Stand each in a glass and drape napkin around to hide the glass.

GOURD GHOST FAMILY

This frightful family is a simple centerpiece that's bound to get your guests in the "spirit" of the holiday.

1. Cover a Styrofoam disk with dried moss.

2. Use a black marker to draw two small oval eyes and a larger oval mouth on one side of each white gourd as shown in photo above.

3. Press each gourd into moss-covered disk, making sure each stands upright. Glue as needed to hold.

freaky fact

For retailers, Halloween is a $7 billion industry, with $2 billion coming from the sale of candy.

Bewitching Bashes

CONTENTS

Bewitching Bashes

SPECIAL THANKS
Costumes/Face Painting Photography: Christine Bronico, RR Donnelly; **Additional Photography:** Getty Images, PhotoDisc, JupiterImages, Veer, Punchstock, Doug Croll; **Costume/Face Paint Models:** Alex D., Alex V., Anneli, Davis, Emily, Erin, Hayley, Leo, Luca, Lucy, Mackenzie, Mikaela, Nicholas, Pasquale, Rebecca, Samantha; **Makeup Styling/Face Painting:** Joel Mendenhall and Sadiya Sellers; **Face Painting Kits:** Douglas Drake at Wolfe Brothers Face Art & FX (available at retail outlets and on-line at www.wolfefxproducts.com); **Costume Creation:** Catherine Alston; **Donations:** Julie Ewert and Jeanne Jansch from Michaels, The Arts and Crafts Store (www.michaels.com) for the craft pumpkins and gourds; **Craft Designers:** Alison Palmer Dupree, Richard Erdman II, Suzanne Gaffney, Patricia Graham, Tamara Kirkman, Diane Napolitano; **Additional Thanks To:** Chris Tipton, Deborah Bechtler, Kirk Beason, Roxanne Knoll, Connie Tuccito, Erick Swindell, Elizabeth Tunnicliffe

SNACKS & BEVERAGES

Keep your BOO-rific party guests mingling by providing them with an array of these simple-to-make finger foods. Add a spooky or warming fall beverage to top it all off. You'll win raves and have time to enjoy yourself, too.

BOO-rific black bean dip with chips

Taste of Home Test Kitchen

Your goblin guests will devour this cute chips and dip combo from our home economists. The peppers add a little kick and the beans pack a nutritional punch—much needed on a holiday centered around sweets! Try different Halloween cookie cutters to add a variety of shapes to the chip selection.

9	flour tortillas (7 inches)
2-1/4	teaspoons Mexican seasoning
4	bacon strips, diced
1/4	cup each chopped onion, sweet red and green pepper
2	garlic cloves, minced
2	cans (15 ounces each) black beans, rinsed and drained, *divided*
2/3	cup picante sauce
2	tablespoons lime juice
2	teaspoons minced chipotle pepper in adobo sauce
1	teaspoon ground cumin
1/2	teaspoon salt
2	tablespoons minced fresh cilantro

1 Carefully cut tortillas with a 3-in. ghost-shaped cookie cutter. Place on baking sheets coated with nonstick cooking spray. Spritz tortillas with nonstick cooking spray; sprinkle with Mexican seasoning. Bake at 350° for 8-10 minutes or until edges just begin to brown. Remove to wire racks to cool.

2 In a skillet, cook bacon over medium heat until crisp. Remove to paper towels; drain, reserving 2 teaspoons drippings. In the drippings, saute onion and peppers until tender. Add garlic; saute 1 minute longer.

3 Add one can of beans and mash. Add the picante sauce, lime juice, chipotle peppers, cumin, salt and remaining beans; heat through. Stir in bacon and cilantro. Serve with ghost chips.

Yield: 3 cups dip and 3 dozen chips.

magic potion punch

Michelle Thomas, Bangor, Maine

At a Halloween party, the more creepy the food, the better! I like to tuck gummy worms into an ice ring when I make this great green punch.

2	packages (3 ounces *each*) lime gelatin
1/2	cup sugar
1	cup boiling water
3	cups cold water
1	quart non-carbonated lemon-lime drink, chilled
1-1/2	quarts lemon-lime soda, chilled

1 Dissolve gelatin and sugar in boiling water; add cold water. Transfer to a punch bowl. Stir in lemon-lime drink and soda.

Yield: about 4 quarts.

confetti cheese salsa

Deidra Engle, Aledo, Illinois

This creamy cheese dip is so quick and easy that it can be served in any season, but it's always a big hit at Fourth of July picnics. I never have to worry about covering the dish on the picnic table because the mixture disappears in a snap.

2	cups (8 ounces) finely shredded cheddar cheese
2	cups (8 ounces) shredded part-skim mozzarella cheese
2	large tomatoes, seeded and chopped
1	medium green pepper, diced
1	small cucumber, seeded and diced
1	small onion, chopped
1	bottle (8 ounces) ranch salad dressing
2	tablespoons salsa

Corn *or* tortilla chips

1 In a large bowl, combine the first six ingredients. Combine the salad dressing and salsa; pour over cheese mixture and toss gently. Serve with chips. Refrigerate leftovers.

Yield: 7 cups.

festive pumpkin dip

Evelyn Kennell, Roanoke, Illinois

Surprise party guests with this festive fall hors d'oeuvre. Served in a round bread bowl, it'll make an attractive addition to your buffet table. Surround the bread bowl with veggies (as shown) and place a basket of assorted crackers next to it. You'll find that the dip will be gone in no time at all!

12	ounces cream cheese, softened
3/4	cup canned pumpkin
2	tablespoons taco seasoning mix
1/8	teaspoon garlic powder
1/3	cup chopped dried beef
1/3	cup chopped green pepper
1/3	cup chopped sweet red pepper
1	can (2-1/4 ounces) sliced ripe olives, drained
1	round loaf (1 pound) Italian *or* pumpernickel bread

Fresh vegetables, crackers *or* corn chips

1 In a mixing bowl, beat cream cheese, pumpkin, taco seasoning and garlic powder until smooth. Stir in beef, peppers and olives. Cover and refrigerate until ready to serve.

2 Just before serving, cut top off bread; scoop out bread from inside, leaving a 1/2-in. shell (save the bread from inside to make croutons or bread crumbs or save for another use). Fill shell with cream cheese mixture. Serve with vegetables, crackers or corn chips.

Yield: 3 cups.

FUNNY BONE!

What did one ghost say to the other ghost? "Do you believe in people?"

orange-glazed chicken wings

Holly Mann, Amherst, New Hampshire

I normally don't care for wings, but after I tried this recipe that was shared by a co-worker, it changed my mind. A simple overnight marinade coats the wings to create a lovely glaze when baked.

3	pounds chicken wings
1-1/2	cups soy sauce
1	cup orange juice
1	teaspoon garlic powder

1 Cut chicken wings into three sections; discard wing tips. In a large resealable plastic bag, combine the soy sauce, orange juice and garlic powder; add wings. Seal bag and turn to coat. Refrigerate overnight.

2 Drain and discard marinade. Place chicken wings in a greased foil-lined 15-in. x 10-in. x 1-in. baking pan. Bake at 350° for 1 hour or until juices run clear and glaze is set, turning twice.

Yield: 2-1/2 dozen.

Editor's Note: 3 pounds of uncooked chicken wing sections (wingettes) may be substituted for the whole chicken wings. Omit the first step.

Trick-or-Treat

The tradition of trick-or-treating probably dates back to the early All Souls' Day parades in England. During the festivities, poor citizens begged for food and wealthier families would give them pastries called "soul cakes" in return for a promise to pray for the family's dead relatives.

orange party punch

Brenda Rupert, Clyde, Ohio

This citrus punch was served at every birthday party I had when I was growing up. Now I prepare this fun, frothy drink for my kids.

1	can (12 ounces) frozen orange juice concentrate, thawed
2	liters lemon-lime soda, chilled
1	can (46 ounces) pineapple juice, chilled
1	quart orange *or* pineapple sherbet

1 Prepare orange juice according to package directions; pour into a punch bowl. Stir in soda and pineapple juice. Top with scoops of sherbet. Serve immediately.

Yield: 5-1/2 quarts.

Editor's Note: If you plan on serving this punch in a cauldron, (as shown) make sure it's plastic, not metal. Metal will react with the citrus in the punch resulting in a metallic flavor.

scarecrow veggie pizza

Taste of Home Test Kitchen

At harvest parties, fall festivals or any autumn event, the flavorful fellow here will raise a crop of smiles! Our cooks shaped a scarecrow using red peppers, carrots, broccoli and lots of other fresh veggies. Since you can make the crust with refrigerated dough and quickly prepare a cream cheese spread to put on top, you'll be ready to form your own colorful character in no time.

1	tube (10 ounces) refrigerated pizza dough
1	package (8 ounces) cream cheese, softened
6	tablespoons mayonnaise
3/4	teaspoon dill weed
1/2	teaspoon garlic salt
1/2	teaspoon dried minced onion
1/4	teaspoon onion salt
1	small sweet red pepper
1	small green pepper
1/4	cup shredded Swiss cheese
1	small carrot, chopped
10	fresh green beans
5	pieces Wheat Chex
1	large mushroom, halved
1	small head cauliflower, chopped
1/2	cup chopped broccoli
1	pattypan squash, halved
2	green onion tops, cut into strips
1/4	cup chow mein noodles

1 Press pizza dough onto a greased 14-in. pizza pan. Bake at 400° for 10 minutes or until golden brown. Cool on a wire rack.

2 In a small mixing bowl, combine the cream cheese, mayonnaise, dill, garlic salt, onion and onion salt. Spread over cooled crust.

3 To make the scarecrow, refer to the photo at left for the size of vegetable pieces and the position of pieces on pizza.

4 From a small piece of red pepper, cut a narrow smile for mouth and a triangle for nose. Chop remaining red pepper and set aside. Cut one ring from green pepper for the scarecrow's head. Chop remaining green pepper and set aside.

5 Position green pepper ring on pizza for the scarecrow's head. Fill with shredded Swiss cheese. Place two carrot pieces on face for eyes. Add red pepper nose and mouth on face.

6 Use green beans to create the outline of a shirt and bib overalls below head where shown in the photo.

7 Combine chopped red pepper and remaining chopped carrot. Sprinkle on pizza to fill in the shirt. Use chopped green pepper to fill in bib overalls.

8 Place cereal on the elbows, knees and bib of overalls for patches. Add a mushroom half at the bottom of each pants leg for shoes. Arrange cauliflower around scarecrow for sky. Arrange broccoli at the bottom for grass.

9 Place one squash half above head for hat. Cut the remaining portion of squash in half again. Place green onion strips and one squash quarter on each side of scarecrow for corn and husks.

10 For straw, place chow mein noodles below hat, on each side of neck, at the end of each arm and above shoes.

Yield: 10-12 servings.

Halloween Facts

The U.S. Census Bureau estimated that there were 36 million potential trick-or-treaters (5- to 13-year-olds) ready to go in 2009. Of course, many other children—older than 13 and younger than age 5—also go trick-or-treating. This mob of candy-loving kids has 111.3 million (the number of occupied housing units across the nation in 2009) possible stops to make.

cider cheese fondue

Kim Marie Van Rheenen, Mendota, Illinois

Cheese lovers are sure to enjoy dipping into this creamy, quick-to-fix fondue that has just a hint of apple. You can also serve this appetizer with apple or pear wedges.

3/4	cup apple cider *or* apple juice
2	cups (8 ounces) shredded cheddar cheese
1	cup (4 ounces) shredded Swiss cheese
1	tablespoon cornstarch
1/8	teaspoon pepper
1	loaf (1 pound) French bread, cut into cubes

1 In a large saucepan, bring cider to a boil. Reduce heat to medium-low. Toss the cheeses with cornstarch and pepper; stir into cider. Cook and stir for 3-4 minutes or until cheese is melted. Transfer to a small ceramic fondue pot or slow cooker; keep warm. Serve with bread cubes.

Yield: 2-2/3 cups.

hot spiced cider

Kim Wallace, Dover, Ohio

Next time you're entertaining, stir up a batch of this nicely spiced cider. The wonderful aroma will make your guests feel welcome on a chilly day.

1	gallon apple cider *or* apple juice
1	cup orange juice
1/4	cup maple syrup
1/2	teaspoon orange extract
1/2	teaspoon lemon extract
4	cinnamon sticks
2	teaspoons whole cloves
1	teaspoon whole allspice

1 In a Dutch oven, combine the first five ingredients. Place the cinnamon sticks, cloves and allspice on a double thickness of cheesecloth; bring up corners of cloth and tie with string to form a bag. Add to the pan. Cook, uncovered, over medium heat for 10-15 minutes or until flavors are blended (do not boil). Discard spice bag.

Yield: 4-1/2 quarts.

FUNNY BONE!
What is a skeleton's favorite musical instrument? A trombone.

roasted pumpkin seeds

Taste of Home Test Kitchen

Try this zippy twist on a Halloween tradition from our home economists. It's got just enough heat to take the chill off autumn afternoons.

2	cups pumpkin seeds
5	teaspoons butter, melted
1	teaspoon Worcestershire sauce
1	teaspoon sugar
1/2	teaspoon salt
1/4	teaspoon garlic powder
1/8	to 1/4 teaspoon cayenne pepper

1 In a bowl, toss pumpkin seeds with butter and Worcestershire sauce. Combine the sugar, salt, garlic powder and cayenne; sprinkle over seeds and toss to coat.

2 Line a 15-in. x 10-in. x 1-in. baking pan with foil; coat the foil with nonstick cooking spray. Spread seeds in pan. Bake at 250° for 45-60 minutes or until seeds are dry and lightly browned, stirring every 15 minutes. Cool completely. Store in an airtight container.

Yield: 2 cups.

hot 'n' spicy cranberry dip

Marian Platt, Sequim, Washington

If you want to make this appetizer for a large buffet crowd, double the recipe and use a 16-ounce can of cranberry sauce. Be sure to have extra copies of the recipe—guests will ask for it!

3/4	cup jellied cranberry sauce
1	to 2 tablespoons prepared horseradish
1	tablespoon honey
1-1/2	teaspoons lemon juice
1-1/2	teaspoons Worcestershire sauce
1/8	to 1/4 teaspoon cayenne pepper
1	garlic clove, minced

Miniature hot dogs *or* smoked sausage links, warmed

Sliced apples *or* pears

1 In a small saucepan, combine the first seven ingredients; bring to a boil, stirring constantly. Reduce heat. Cover and simmer for 5 minutes, stirring occasionally. Serve warm with sausage and/or fruit.

Yield: 3/4 cup.

FUNNY BONE!

What do you use to mend a broken jack-o'-lantern? A pumpkin patch.

lime fruit slushies

Linda Horst, Newville, Pennsylvania

These frosty drinks have a bright green color and refreshing flavor. Divide the mixture between two plastic containers before freezing. They'll thaw to a nice slushy consistency.

3/4	cup sugar
1	package (3 ounces) lime gelatin
1	cup boiling water
3	cups cold water
3	cups unsweetened pineapple juice
1	can (6 ounces) frozen orange juice concentrate, thawed
1	liter ginger ale, chilled

1 In a large container, dissolve sugar and gelatin in boiling water. Stir in the cold water, pineapple juice and orange juice concentrate. Freeze.

2 Remove from the freezer 1-2 hours before serving. Transfer to a punch bowl; stir in the ginger ale.

Yield: 12 servings.

shrunken apple heads in citrus cider

Annette Engelbert, Bruce Crossing, Michigan

Granny Smith apples shaped like shrunken heads will surprise even the scariest goblins at your Halloween bash. And the cool cider is so refreshing.

1	cup lemon juice
1	tablespoon salt
4	large Granny Smith apples
16	whole cloves
1	gallon apple cider
1	can (12 ounces) frozen lemonade concentrate, thawed

1 In a small bowl, combine lemon juice and salt; set aside. Peel apples. Cut each apple from the stem to the blossom end; discard seeds and core. Using a sharp knife, carefully carve a face on the rounded side of each apple half. After carving, dip each apple in lemon juice mixture for 1 minute. Drain on paper towels.

2 Arrange apple heads on a rack in a shallow baking pan. Bake at 250° for 2 hours or until apples begin to dry and shrink and are lightly browned on the edges. Cool on a wire rack. Insert cloves for eyes. Store in the refrigerator.

3 Just before serving, combine cider and lemonade in a punch bowl. Float shrunken apple heads in cider.

Yield: 4 apple heads and about 1 gallon cider.

festive cranberry drink

Dixie Terry, Goreville, Illinois
Served hot or cold, this cranberry drink is so delicious. I found the recipe in my late mother-in-law's collection, handwritten, probably by one of her woman's club friends.

4	cups fresh *or* frozen cranberries
3	quarts water, *divided*
1-3/4	cups sugar
1	cup orange juice
2/3	cup lemon juice
1/2	cup red-hot candies
12	whole cloves

1 In a Dutch oven or large kettle, combine cranberries and 1 qt. water. Cook over medium heat until the berries pop, about 15 minutes. Remove from the heat. Strain through a fine strainer, pressing mixture with a spoon; discard skins. Return cranberry pulp and juice to the pan.

2 Stir in the sugar, juices, red-hots and remaining water. Place cloves on a double thickness of cheesecloth. Bring up corners of cloth and tie with kitchen string to form a bag; add to juice mixture. Bring to a boil; cook and stir until sugar and red-hots are dissolved.

3 Remove from the heat. Strain through a fine mesh sieve or cheesecloth. Discard spice bag. Serve drink warm or cold.

Yield: 3 quarts.

mummy man cheese spread

Rebecca Eremich, Barberton, Ohio
My annual Halloween bash wouldn't be the same without the now famous Mummy Man. When kids first see Mummy Man, they wonder if they can actually eat him. I assure them they can, and we hack off a foot or an arm with some crackers.

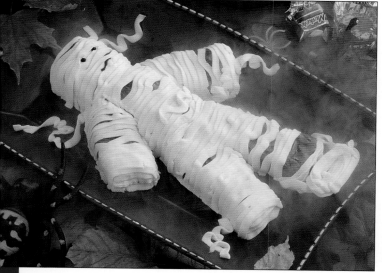

2	port wine cheese logs (12 ounces *each*)
1	package (8 ounces) cream cheese, softened
1	tablespoon milk
2	whole peppercorns
1	pimiento strip

1 Cut cheese logs into pieces for mummy's head, body, arms and legs; arrange on a serving plate.

2 In small mixing bowl, beat cream cheese and milk. Cut a small hole in the corner of a pastry or plastic bag; insert basket weave tip #47. Pipe rows across the mummy, creating bandages. Add peppercorns for eyes and pimiento strip for mouth. Chill until serving.

Yield: 24 servings.

slow cooker mexican dip

Heather Courtney, Ames, Iowa

My husband, Jamie, and I love to entertain, and this hearty, 7-ingredient dip is always a hit...as well as a request. It couldn't be much easier to put together, and using our slow cooker leaves us free to share some quality time with our guests. After all, isn't that the purpose of a party?

1-1/2	pounds ground beef
1	pound bulk hot Italian sausage
1	cup chopped onion
1	package (8.8 ounces) ready-to-serve Spanish rice
1	can (16 ounces) refried beans
1	can (10 ounces) enchilada sauce
1	pound process cheese (Velveeta), cubed
1	package tortilla chip scoops

1 In a Dutch oven, cook the beef, sausage and onion over medium heat until meat is no longer pink; drain. Heat rice according to the package directions.

2 In a 3-qt. slow cooker, combine the meat mixture, rice, beans, enchilada sauce and cheese. Cover and cook on low for 1-1/2 to 2 hours or until cheese is melted. Serve with tortilla scoops.

Yield: 8 cups.

parmesan party mix

Karen Smith, Thornton, Colorado

This is our favorite mix. The combination of seasonings gives it just the right flavor, and it's a snap to toss together.

7	cups Crispix
2	cups cheese-flavored snack crackers
1	cup pretzel sticks
3	tablespoons olive oil
1	teaspoon Italian seasoning
1/4	teaspoon fennel seed, crushed
1/8	teaspoon hot pepper sauce
1/2	cup grated Parmesan *or* Romano cheese

1 In a 2-gal. resealable plastic bag, combine the cereal, crackers and pretzels. In a small bowl, combine the oil, Italian seasoning, fennel seed and hot pepper sauce. Pour over cereal mixture; seal bag and toss to coat. Add Parmesan or Romano cheese; seal bag and toss to coat. Store in an airtight container.

Yield: 8 cups.

FUNNY BONE!
What is a ghost's favorite brand of automobile? A Boo-ick.

BUFFETS

Your party spread will be unforgettable when you use recipes from this special, Halloween-only chapter. From sweet treats to hearty, savory dishes, you'll find what you need to satisfy your Halloween crowd.

the great pumpkin cakes

Sharon Skildum, Maple Grove, Minnesota
This is the ultimate confectionery tribute to Charlie Brown's Great Pumpkin. These little round cakes are surprisingly easy—they're just two cupcakes put together! Just frost and decorate with vines and leaves. Create a pumpkin patch scene (as shown) by sprinkling crushed chocolate wafer cookies on top of a prepared sheet cake. You'll win raves!

1	package (18-1/4 ounces) yellow cake mix *or* cake mix of your choice
2	cans (16 ounces *each*) vanilla frosting, *divided*
1	to 1-1/2 teaspoons orange paste food coloring
12	green gumdrops
1/2	teaspoon green paste food coloring

1 Prepare cupcakes according to package directions. Fill 24 greased muffin cups two-thirds full. Bake at 350° for 15-18 minutes or until a toothpick comes out clean. Cool for 5 minutes before removing from pans to wire racks to cool completely.

2 For frosting, in a small bowl, combine 1-1/2 cans frosting; tint orange. Cut a thin slice off the top of each cupcake. Spread frosting on 12 cupcakes. Invert remaining cupcakes and place on top; frost top and sides.

3 For stems, place one gumdrop on top of each pumpkin.

4 Tint remaining frosting green. Cut a small hole in the corner of a pastry or plastic bag; insert #5 round tip and fill with a third of green frosting. Pipe curly vines from pumpkin stems. Using remaining green frosting and a #352 leaf tip, pipe leaves randomly along the vines.

Yield: 1 dozen.

halloween gelatin cutouts

Taste of Home Test Kitchen
Kids just love these simple-to-make cutouts. The addition of pudding makes them special, too.

4	packages (3 ounces *each*) orange gelatin
5	cups boiling water, *divided*
4	packages (3 ounces *each*) grape gelatin
2	cups cold milk
2	packages (3.4 ounces *each*) instant vanilla pudding mix

1 In a large bowl, dissolve orange gelatin in 2-1/2 cups boiling water. In another bowl, dissolve grape gelatin in remaining boiling water; set both aside for 30 minutes.

2 In a bowl, whisk milk and pudding mixes until smooth, about 1 minute. Quickly pour half of the pudding into each bowl of gelatin; whisk until well blended. Pour into two 13-in. x 9-in. x 2-in. dishes coated with nonstick cooking spray. Chill for 3 hours or until set. Cut with 2-in. Halloween cookie cutters.

Yield: 4 dozen.

sweet and sour spareribs

Ruth Ann Stelfox, Raymond, Alberta

Just the tempting aroma of these ribs will get your party going. Your guests will especially like the thick, tangy sauce.

5	to 6 pounds pork spareribs
1/2	cup *each* sugar and packed brown sugar
2	tablespoons cornstarch
1	cup ketchup
2/3	cup cider vinegar
1/2	cup cold water

1 Place ribs on a rack in a large shallow roasting pan. Bake, uncovered, at 350° for 1-1/2 hours.

2 Meanwhile, in a small saucepan, combine the sugar, brown sugar, cornstarch, ketchup, vinegar and water until smooth. Bring to a boil. Cook and stir for 1-2 minutes or until thickened. Remove ribs and rack from pan. Drain and discard fat. Return ribs to roasting pan; drizzle 1-1/2 cups sauce over ribs. Bake 30 minutes longer. Cut ribs into serving-size pieces; brush with remaining sauce.

Yield: 5 to 6 servings.

freaky hand sandwiches

Anna Mowan, Spencerville, Indiana

Serve your guests these fun sandwiches and they'll be sure to "hand" out compliments!

2	cups finely chopped cooked chicken
1	small cucumber, finely chopped
2	hard-cooked eggs, finely chopped

1	celery rib, finely chopped
1/3	cup mayonnaise
1/4	teaspoon salt
1/8	teaspoon *each* ground mustard and white pepper
24	slices thin sandwich bread, crusts removed
Sliced almonds	
1	tablespoon spreadable cream cheese
Neon green food coloring	

1 In a small bowl, combine the first eight ingredients. Spread 1/4 cup chicken salad onto 12 bread slices; top with remaining bread.

2 For fingers, cut each of six sandwiches into four 3/4-in. strips. With a small knife, trim one end of each strip, forming a point. For fingernails, attach an almond to each strip with a dab of cream cheese. With a clean paint brush, paint almond nails with green food coloring.

3 From each of the remaining sandwiches, cut out one strip for the thumb and one 2-in. oval for the palm. Trim strips; attach almonds and paint the thumbnails. Arrange one palm, four fingers and a thumb on each plate.

Yield: 6 sandwiches.

FUNNY BONE!

How do you tell twin witches apart? You can't tell which witch is which.

italian vegetable salad

Debbie Laubach, La Prairie, Minnesota

Even our two small children eat their vegetables when I serve this colorful, nutritious combination. To make it a main dish, I'll stir pepperoni slices and cooked cooled pasta into the crunchy, creamy blend.

5	cups fresh broccoli florets (1 large bunch)
5	cups fresh cauliflowerets (1 small head)
4	plum tomatoes, chopped
1	medium cucumber, peeled and sliced
1	medium sweet onion, thinly sliced
1	cup sliced fresh carrots
2	cans (2-1/4 ounces *each*) sliced ripe olives, drained
1/2	cup pimiento-stuffed olives
1	bottle (8 ounces) Italian salad dressing
1	bottle (8 ounces) creamy Italian salad dressing
2	cups (8 ounces) shredded part-skim mozzarella cheese

1 In a large salad bowl, combine the first eight ingredients. Combine salad dressings; pour over vegetable mixture and toss to coat. Cover and refrigerate for at least 4 hours. Stir in cheese just before serving.

Yield: 14 servings.

Halloween Destinations

Traveling for Halloween? North Carolina seems like a great spot, with Transylvania County, Pumpkin Center, and Cape Fear Township in New Hanover County and Cape Fear Township in Chatham County. If you aren't headed there, try Boneyard or Tombstone, Arizona; Skull Creek, Nebraska; Deadwood, California; Frankenstein, Missouri or River Styx, Ohio.

pumpkin cookie dip

Gloria Kirchman, Eden Prairie, Minnesota

A few moments are all you need to whip up this creamy dip that goes perfectly with store-bought gingersnaps.

1	package (8 ounces) cream cheese, softened
2	jars (7 ounces *each*) marshmallow creme
1	can (15 ounces) solid-pack pumpkin
1	teaspoon ground cinnamon
1	teaspoon grated orange peel

Gingersnaps *or* vanilla wafers

1 In a large mixing bowl, beat the cream cheese and marshmallow creme until smooth. Stir in pumpkin, cinnamon and orange peel. Serve as a dip with cookies. Store in the refrigerator.

Yield: 4 cups.

graveyard veggie pizza

Taste of Home Test Kitchen

Scare your guests with this delicious, yet good-for-you addition to your next Halloween party!

- 2 cups all-purpose flour
- 2 teaspoons baking powder
- 1 teaspoon salt
- 2/3 cup milk
- 1/4 cup plus 1 tablespoon canola oil, *divided*

TOPPING:

- 3 cups (24 ounces) cottage cheese
- 1 envelope ranch salad dressing mix
- 1/2 cup mayonnaise
- 1/4 cup milk
- 2 cups (8 ounces) shredded part-skim mozzarella cheese
- 1 cup chopped fresh broccoli
- 1 cup chopped fresh cauliflower
- 2 cans (2-1/4 ounces *each*) chopped ripe olives
- 1/2 cup chopped celery
- 1/3 cup shredded carrot
- 1/4 cup chopped onion
- 1 jar (2 ounces) sliced pimientos, drained
- 1 package (3 ounces) cream cheese, softened
- 4 teaspoons sour cream
- 10 to 15 crackers

1 For crust, in a bowl, combine the flour, baking powder and salt. Add milk and 1/4 cup oil; mix well. Shape into a ball; knead 10 times. On a lightly floured surface, roll into a 15-in. x 10-in. rectangle. Transfer to an ungreased 15-in. x 10-in. x 1-in. baking pan. Press onto the bottom and up the sides of pan. Prick with fork; brush with remaining oil. Bake at 425° for 12-14 minutes or until edges are lightly browned. Cool completely on a wire rack.

2 In a small mixing bowl, combine the cottage cheese, ranch dressing mix, mayonnaise and milk; spread over crust. Sprinkle with the cheese, broccoli, cauliflower, olives, celery, carrot, onion and pimientos.

3 For tombstones, in another small mixing bowl, beat cream cheese and sour cream until fluffy. Place mixture in a resealable plastic bag; cut a small hole in a corner of bag. Pipe "RIP" onto crackers. Insert into pizza. Refrigerate until serving.

Yield: 15 servings.

Costumes and Customs

Some think that the tradition of wearing costumes on this spooky holiday can be traced back hundreds of years to the Europeans and Celts. People feared the long, dark autumn nights and believed that ghosts came back from the dead on Halloween. To avoid being recognized by the ghosts, they wore masks and placed bowls of food outside their doors to keep the ghosts from entering their homes.

As Europeans came to America, they brought their customs with them, but the rigid beliefs of many of the settlers prevented the ideas of Halloween from becoming popular. As time went on, the autumnal celebrations of New England began to blend with the beliefs of the new immigrants. By the 1920s Halloween parades were popular, and by the 1950s, kids were trick-or-treating. Today, it's the second largest commercial holiday!

ham 'n' cheese spiders

Kendra Barclay, De Kalb, Illinois
These creepy sandwiches are sure to scare up some fun at Halloween time! Kids really enjoy eating the spider-shaped sandwiches.

1	tube (12 ounces) refrigerated flaky buttermilk biscuits, separated into 10 biscuits
1	tube (11 ounces) refrigerated breadsticks, separated into 12 breadsticks
1	cup chopped fully cooked ham
2	tablespoons finely chopped onion
2	tablespoons butter, softened
1-1/2	teaspoons prepared mustard
5	slices process American cheese
1	egg yolk
1	teaspoon water
2	tablespoons sliced ripe olives
1	tablespoon diced pimientos
1	teaspoon poppy seeds

1 On two greased baking sheets, pat five biscuits into 3-1/2-in. circles. Cut one breadstick in half lengthwise, then in half widthwise, creating four strips. Repeat nine times (save remaining breadsticks for another use). Position eight strips of dough around each biscuit to resemble spider legs; twist and press lightly onto baking sheet. Tuck a 1/2-in. foil ball under each dough strip so it stands up in the center.

2 Combine the ham, onion, butter and mustard; spoon 3 tablespoons onto each biscuit circle. Fold cheese slices into quarters and place over ham mixture. Pat remaining biscuits into 4-in. circles; place over filling. Pinch edges to seal.

3 In a small bowl, beat egg yolk and water. Brush over tops of biscuits and breadsticks. On each spider, position two olive slices for eyes; place pimientos in center of olives. Sprinkle with poppy seeds. Bake at 375° for 15-20 minutes or until browned.

Yield: 5 sandwiches.

FUNNY BONE!
What do birds give out on Halloween night? Tweets.

monkey bread

Carol Allen, McLeansboro, Illinois

When my boys hear I'm planning to make Monkey Bread, they're eager to help. Both boys really enjoy helping me, and it seems to taste twice as good when they've helped fix it. It's one of our favorite snacks.

1	package (3-1/2 ounces) cook-and-serve butterscotch pudding mix
3/4	cup sugar
1	tablespoon ground cinnamon
1/2	cup finely chopped pecans, optional
1/2	cup butter, melted
3	tubes (10 ounces *each*) refrigerated biscuits

1 In a large resealable plastic bag, combine the pudding mix, sugar, cinnamon and pecans if desired. Pour the butter into a shallow bowl. Cut the biscuits into quarters. Dip several pieces into the butter, then place in bag and shake to coat.

2 Arrange in a greased 10-in. fluted tube pan. Repeat until all the biscuit pieces are coated. Bake at 350° for 30-35 minutes or until browned. Cool for 30 minutes before inverting onto a serving plate.

Yield: 10-12 servings.

mummies on a stick

Taste of Home Test Kitchen

These little hot dogs are all "wrapped-up" in Halloween fun. Kids especially enjoy them!

1	package (11 ounces) refrigerated breadsticks
10	Popsicle sticks
10	hot dogs
Prepared mustard	

1 Separate dough; roll 10 pieces into a 24-in. rope. Insert sticks into hot dogs. Starting at the stick end, wrap one dough rope around each hot dog, leaving 2 in. of the hot dog uncovered at the top for the mummy head.

2 Place mummies 1 in. apart on a greased baking sheet. Place remaining breadsticks on another baking sheet. Bake at 350° for 18-20 minutes. Add dots of mustard for eyes. Save leftover breadsticks for another use.

Yield: 10 servings.

FUNNY BONE!
What kind of streets do mummies live on? Dead ends.

sweet potato biscuits

Lauren McMann, Blairsville, Georgia
Fresh from the oven, these biscuits are a perfect complement to a hearty casserole or stew—yum!

1-1/2	cups self-rising flour
2	teaspoons brown sugar
1/3	cup shortening
1	egg
1/2	cup mashed cooked sweet potatoes (without added butter or milk)
2	tablespoons milk

1 In a bowl, combine the flour and brown sugar; cut in shortening until mixture resembles coarse crumbs. In another bowl, combine the egg, sweet potatoes and milk. Stir into crumb mixture just until moistened.

2 Turn onto a floured surface knead 10-12 times or until smooth. Roll dough to 1/2-in. thickness. Cut with a 2-1/2-in. biscuit cutter; place on an ungreased baking sheet.

3 Bake at 425° for 10-12 minutes or until bottoms are lightly browned. Serve warm.

Yield: 10 biscuits.

halloween tuna cheese melts

Bernadine Dirmeyer, Harpster, Ohio
Adult and little goblins alike are sure to enjoy these easy, cheesy sandwiches at your next Halloween party.

8	slices light rye bread
1/4	cup butter, softened
1	can (6 ounces) tuna, drained
1/2	cup sour cream
2	tablespoons mayonnaise
1/2	teaspoon garlic salt
4	slices process American cheese
1	thin slice green pepper

1 With a 2-in. pumpkin-shaped cookie cutter, cut a pumpkin from the center of four slices of bread (discard cutouts or save for another use). Butter one side of bread; place buttered side up on a greased baking sheet. Bake at 425° for 5-8 minutes or until lightly browned.

2 Butter one side of remaining solid slices of bread. In a bowl, combine the tuna, sour cream, mayonnaise and garlic salt. Spread over unbuttered side of solid bread; top with cheese. Place on baking sheet.

3 Place cutout bread slices over cheese; press down gently. Cut green pepper into small pieces; place on cheese for pumpkin stems. Bake 5-8 minutes longer or until golden brown.

Yield: 4 servings.

sweet 'n' savory snack treat

Betty Sitzman, Wray, Colorado
Serve this yummy Halloween mix in colorful snack cups, ice cream cones or in cellophane treat bags.
You can use different colored M&M's for other festive parties.

- 3 cups *each* Wheat Chex; Rice Chex and miniature cheese crackers
- 1 cup fresh pumpkin seeds, washed and dried
- 1/4 cup butter
- 1-1/2 teaspoons seasoned salt
- 1-1/2 teaspoons Worcestershire sauce
- 1/4 teaspoon garlic powder
- 1/4 teaspoon hot pepper sauce
- 2 cups milk chocolate M&M's

1 In a large bowl, combine the cereal, crackers and pumpkin seeds. In a small saucepan, melt butter. Stir in the seasoned salt, Worcestershire sauce, garlic powder and hot pepper sauce. Drizzle over cereal mixture and toss to coat.

2 Spread into a greased 15-in. x 10-in. x 1-in. baking pan. Bake at 250° for 1 hour, stirring every 15 minutes. Cool completely on a wire rack. Transfer to a large bowl; stir in M&M's. Store in an airtight container.

Yield: 11 cups.

shattered crystal ball

Taste of Home Test Kitchen
Kids love the sweet gelatin and whipped topping dessert from our home economists. Use different flavors of gelatin for color variety. The green and orange colors are perfect for Halloween.

- 2 packages (3 ounces *each*) lime gelatin
- 6 cups boiling water, *divided*
- 2 packages (3 ounces *each*) orange gelatin
- 2 envelopes unflavored gelatin
- 1/3 cup cold water
- 1-1/2 cups white grape juice
- 1 carton (12 ounces) frozen whipped topping, thawed

1 In a bowl, dissolve the lime gelatin in 3 cups boiling water. Pour into an 8-in. square dish coated with nonstick cooking spray. In another bowl, dissolve orange gelatin in remaining boiling water. Pour into another 8-in. square dish coated with nonstick cooking spray. Refrigerate for 4 hours or until very firm.

2 In a small saucepan, sprinkle unflavored gelatin over cold water; let stand for 1 minute. Add grape juice. Heat over low heat, stirring until gelatin is completely dissolved. Pour into a large bowl; refrigerate for 45 minutes or until slightly thickened. Fold in whipped topping.

3 Cut green gelatin into 1/2-in. cubes and orange gelatin into 1-in. cubes. Set aside 8-10 cubes of each color for garnish. Place 2 cups whipped topping mixture in a bowl; fold in remaining green cubes. Spread into a 13-in. x 9-in. x 2-in. dish coated with nonstick cooking spray. Fold remaining orange cubes into remaining whipped topping mixture; spread over bottom layer. Sprinkle with reserved green and orange gelatin cubes. Refrigerate for 2 hours or until set. Cut into squares.

Yield: 12-15 servings.

pumpkin bread

Joyce Jackson, Bridgetown, Nova Scotia
This is definitely a deliciously spicy, pumpkin-rich quick bread. I keep my freezer stocked with it.

1-1/2	cups sugar
1	cup canned pumpkin
1/2	cup *each* canola oil and water
2	eggs
1-2/3	cups all-purpose flour
1	teaspoon *each* baking soda and ground cinnamon
3/4	teaspoon salt
1/2	teaspoon *each* baking powder and ground nutmeg
1/4	teaspoon ground cloves
1/2	cup *each* chopped walnuts and raisins

1 In a large mixing bowl, combine sugar, pumpkin, oil, water and eggs; beat well. Combine dry ingredients; gradually add to pumpkin mixture and mix well. Stir in nuts and raisins.

2 Pour into a greased 9-in. x 5-in. x 3-in. loaf pan. Bake at 350° for 65-70 minutes or until a toothpick comes out clean. Cool in pan 10 minutes before removing to a wire rack.

Yield: 1 loaf.

tex-mex dip with spooky tortilla chips

Mary Anne McWhirter, Pearland, Texas
These spooky ghost- or pumpkin-shaped chips, with a flavorful Tex-Mex dip, are perfect for Halloween.

20	flour tortillas (8 inches)
1/2 to 1	teaspoon seasoned salt
2	cans (9 ounces *each*) bean dip

3	medium ripe avocados, peeled
2	tablespoons lemon juice
1/2	teaspoon salt
1/4	teaspoon pepper
1	cup (8 ounces) sour cream
1/2	cup mayonnaise
1	envelope taco seasoning
2	cups (8 ounces) shredded cheddar cheese
1	cup sliced ripe olives
4	green onions, sliced
1	large tomato, seeded and chopped

1 Cut tortillas with a ghost- or pumpkin-shaped 3-1/2-in. cookie cutter. Place on baking sheets coated with nonstick cooking spray. Spritz tortillas with nonstick cooking spray; sprinkle with seasoned salt. Bake at 350° for 5-8 minutes or until edges just begin to brown. Remove to wire racks.

2 Spread bean dip onto a 12-in. serving plate. In a bowl, mash avocados with lemon juice, salt and pepper; spread over bean dip. Combine the sour cream, mayonnaise and taco seasoning; spread over avocado layer. Sprinkle with cheese, olives, onions and tomato.

Yield: about 9 cups dip and 5 dozen chips.

FUNNY BONE!
What does a mommy ghost say to her kids when they get in the car? "Fasten your sheet belts."

SWEET TREATS

What would the spooky season be without sweets? It would be far less fun, that's for sure! Whether you're looking for a school treat or the perfect dessert for a party, you'll find the most creative recipes in these pages.

pumpkin cookie pops

Taste of Home Test Kitchen

These cookie pops from our very own home economists are a great way to liven up a Halloween party. Kids love them. Serve them standing upright in a bowl of candy (as shown at left), or place them flat on pieces of waxed paper all around your Halloween buffet.

1/2	cup butter, softened
3/4	cup packed brown sugar
1/2	cup sugar
1	egg
1	teaspoon vanilla extract
1	cup canned pumpkin
2-1/2	cups all-purpose flour
1	teaspoon baking powder
1	teaspoon baking soda
1	teaspoon ground cinnamon
30	Popsicle sticks
1/3	cup green gumdrops, quartered lengthwise

ICING:

4	cups confectioners' sugar
1/4	cup water

Orange and black paste *or* gel food coloring

1 In a mixing bowl, cream butter and sugars. Beat in egg and vanilla. Beat in pumpkin. Combine the flour, baking powder, baking soda and cinnamon; gradually add to creamed mixture (dough will be soft).

2 Drop by rounded tablespoonfuls 2 in. apart onto greased or parchment paper-lined baking sheets. Insert Popsicle sticks into dough. Insert a gumdrop piece into the top of each for stem. Bake at 350° for 14-16 minutes or until set and lightly browned around the edges. Remove to wire racks to cool.

3 For icing, combine confectioners' sugar and water until smooth. Remove 1/2 cup to another bowl; cover and set aside. Stir orange food coloring into remaining icing. Spread or pipe over cookies. Let stand for 30 minutes or until icing is set and dry.

4 Stir black food coloring into reserved icing. Transfer to a heavy-duty resealable plastic bag; cut a small hole in a corner of bag. Pipe icing over cookies to create jack-o'-lantern faces.

Yield: 2-1/2 dozen.

Pumpkin Primer

Pumpkins, which are actually berries, are cousins to melons, cucumbers, squash and gourds. They're not always orange, either. Some varieties are white, blue or green! All pumpkins are native to Central America. They quickly became popular in Europe when explorers "discovered" them in the New World.

ghostly pirate cake

Taste of Home Test Kitchen

This moist white cake is a snap to prepare because it starts with a mix. Have fun decorating it—we sure did!

1	package (18-1/4 ounces) white cake mix
1/2	cup butter, softened
4-1/2	cups confectioners' sugar
5	tablespoons milk
1-1/2	teaspoons vanilla extract

3	red Fruit Roll-Ups, unrolled

Shredded coconut and black food coloring

Assorted candies of your choice: Fruit by the Foot fruit roll, M&M's, black licorice twists, caramels, plain chocolate bar, dark purple Gummi Life Saver, red-hot candy and gold candy coins

1 Prepare and bake cake according to package directions, using two greased 9-in. round baking pans. Cool for 10 minutes before removing from pans to cool completely. Cut two pieces from the lower edges of each cake, forming a pirate's head (save small pieces for another use).

2 For frosting, in a mixing bowl, beat butter until creamy. Gradually beat in the confectioners' sugar, milk and vanilla until smooth and fluffy. Place one cake on a serving platter. Spread with 1/2 cup frosting; top with second cake. Spread top and sides with remaining frosting.

3 For pirate's bandanna, place Fruit Roll-Ups over top edge of cake. Tint coconut with black food coloring; sprinkle over chin for goatee. Decorate pirate's features with assorted candies.

Yield: 10-12 servings.

bloodshot eyeballs

Taste of Home Test Kitchen

Your party guests will be surprised to find that these aren't eyeballs at all—they're peanut butter balls!

2	cups confectioners' sugar, *divided*
1/2	cup creamy peanut butter
3	tablespoons butter, softened
1/2	pound white candy coating

24	brown Reese's pieces or milk chocolate M&M's
1	tablespoon water
1/4	to 1/2 teaspoon red food coloring

1 In a small mixing bowl, combine 1 cup confectioners' sugar, peanut butter and butter. Shape into 1-in. balls; place on a waxed paper-lined pan. Chill for 30 minutes or until firm.

2 In a microwave-safe bowl, melt white candy coating; stir until smooth. Dip balls in coating and place on waxed paper. Immediately press a candy onto the top of each eyeball for pupil. Let stand for 30 minutes or until set.

3 In a small bowl, combine the water, food coloring and remaining confectioners' sugar. Transfer to a heavy-duty resealable plastic bag; cut a small hole in a corner of bag. Pipe wavy lines downward from pupil, creating the look of bloodshot eyes. Store in an airtight container.

Yield: 2 dozen.

FUNNY BONE!
How do witches keep their hair in place while flying? They use scare spray.

carnival caramel apples

Gail Prather, Bethel, Minnesota

With four kids, we celebrate Halloween in style around our house. These caramel apples are a tried-and-true favorite year after year.

1/2	cup butter, cubed
2	cups packed brown sugar
1	cup light corn syrup
Dash	salt
1	can (14 ounces) sweetened condensed milk
1	teaspoon vanilla extract
10	to 12 Popsicle sticks
10	to 12 medium tart apples, washed and dried
1	cup salted peanuts, chopped

1 In a large heavy saucepan, melt butter; add the brown sugar, corn syrup and salt. Cook and stir over medium heat until mixture comes to a boil, about 10-12 minutes. Stir in milk. Cook and stir until a candy thermometer reads 248° (firm-ball stage). Remove from the heat; stir in vanilla.

2 Insert Popsicle sticks into apples. Dip each apple into hot caramel mixture; turn to coat. Dip bottom of apples into peanuts. Set on greased waxed paper to cool.

Yield: 10-12 apples.

Editor's Note: We recommend that you test your candy thermometer before each use by bringing water to a boil; the thermometer should read 212°. Adjust your recipe temperature up or down based on your test.

chocolate skeleton cookies

Lisa Rupple, Keenesburg, Colorado

Put these cute treats out for your next ghost and goblin party and watch them disappear.

1	cup butter, softened
1	cup sugar
1/2	cup packed brown sugar
1	egg
1	teaspoon vanilla extract
2-3/4	cups all-purpose flour
1/2	cup baking cocoa
1	teaspoon baking soda
1-1/2	cups confectioners' sugar
2	tablespoons milk

1 In a large mixing bowl, cream butter and sugars until light and fluffy. Beat in egg and vanilla. Combine the flour, cocoa and baking soda; gradually add to creamed mixture. Cover and refrigerate for 1-2 hours or until easy to handle.

2 On a lightly floured surface, roll the dough to 1/8-in. thickness. Cut with a floured 3-in. gingerbread boy cookie cutter. Place on greased baking sheets.

3 Bake at 375° for 7-8 minutes or until set. Cool for 1 minute before removing from pans to wire racks to cool completely.

4 For icing, in a small bowl, combine confectioners' sugar and milk until smooth. Cut a small hole in the corner of a resealable plastic bag; fill with icing. Pipe skeleton bones on cookies.

Yield: 3 dozen.

Crazy for Cupcakes!

These little cakes are taking the party world by storm, so this Halloween, don't be caught behind the curve without any on your buffet. All of these treats start with easy-to-make cake mixes and canned frosting, and the home economists in our Test Kitchen made sure that the decorations are simple, too. Get the kids in on the fun by having them add cat whiskers, creepy tombstone "fingers" or even the wart on the witch's nose!

FUNNY BONE!

How can you predict the future on Halloween? Read the horror-scope.

tombstone cupcakes

- 1 package (18-1/4 ounces) cake mix of your choice
- 1/3 cup semisweet chocolate chips
- 24 Milano cookies
- 1 can (16 ounces) vanilla frosting
- 1/2 cup chocolate wafer crumbs
- 1 cup chow mein noodles
- 24 orange gumdrops
- 3 green gumdrops, cut into small pieces

1 Prepare and bake cake mix according to package directions for cupcakes; cool completely.

2 For tombstones, in the microwave, melt chocolate chips. Pipe "RIP" onto cookies; place on waxed paper to dry.

3 Frost cupcakes; sprinkle with chocolate wafer crumbs. Carefully insert tombstones into cupcakes. Arrange chow mein noodles to resemble fingers. Use gumdrops to make pumpkins; place in front of tombstones. **Yield:** 2 dozen.

scaredy-cat cupcakes

- 1 package (18-1/4 ounces) cake mix of your choice
- 1 can (16 ounces) vanilla frosting

Orange paste food coloring

- 1 cup chow mein noodles
- 2 teaspoons sugar
- 2 teaspoons baking cocoa
- 48 nacho tortilla chips, broken

Assorted candies: green M&M's, miniature semisweet chocolate chips, black licorice twists and shoestring licorice

1 Prepare and bake cake mix according to package directions for cupcakes; cool completely. Tint vanilla frosting orange. Using a star tip, pipe orange frosting onto cupcakes.

2 For whiskers, in a small bowl, combine the chow mein noodles, sugar and cocoa; set aside.

3 For cats' ears, insert nacho chips with pointed tips up. Use M&M's and miniature chocolate chips for eyes, pieces of licorice twists for noses and shoestring licorice for mouths. Arrange reserved chow mein noodles on cupcakes for whiskers. **Yield:** 2 dozen.

wicked witch cupcakes

- 1 package (18-1/4 ounces) cake mix of your choice
- 1-1/2 cups semisweet chocolate chips
- 1 tablespoon shortening
- 24 Bugles
- 24 chocolate wafers
- 1 cup chow mein noodles
- 2 teaspoons sugar
- 2 teaspoons baking cocoa
- 1 can (16 ounces) vanilla frosting

Green paste food coloring

- 1/3 cup miniature marshmallows

Miniature chocolate chips

Assorted candies: black licorice twists, black shoestring licorice and purple Nerds

1 Prepare and bake cake mix according to package directions for cupcakes; cool completely.

2 For witches' hats, in a microwave-safe bowl, melt chocolate chips and shortening; stir until smooth. Dip a Bugle in chocolate, allowing excess to drip off. Position on a chocolate wafer, forming a witch's hat. Place on waxed paper to dry. Repeat with remaining chocolate, Bugles and wafers.

3 For hair, in a small bowl, combine the chow mein noodles, sugar and cocoa; set aside. Tint frosting green; frost cupcakes. Insert brim of witches' hats into cupcakes.

4 For eyes, cut miniature marshmallows in half and pinch slightly; attach miniature chocolate chips with frosting for pupils. Place on cupcakes. Add pieces of licorice twists for noses, shoestring licorice for mouths and Nerds for warts. Arrange reserved chow mein noodles on cupcakes for hair. **Yield:** 2 dozen.

Safety First

Teach your kids these smart practices and they'll have a fun and safe Trick-or-Treat. If possible, always use sidewalks to get from house to house and cross only at street corners. Visit only houses that have a porch light on. Never go into a stranger's house. Carry a flashlight to light the way and bring a watch, too. Be cautious of animals—they're often nervous because of all the commotion. Take masks off when crossing streets and walking from house to house, or better yet, wear face paint (see ideas beginning on page 250). Say "Trick-or-Treat!" and don't forget to say "Thank you!"

Jack-o'-Lantern Origins

Today's jack-o'-lanterns are said to have their origins in Ireland, where people hollowed out turnips and beets and placed candles in them in an attempt to frighten bad spirits. Orange and black are the classic colors of Halloween. Orange represents the bounty of the fall harvest and black represents the darkness of death and the coming winter.

spiderweb cupcakes

Janis Plourde, Smooth Rock Falls, Ontario
The cupcake batter and frosting contain orange flavors for a special, made-from-scratch taste.

6	tablespoons butter, softened
1	cup packed brown sugar
1	egg
1/2	cup unsweetened applesauce
1	teaspoon vanilla extract
1	teaspoon grated orange peel
1	cup all-purpose flour
1	teaspoon baking powder
1/2	teaspoon salt
1/4	teaspoon baking soda
1/2	cup chopped pecans

FROSTING:

1/4	cup butter, softened
2	cups confectioners' sugar
1-1/2	teaspoons grated orange peel
Orange paste food coloring	
2	to 4 teaspoons orange juice
1/2	cup chocolate frosting
Black shoestring licorice	
12	black gumdrops

1 In a small mixing bowl, cream butter and brown sugar until light and fluffy. Add egg; beat well. Beat in the applesauce, vanilla and orange peel. Combine the flour, baking powder, salt and baking soda; gradually add to the creamed mixture. Stir in pecans.

2 Fill paper-lined muffin cups half full. Bake at 350° for 20-25 minutes or until a toothpick comes out clean. Cool for 10 minutes before removing from pan to a wire rack to cool completely.

3 For frosting, in a small mixing bowl, cream butter and confectioners' sugar. Add orange peel, food coloring and enough orange juice to achieve spreading consistency. Set aside 1/4 cup orange frosting. Frost cupcakes.

4 Transfer chocolate frosting to a heavy-duty resealable bag; cut a small hole in a corner of bag. Pipe a circle of chocolate in center of each cupcake. Pipe evenly spaced thin concentric circles about 1/4 in. apart. Beginning with the center circle, gently pull a toothpick through circles toward outer edge. Wipe toothpick clean. Repeat to complete web pattern.

5 Cut licorice into 2-in. pieces; press eight pieces into each gumdrop for legs. Place reserved orange frosting in a heavy-duty resealable bag; cut a small hole in a corner of the bag. Pipe eyes on each spider gumdrop. Position on cupcakes.

Yield: 1 dozen.

FUNNY BONE!
What's Dracula's favorite breed of dog? The bloodhound.

spiderweb brownies

Sandy Pichon, Slidell, Louisiana

To decorate these moist brownies for Halloween, I drizzle a chocolate spiderweb on the white icing.

3/4	cup butter, cubed
4	squares (1 ounce *each*) unsweetened chocolate
2	cups sugar
3	eggs, beaten
1	teaspoon vanilla extract
1	cup all-purpose flour
1	cup chopped pecans *or* walnuts
1	jar (7 ounces) marshmallow creme
1	square (1 ounce) semisweet chocolate

1 In a large saucepan over low heat, stir butter and unsweetened chocolate until melted. Remove from the heat; stir in sugar. Cool for 10 minutes. Whisk in eggs and vanilla. Stir in flour and nuts. Pour into a greased foil-lined 13-in. x 9-in. x 2-in. baking pan.

2 Bake at 350° for 25-30 minutes or until a toothpick inserted near the center comes out clean (do not overbake). Immediately drop marshmallow cream by spoonfuls over hot brownies; spread evenly. Cool on a wire rack.

3 Lift out of the pan; remove foil. For web decoration, melt semisweet chocolate and place in a small resealable plastic bag. Cut a small hole in one corner of the bag; drizzle chocolate over top in a spiderweb design. Cut into bars.

Yield: 2 dozen.

pumpkin-shaped rollouts

Margaret Hancock, Camp Verde, Arizona

These cookies have a bit of orange peel added. Yum!

2/3	cup shortening
3/4	cup sugar
1/2	to 1 teaspoon grated orange peel
1	egg
4	teaspoons milk
1/2	teaspoon vanilla extract
2	cups all-purpose flour
1-1/2	teaspoons baking powder
1/4	teaspoon salt

FROSTING:

1/2	cup butter, softened
4	cups confectioners' sugar
1	teaspoon vanilla extract
1/2	teaspoon grated orange peel
2	to 4 tablespoons orange juice

Green and orange food coloring

1 In a large mixing bowl, cream the shortening, sugar and orange peel until light and fluffy. Beat in the egg, milk and vanilla. Combine the flour, baking powder and salt; gradually add to the creamed mixture.

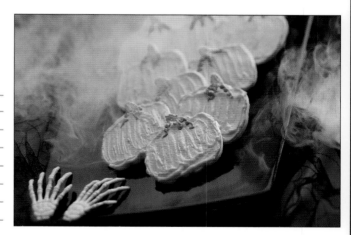

2 On a lightly floured surface, roll out to 1/4-in. thickness. Cut with 2-1/2-in. pumpkin cookie cutters dipped in flour. Place 1 in. apart on greased baking sheets. Bake at 375° for 6-8 minutes or until lightly browned. Remove to wire racks to cool.

3 In a small mixing bowl, combine the butter, confectioners' sugar, vanilla, orange peel and enough orange juice to achieve spreading consistency. Remove 1/2 cup frosting; tint green. Tint remaining frosting orange. Frost cookies with orange frosting; add leaves and vines with green frosting.

Yield: about 3-1/2 dozen.

magic wands

Renee Schwebach, Dumont, Minnesota
These fun and colorful magic wands don't take a magician to make. You can change the colors for any theme party, too!

1-1/2	cups vanilla *or* white chips
1	package (10 ounces) pretzel rods

Colored candy stars *or* sprinkles

Colored sugar *or* edible glitter

1. In a microwave, melt chips; stir until smooth. Dip each pretzel rod halfway into melted chips; shake off excess.
2. Sprinkle with candy stars and colored sugar. Place on a wire rack for 15 minutes or until set. Store in an airtight container.

Yield: 2 dozen.

halloween mini-cakes

Taste of Home Test Kitchen
These little cakes are sure to please everyone at your Halloween get-together.
Make a double batch, though, because these one- (or two-) bite wonders are sure to be a hit!

1	package (18-1/4 ounces) yellow cake mix
9	cups confectioners' sugar, *divided*
9	tablespoons milk, *divided*
4	tablespoons plus 1 teaspoon light corn syrup, *divided*

Orange and black paste *or* gel food coloring

1. Grease two 13-in. x 9-in. x 2-in. baking pans; line with parchment paper and set aside. Prepare cake batter according to package directions. Pour into prepared pans.
2. Bake at 350° for 20-25 minutes or until a toothpick inserted near the center comes out clean. Cool for 10 minutes. Using parchment paper, remove cakes from pans and invert onto wire racks; carefully peel off parchment paper. Cool completely. Cut one cake into pumpkin shapes and the second cake into ghost shapes using 3-in. cookie cutters dipped in confectioners' sugar. Carefully arrange individual cakes on wire racks over waxed paper.
3. For icing, in each of two large bowls, combine 4 cups confectioners' sugar, 4 tablespoons milk and 2 tablespoons corn syrup until smooth. Tint icing in one bowl orange. Place orange icing in a heavy-duty resealable plastic bag; cut a small hole in a corner of bag. Pipe over top of pumpkin shapes, allowing icing to drape over cake sides. Repeat with white icing and ghost cakes. Let stand for 30 minutes or until icing is set and dry.

4. In a small bowl, combine the remaining confectioners' sugar, milk and corn syrup. Tint black. Pipe faces onto pumpkin and ghost cakes.

Yield: 1-1/2 dozen.

frankenstein cake

Nancy Fresler, Kinde, Michigan

Convenience items like a cake mix and canned frosting make this clever dessert a breeze to prepare. It always elicits oohs and aahs at Halloween parties.

Frankenstein Fact

Mary Shelley spent the stormy summer of 1816 with her poet husband, Percy Byshe Shelley, and their friend, Lord Byron. Both men were already established poets. To pass the time, they came up with a contest—write a ghost story. Mary's story, inspired by a dream, won the contest and became the famous novel Frankenstein.

1 package (18-1/4 ounces) chocolate cake mix
1 package (8 ounces) cream cheese, softened
1/2 cup sour cream
1/2 cup sugar
1 egg
1/2 teaspoon vanilla extract
1 carton (8 ounces) frozen whipped topping, thawed
Moss green paste food coloring
1 can (16 ounces) chocolate frosting
1 Swiss cake roll *or* Ho Ho

1 Prepare cake batter according to package directions. Pour into a greased and waxed paper-lined 13-in. x 9-in. x 2-in. baking pan. In a small mixing bowl, beat the cream cheese, sour cream, sugar, egg and vanilla until smooth. Drop by tablespoonfuls about 1 in. apart onto batter.

2 Bake at 350° for 40-45 minutes or until center is firm when lightly touched. Cool for 10 minutes before removing from pan to a wire rack to cool completely.

3 To make Frankenstein, cut a piece of cake for the head (about 10 in. x 7-3/4 in.) and neck (about 2-1/2 in. x 4-1/2 in.). Cut two pieces for ears (about 2-3/4 in. x 1/2 in.). Save remaining cake for another use. Position head, neck and ears on a covered board.

4 Place 1/4 cup whipped topping in a small bowl; tint dark green with moss green food coloring. Cut a small hole in the corner of a small plastic bag; insert round pastry tip #3 and fill with tinted topping. Set aside.

5 Tint remaining whipped topping moss green. Frost face, neck and ears, building up areas for the forehead, nose and cheeks. With reserved dark green topping, pipe mouth, stitches on neck and forehead, and eyes with pupils.

6 Cut a hole in the corner of a pastry or plastic bag; insert pastry tip #233. Fill with chocolate frosting; pipe hair 1-1/4 in. from top of head to forehead and about 4 in. down sides of head. Cut cake roll in half widthwise; place on each side of neck for bolts. Store in the refrigerator.

Yield: 12-15 servings.

FUNNY BONE!
What do polite skeletons say before eating a meal? Bone appetit!

FALL FARE

When the weather cools and the bounty of the fall harvest is upon us, we crave hearty, warming comfort foods like these. Try one on your family when the autumn winds start to blow, and you'll be sure to win compliments.

harvest vegetable bake

Janet Weisser, Seattle, Washington

This delicious dish is packed with a large assortment of vegetables. Served with a green salad, it makes an excellent entree in the autumn months.

2-1/2	to 3 pounds skinless chicken thighs
2	bay leaves
4	small red potatoes, cut into 1-inch pieces
4	small onions, quartered
4	small carrots, cut into 2-inch pieces
2	celery ribs, cut into 2-inch pieces
2	small turnips, peeled and cut into 1-inch pieces
1	medium green pepper, cut into 1-inch pieces
12	small fresh mushrooms
2	teaspoons salt
1	teaspoon dried rosemary, crushed
1/2	teaspoon pepper
1	can (14-1/2 ounces) diced tomatoes, undrained

1 Place chicken in a greased 13-in. x 9-in. x 2-in. baking dish; add bay leaves. Top with the potatoes, onions, carrots, celery, turnips, green pepper and mushrooms. Sprinkle with salt, rosemary and pepper. Pour tomatoes over all.

2 Cover and bake at 375° for 1-1/2 hours or until chicken juices run clear and vegetables are tender. Discard bay leaves before serving.

Yield: 6-8 servings.

spiced pot roast

Loren Martin, Big Cabin, Oklahoma

Just pour these ingredients over your pot roast and let the slow cooker do the work. Herbs and spices give the beef an excellent taste. I often serve this roast over noodles or with mashed potatoes, using the juices as a gravy.

1	boneless beef chuck roast (2-1/2 pounds)
1	medium onion, chopped
1	can (14-1/2 ounces) diced tomatoes, undrained
1/4	cup white vinegar
3	tablespoons tomato puree
2	teaspoons Dijon mustard
1/2	teaspoon lemon juice
4-1/2	teaspoons poppy seeds
2	garlic cloves, minced
2-1/4	teaspoons sugar
1/2	teaspoon *each* ground ginger, salt and dried rosemary (crushed)
1/4	teaspoon *each* ground turmeric and cumin
1/4	teaspoon crushed red pepper flakes
1/8	teaspoon ground cloves
1	bay leaf
Hot cooked noodles	

1 Place roast in a 3-qt. slow cooker. In a large bowl, combine the onion, tomatoes, vinegar, tomato puree, mustard, lemon juice and seasonings; pour over roast. Cover and cook on low for 8-9 hours or until meat is tender. Discard bay leaf. Thicken cooking juices if desired. Serve over noodles.

Yield: 6-8 servings.

turkey hash

Edna Hoffman, Hebron, Indiana
This mild-tasting dish comes highly recommended by my family, and it's a good use for leftover turkey, too.

1	medium onion, chopped
1/2	cup chopped green pepper
1/2	cup chopped sweet red pepper
2	tablespoons butter
6	cups diced cooked potatoes
2	cups cubed cooked turkey
1/2	teaspoon salt, optional
1/8	teaspoon cayenne pepper
1/8	teaspoon ground nutmeg

1 In a skillet, saute onion and peppers in butter until tender. Add the potatoes, turkey, salt if desired, cayenne and nutmeg. Cook and stir over low heat for 20 minutes or until lightly browned and heated through.

Yield: 8 servings.

golden harvest cookies

Florence Pope, Denver, Colorado
Folks may be skeptical when you tell them the ingredients in these cookies. But what a tantalizing treat for the taste buds! These unique cookies are just slightly sweet and great for fall.

2/3	cup butter, softened
1/3	cup packed brown sugar
1	egg
1	teaspoon vanilla extract
3/4	cup self-rising flour
1	teaspoon ground cinnamon
1/8	teaspoon ground cloves
1-1/2	cups quick-cooking oats
1	cup shredded carrots
1	cup (4 ounces) shredded cheddar cheese
1	cup chopped pecans
1/2	cup raisins

1 In a large mixing bowl, cream butter and brown sugar until light and fluffy. Beat in egg and vanilla. Combine the flour, cinnamon and cloves; gradually add to the creamed mixture. Stir in remaining ingredients.

2 Drop by heaping tablespoonfuls 2 in. apart onto ungreased baking sheets. Bake at 375° for 12-14 minutes or until golden brown. Remove to wire racks to cool. Store in the refrigerator.

Yield: 3-1/2 dozen.

FUNNY BONE!
What kind of music do mummies listen to? Wrap.

southwestern stew

Virginia Price, Cheyene, Wyoming

Slow-cooking allows the flavors in this recipe to blend beautifully. It's perfect for either before or after trick-or-treating.

1-1/2	pounds boneless pork, cut into 1/2-inch cubes
2	tablespoons canola oil
1	medium onion, chopped
1	can (15-1/2 ounces) yellow hominy, drained
1	can (14-1/2 ounces) diced tomatoes, undrained
1	can (4 ounces) chopped green chilies
1/2	cup water
1/2	teaspoon chili powder
1/4	teaspoon garlic powder
1/4	teaspoon ground cumin
1/4	teaspoon salt
1/4	teaspoon pepper

1 In a large skillet over medium-high heat, brown pork in oil. Add onion and cook for 2 minutes or until tender.

2 Transfer to a 3-qt. slow cooker; add remaining ingredients. Cover and cook on high for 2 hours. Reduce heat to low and cook 4 hours longer.

Yield: 4-6 servings.

crowd chicken casserole

Marna Dunn, Bullhead City, Arizona

If you need to feed a big group, this is the answer! It's full of the creamy, ooey-gooey goodness that will hit the spot on a cool fall day. The potato chips add a kid-friendly crunch, too.

10	cups diced cooked chicken
10	cups chopped celery
2	cups slivered almonds
2	bunches green onions with tops, sliced
2	cans (4 ounces *each*) chopped green chilies
2	cans (2-1/4 ounces *each*) sliced ripe olives, drained
5	cups (20 ounces) shredded cheddar cheese, *divided*
2	cups mayonnaise
2	cups (16 ounces) sour cream
5	cups crushed potato chips

1 In a very large bowl, combine the first six ingredients; add 2 cups cheese. In a small bowl, mix mayonnaise and sour cream; add to chicken mixture and toss to coat.

2 Transfer to two greased 3-qt. baking dishes. Sprinkle with chips and remaining cheese. Bake, uncovered, at 350° for 20-25 minutes or until heated through.

Yield: 2 casseroles (12 servings each).

cheesy tortilla soup

LaVonda Owen, Marlow, Oklahoma

My daughter came up with this dish when trying to duplicate a soup she sampled at a restaurant. I always pass on to her the rave reviews whenever this is served.

1	envelope fajita marinade mix
4	boneless skinless chicken breast halves, diced
2	tablespoons canola oil
1/2	cup chopped onion

1/4	cup butter
1/3	cup all-purpose flour
2	cans (14-1/2 ounces *each*) chicken broth
1/3	cup canned diced tomatoes with chilies
1	cup cubed process cheese (Velveeta)
1-1/2	cups (6 ounces) shredded Monterey Jack cheese, *divided*
1-1/2	cups half-and-half cream

Guacamole

1/2	cup shredded cheddar cheese

Tortilla chips

1 Prepare fajita mix according to package directions; add chicken and marinate as directed. In a large skillet, cook chicken in oil until juices run clear; set aside.

2 In a large saucepan, cook onion in butter until tender. Stir in flour until blended. Gradually stir in broth. Bring to a boil. Cook and stir for 2 minutes until thickened and bubbly. Add tomatoes, process cheese and 1 cup Monterey Jack; cook and stir until cheese is melted. Stir in cream and chicken; heat through (do not boil). Spoon into bowls. Garnish with guacamole, cheddar cheese and remaining Monterey Jack cheese; add tortilla chips.

Yield: 8 servings (2 quarts).

sweet potato pineapple bake

Ruth Beers, Larkspur, Colorado

Pineapple turns this hearty casserole into a side dish with a tropical twist. It's sure to be a big hit during the holidays when served along with roasted poultry or a festive baked ham.

3	cups cooked mashed sweet potatoes
1/2	cup *each* sugar and milk
1/4	cup butter, melted
2	eggs, lightly beaten
1	teaspoon vanilla extract

Dash salt

TOPPING:

1/4	cup *each* sugar and all-purpose flour
1	can (8 ounces) crushed pineapple, undrained
1/4	cup butter, melted
2	eggs

1 In a large bowl, combine the first seven ingredients. Pour into a lightly greased 9-in. square baking dish. Combine the topping ingredients; pour over potato mixture.

2 Bake, uncovered, at 350° for 45-50 minutes or until a knife inserted near the center comes out clean.

Yield: 8-10 servings.

apple pizza

Brenda Mowrey, Taylors, South Carolina

Pizza is a favorite at our house, so when I had some apples to use up, I started searching for an apple pizza recipe. I tailored this one to fit my family's tastes.

2-1/3	to 3 cups all-purpose flour
3	tablespoons sugar
1	package (1/4 ounce) active dry yeast
1/2	teaspoon salt
1/2	cup water
1/4	cup milk
1/4	cup butter, cubed

APPLE TOPPING:

4	cups sliced peeled Granny Smith apples
2	tablespoons butter
1/2	cup sugar
2	tablespoons all-purpose flour
1	teaspoon ground cinnamon

CHEESE TOPPING:

4	ounces cream cheese, softened
1/4	cup packed brown sugar
2	tablespoons caramel ice cream topping

STREUSEL:

2/3	cup all-purpose flour
1/3	cup sugar
1/4	cup cold butter

1 In a large mixing bowl, combine 1-1/2 cups flour, sugar, yeast and salt. In a saucepan, heat water, milk and butter to 120°-130°. Add to dry ingredients; beat for 2 minutes. Stir in enough remaining flour to form a firm dough. Turn onto a floured surface; cover and let rest for 15 minutes.

2 Meanwhile, in a large skillet, cook and stir apples in butter over medium heat for 2 minutes. Combine sugar, flour and cinnamon; stir into skillet. Cook 3 minutes longer. Reduce heat to low; cook, uncovered, for 4-6 minutes or until apples are tender, stirring frequently.

3 In a small mixing bowl, combine the cheese topping ingredients. For streusel, in a small bowl, combine flour and sugar; cut in butter until crumbly.

4 Pat dough onto a greased 14-in. pizza pan, building up edges slightly. Spread with cheese topping, then apple topping. Sprinkle with streusel. Bake at 375° for 20-25 minutes or until crust is golden brown. Serve warm or cold.

Yield: 10-12 servings.

FUNNY BONE!
Who won the skeleton beauty contest? No body.

curried lamb stew

Lorna Irving, Holberg, British Columbia
This is without a doubt the yummiest stew I've ever tasted. You can make it ahead and reheat before serving, so it's great for a get-together.

2	pounds lean lamb stew meat, cut into 3/4-inch cubes
4	teaspoons olive oil
1	medium onion, chopped
2	garlic cloves, minced
1	tablespoon curry powder
1	teaspoon salt
1/4	teaspoon pepper
1/8	teaspoon *each* ground coriander, cumin and cinnamon
1/8	teaspoon cayenne pepper
1/4	cup all-purpose flour
1-1/4	cups water
1	cup unsweetened pineapple juice
1	medium tart apple, peeled and chopped
1/4	cup tomato sauce
1/2	cup sour cream

Hot cooked noodles *or* rice, optional

1 In a Dutch oven, brown meat in oil in batches. Cook onion and garlic in drippings until onion is tender. Add the curry, salt, pepper, coriander, cumin, cinnamon and cayenne; cook and stir for 2 minutes. Sprinkle with flour; cook and stir for 2-3 minutes. Stir in the water, pineapple juice, apple and tomato sauce.

2 Return meat to Dutch oven. Bring to boil. Reduce heat; cover and simmer for 1 hour or until meat is tender. Remove from the heat. Stir in sour cream. Serve with noodles or rice if desired.

Yield: 6 servings.

FUNNY BONE!
How do young ghosts get to school? They take the ghoul bus.

crunch top ham and potato casserole

Nancy Schmidt, Delhi, California

Hash browns, ham and cheese are what make this a dish that's sure to satisfy. Serve your kids this hearty casserole before they head off trick-or-treating and you'll find that they'll eat a lot less candy!

2	pounds frozen Southern-style hash brown potatoes, thawed
2	cups cubed cooked ham
2	cups (16 ounces) sour cream
1-1/2	cups (6 ounces) shredded cheddar cheese
1	can (10-3/4 ounces) cream of chicken soup, undiluted
1/2	cup butter, melted
1/3	cup chopped green onions
1/2	teaspoon pepper

TOPPING:

2	cups crushed cornflakes
1/4	cup melted butter

1 In a bowl, combine the first eight ingredients. Transfer to a greased 13-in. x 9-in. x 2-in. baking dish. Combine topping ingredients; sprinkle over top. Bake, uncovered, at 350° for 1 hour or until heated through.

Yield: 10 servings.

corny chili

Marlene Olson, Hoople, North Dakota

This is so delicious and simple that I had to share it. I'm sure busy moms will be just as happy as I am with the taste and time-saving convenience of this pleasant chili.

1	pound ground beef
1	small onion, chopped
1	can (16 ounces) kidney beans, rinsed and drained
2	cans (14-1/2 ounces *each*) diced tomatoes, undrained
1	can (11 ounces) whole kernel corn, drained
3/4	cup picante sauce
1	tablespoon chili powder
1/4	to 1/2 teaspoon garlic powder

Corn chips, sour cream and shredded cheddar cheese, optional

1 In a large skillet, cook beef and onion over medium heat until meat is no longer pink; drain.

2 Transfer to a 3-qt. slow cooker. Stir in the beans, tomatoes, corn, picante sauce, chili powder and garlic powder. Cover and cook on low for 3-4 hours or until heated through. Serve with corn chips, sour cream and cheese if desired.

Yield: 4-6 servings.

simple sausage ring

Jean Wilkins, Cabot, Arkansas

I received this recipe from our son, who fixed it for the family one Saturday morning. We were all pleased.

1	pound bulk pork sausage
2	tubes (12 ounces *each*) refrigerated biscuits
2	cups (8 ounces) shredded Monterey Jack cheese

1 In a skillet, cook sausage over medium heat until no longer pink; drain and set aside.

2 Flatten each biscuit to a 3-in. diameter. Press half of the biscuits onto the bottom and 2 in. up the sides of a greased 10-in. fluted tube pan. Spoon sausage over dough; sprinkle with cheese. Top with remaining biscuits.

3 Bake at 350° for 20-25 minutes or until golden brown. Let stand 10 minutes before inverting onto a serving plate.

Yield: 8-10 servings.

apple butter pumpkin pie

Edna Hoffman, Hebron, Indiana

The addition of apple butter gives this pumpkin pie a slightly fruity flavor for a special variation of the classic dessert.

3	eggs
1	cup canned pumpkin
1	cup apple butter
3/4	cup packed brown sugar
1	can (5 ounces) evaporated milk
1/3	cup milk
1	teaspoon vanilla extract
1/2	teaspoon salt
1/2	teaspoon ground cinnamon
1/8	teaspoon *each* ground ginger, cloves and nutmeg
1	unbaked pastry shell (9 inches)

Whipped cream, optional

1 In a bowl, combine first seven ingredients. Whisk in the salt and spices until well blended. Pour into pastry shell.

2 Bake at 400° for 50-55 minutes or until a knife inserted near the center comes out clean. Cover edges loosely with foil during the last 20 minutes if necessary. Cool on wire rack. Garnish with whipped cream if desired. Refrigerate leftovers.

Yield: 6-8 servings.

caramel apple crisp

Michelle Brooks, Clarkston, Michigan

When my children and I make this scrumptious layered dessert at home, we use a variety of apples to give it a nice combination of flavors.

3	cups old-fashioned oats
2	cups all-purpose flour
1-1/2	cups packed brown sugar
1	teaspoon ground cinnamon
1	cup cold butter
8	cups thinly sliced peeled tart apples
1	package (14 ounces) caramels, halved
1	cup apple cider, *divided*

1 In a large bowl, combine the oats, flour, brown sugar and cinnamon; cut in butter until crumbly. Press half of the mixture into a greased 13-in. x 9-in. x 2-in. baking dish. Layer with half of the apples, caramels and 1 cup oat mixture. Repeat layers. Pour 1/2 cup cider over top.

2 Bake, uncovered, at 350° for 30 minutes. Drizzle with remaining cider; bake 15-20 minutes longer or until apples are tender.

Yield: 12-14 servings.

throw-together short ribs

Lamya Asiff, Delburne, Alberta

This recipe takes no time to prepare and results in the most delicious, fall-off-the-bone short ribs. The longer you cook them, the better they get! Serve the ribs on a bed of rice.

1/3	cup water
1/4	cup tomato paste
3	tablespoons brown sugar
1	tablespoon prepared mustard
2	teaspoons seasoned salt
2	teaspoons cider vinegar
1	teaspoon Worcestershire sauce
1	teaspoon beef bouillon granules
2	pounds beef short ribs
1	small tomato, chopped
1	small onion, chopped
1	tablespoon cornstarch
1	tablespoon cold water

1 In a 3-qt. slow cooker, combine the first eight ingredients. Add the ribs, tomato and onion. Cover and cook on low for 4-5 hours or until meat is tender.

2 In a small bowl, combine cornstarch and cold water until smooth; gradually stir into cooking juices. Cover and cook for 10-15 minutes or until thickened.

Yield: 4-5 servings.

FUNNY BONE!
What do ghosts and goblins serve for dessert? Ice scream.

PARTIES

Want to throw a special Halloween bash this year? Whether you want to entertain the kids or adults (or both), there's a party plan for you. There are even menu suggestions, themed games and tips from the experts to make your spooky-season get-together unforgettable!

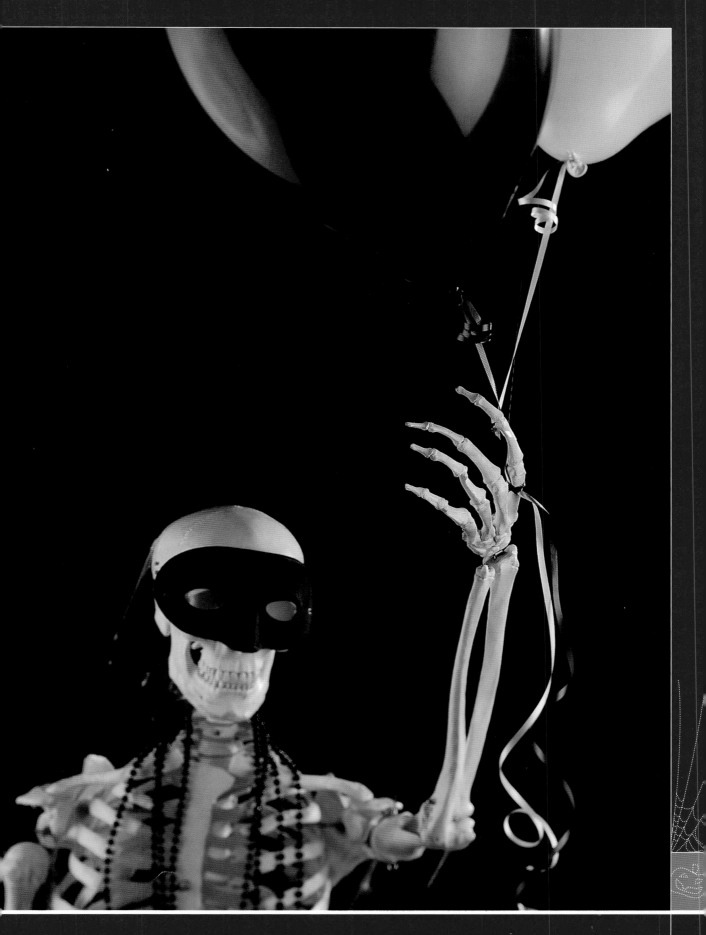

Haunted House Party

Pull out all the scary stops for kids of all ages. Turn your house into a mysterious place where anything can—and probably will—happen. This party is all about atmosphere. You don't need formal activities (kids often entertain themselves!), just a terrific environment for spooky fun.

WHAT YOU'LL NEED

For the most creative Halloween decor, look to our Crafts and Decor sections on pages 54-71, 170-177 and 228-247 for lots of fun ideas, and also think in terms of the following:

Lighting:

You want things dark, but not so dark that people can't see and safety becomes an issue. Colored lights, black lights and creative use of spotlights can all be used to create the right mood.

Surprises:

Follow some of these simple tricks to create smiles and chills.

- Fake bats hanging from the ceiling

- A Frankenstein sitting at the buffet table

- Spiderwebs and black cat cutouts on walls and windows

- White sheets draped over the furniture

- Funny signs and tombstones along the walls

- Ghostly (gray, off-white and black) helium balloons with plastic spiders tied to the end of the ribbon

Space:

While people are often hesitant to dance in public, the combination of costumes, crazy lighting and surprise music may loosen up even the shyest partygoer. So have a room for dancing and a room for sitting and relaxing as well. Yes, you want fun and commotion, but also places where people can escape for a bit to enjoy food and conversation.

For great invitation and party favor ideas, see pages 234-235.

PLAN AHEAD

Invitations should be both creative and detailed. Is it a costume party? Will there be prizes? Will there be dancing? Is a meal being served? Are children invited? Are your plans scary enough that you should offer a warning?

A day or two before the party, have a small pre-party in which you, family members and a few friends get your space ready. Make your crafts, set up your rooms, get food ready and test all the effects. You can pick up inexpensive prizes at a discount store.

For a truly haunted house, you need a few actors. Arrange to have some friends or family members take on particular roles at the party: Frankenstein (and of course, his bride), a mummy, a witch, a zombie and Count Dracula are some options. Help assemble their costumes, and coach them to stay in character throughout the first hour of the party. Their job: joke with guests, give simple scares, make funny noises and set the tone for fun.

Think through sound effects well in advance of the party. CDs are available of nothing but eerie sounds; there are also many collections of Halloween songs. A quick search on-line will reveal what's available. Do you want sound effects in different parts of the house? And if you plan on having dancing, what is the best soundtrack for your friends and family?

menu

Likely, you'll be serving food on a buffet. You want to keep it as simple and as fun as possible. Check out some of the recipes below to get the party started.

SNACKS & BEVERAGES
Hot Spiced Cider, p. 185
Hot 'n' Spicy Cranberry Dip, p. 186
Lime Fruit Slushies, p. 187
Mummy Man Cheese Spread, p. 188
Slow Cooker Mexican Dip, p. 189
Graveyard Veggie Pizza, p. 194

BUFFET MAIN DISHES & SIDES
Sweet and Sour Spareribs, p. 192
Sweet Potato Biscuits, p. 197
Turkey Hash, p. 212
Crowd Chicken Casserole, p. 213
Cheesy Tortilla Soup, p. 214

SWEET TREATS
Pumpkin Cookie Pops, p. 201
Carnival Caramel Apples, p. 203
Chocolate Skeleton Cookies, p. 203
Spiderweb Cupcakes, p. 206
Halloween Mini-cakes, p. 208
Frankenstein Cake, p. 209

SET THE MOOD

Cut a coffin shape from a piece of plywood to use as the serving table top.

Write "Rest in Peace" on serving trays that look like cemetery slabs. Use witch cauldrons, skulls and other Halloween containers as serving pieces.

Make a gallery of ghouls (rent or borrow mannequins from a store or stuff clothing with newspaper): Frankenstein, Dracula, the Headless Horseman, a skeleton or a mummy are some ideas. Keep the lights low and take guests through the gallery while eerie music plays.

Ask guests to come as their favorite horror story character and have a prize for the scariest costume. Of course, they have to tell the story, too!

 FUNNY BONE!
What is a vampire's favorite fruit? Neck-tarines.

Scavenger Hunt

In a treasure hunt, you hide the clues or prizes for people to find. A scavenger hunt is different. Each team (usually three to five people) gets a list of objects to gather, and it is up to them to locate the items.

PLAN AHEAD

Invitees need to know exactly what they are getting into well before they arrive at the party. Will they be hiking through the woods? Driving around town? Asking store clerks or waitresses embarrassing questions? Provide the appropriate details in your invitation.

Sometimes it's fun to let neighbors and even retailers into the fun. Arrange in advance for them to hold on to items, but to not give them to the hunters unless they answer a riddle or do something silly.

+ MAKE MEMORIES

Make it a photo or video scavenger hunt! Instead of gathering items, require a list of digital shots such as the team singing a song to a policeman or dancing through a restaurant; a stranger spelling "pumpernickel" or putting on a wig; the team standing under a sign with the word "black" in it; and so on. Give them the assignments 48 hours in advance and make the party a viewing party with a buffet dinner.

happy haunting

Here are examples of items to include in your scavenger hunt. Be careful in picking them; you want some that are easy to find and some that take ingenuity. Think through the methods people might use for finding the items, estimate the time it will take, and then add an hour to be safe. Better yet, do a dry run yourself! You don't want to find out that your hunt takes 6 hours instead of the 3 you had planned.

- ☐ AAA battery
- ☐ Acorn
- ☐ Apple
- ☐ Black fingernail polish
- ☐ Blood-red lipstick
- ☐ Broom
- ☐ Candy corn
- ☐ Golf ball
- ☐ Gourd
- ☐ Head of garlic
- ☐ Indian corn
- ☐ Lock of black, red or gray hair
- ☐ Map of the U.S.A.
- ☐ Miniature pumpkin
- ☐ Orange sock
- ☐ Pie tin
- ☐ Sewing needle
- ☐ Spider—real or fake
- ☐ Thread
- ☐ Today's newspaper
- ☐ Toothpick
- ☐ Tootsie Roll
- ☐ Whistle

WHAT YOU'LL NEED

Easy: a list of objects to gather. They can be themed or completely random. Make sure you have a copy of the item list, too. See below left for suggestions to get you started!

Get the permission of your neighbors, particularly if the scavenger hunt will be on foot. Let them know the types of things everyone will be searching for and discuss what limits and rules you intend to share.

You'll need a clear set of rules for participants. What are the boundaries of the search? The timetable? Of course, make it clear that stealing is NOT allowed under any circumstances; nor is driving unsafely or running through anyone's hedge or garden.

Don't forget food, drink, prizes and a place to relax when all the teams return.

PARTY IDEAS
FOR BIG KIDS

BE PREPARED

- Scare up witch cauldrons, skulls and other Halloween props as serving containers. Serve Roasted Pumpkin Seeds (p. 186) or Parmesan Party Mix (p. 189) in the creative containers.

- Freeze fake bugs in the ice cubes used for party drinks. Or make Magic Potion Punch (p. 181) or Shrunken Apple Heads in Citrus Cider (p. 187).

- Use Halloween cookie cutters, such as bats, cats or witches, to cut out sandwiches for the buffet. See Freaky Hand Sandwiches (p. 192).

- Collect all the black plates, cups and glasses that you can find for the party. They'll be readily available at party stores around Halloween.

- Prepare all the equipment and special items needed for the games with a few spares for emergencies. Make sure there are prizes!

- Emphasize costumes as well as games for the party. Have prizes for the most ghoulish, the wittiest, the most dazzling, the best couple's costume or the best group costume.

ARE KIDS COMING?

If you have a party that includes both adult guests and children, consider keeping the kids busy so the adults can enjoy themselves, too. Hire a teenage babysitter or two to entertain the kids in a separate room or somewhere on the outskirts of the party. The kids can do inexpensive Halloween crafts, cut and paste construction paper jack-o'-lanterns or scarecrows, play games (see p. 227) or just color in Halloween coloring books. The adults will thank you, and the kids will have a great time, too!

MONSTER PARTY. Decorate your yard and house with signs of a monster. Create huge footprints from the street to the front door. Some doormats are shaped like footprints, and you could use them to make the monster's path or cut the prints out of foam sheets. Set a place for him at the table with a giant place mat, a straight-sided glass vase as a drinking glass and a barbecue fork, butcher knife and large serving spoon for cutlery. His plate can be a large, round tray and his soup bowl, a tureen. Pipe a loud voice down from the attic or up from the basement. Have guests dress as monsters; the scariest gets a prize.

HALLOWEEN BARN DANCE. It's the right time of year for bales of straw for seats, pumpkins and corn stalks for decorations, and country music for getting your feet going. Join with friends to rent a hall and hire a trio of musicians and a caller to get the dancing started. With a caller, even beginners can twirl like pros. Serve cider, beer and chili and have a ball. Friends can bring appetizers, too.

DAY OF THE DEAD PARTY. This November 1 Mexican holiday honors the cycle of life and death. It welcomes deceased ancestors for a yearly visit and uses skeleton-shaped foods, not to scare the living but to celebrate the dead. Serve a mole—a chicken stew with chocolate, bread of the dead shaped like a skeleton, and spicy hot chocolate with cinnamon for a drink.

HAYRIDE PARTY. An increasing number of farms have gotten into the Halloween spirit by offering hayrides, cornfield mazes, pumpkin patches, even hay-bale courses for kids to ride tricycles through. Find a farm in your area that has autumn activities and have a great day with your children and their best friends.

6 Games for BIG Kids

1 **MUMMY WRAP.** Divide guests up in pairs; give each pair a roll of toilet paper. One team member will be the wrapper, the other will be the mummy. The first team to use up its roll wins. Or you can give each team two rolls of toilet paper and after the mummy is wrapped, he or she must wrap his partner.

2 **IDENTIFY WHAT YOU FEEL.** This is a favorite game from childhood but the big kids still like it. Line up five opaque plastic dishes and cover them all with a black cloth. Let each guest stick a hand in each dish, under the cloth so that the contents can't be seen, and try to guess what it really is. You can tell the guest that the first dish holds eyeballs (really peeled grapes) and see what he or she guesses. The second dish is said to hold brains (damp coarse sponge). The third is said to hold veins (cold, cooked spaghetti). The fourth is said to hold cut-off fingers (cocktail sausages) and the fifth to hold skin (pieces of a soft flour tortilla). The person who guesses the most actual contents wins.

3 **APPLE PASS.** Divide guests into teams and line each team up. The first in line for each team is given an apple under his or her chin. Without using any hands, the apple must be passed to under the second team member's chin and from that chin to the next until all the members of the team have held the apple. If the apple drops, it must start at the beginning again. The first team to successfully pass the apple down its row of members wins.

4 **BOBBING FOR APPLES.** This is probably the oldest Halloween game on record. Fill a large tub with cold water and set it on the ground or the floor of a porch. Float some clean, stemmed apples in the tub and invite guests to try to catch an apple with their teeth—no hands allowed. Anyone who gets an apple deserves a prize.

5 **DOUGHNUT RACE.** Divide guests into teams. Hang as many doughnuts as guests from a tree limb or a clothesline by string. Without using hands, each guest must catch and eat a doughnut. The first team to finish its doughnuts wins.

6 **WHAT AM I?** Pin or tape Halloween-themed pictures on each guest's back (without the guest seeing what it is). While others can only give yes or no answers, each guest must guess what he or she is.

6 Games for Young Children

1 **THE HANGING TREE.** In the original game, there were 12 red apples and 1 green apple to match a poem said while spinning the children around. For a small group of children, you don't need so many. Hang the apples by long strings from a tree branch (by twisting the strings you disguise where the green apple is). For each child's turn, blindfold him or her, untwist the apples, and set the youngster toward the branch. If he or she picks the green apple, he or she wins a prize (and the apple). Put up a new green apple and give another child a turn.

2 **PASS THE PUMPKIN.** Have one fewer small pumpkins than players. Sit youngsters in a circle. Play Halloween music while they pass the pumpkins around the circle. When the music stops, the player without a pumpkin is out, but he gets to take a pumpkin with him. The rest of the players continue to play until there is a winner, who will get a prize. Make Pumpkin Cookie Pops (p. 201) to set the mood.

3 **BALLOON SWEEP RELAY RACE.** Set up a course that zigzags across the yard or playroom. Use colored rope tied to stakes (or chairs) to mark it. Divide the guests into two teams. Give each team a small broom and a blown-up balloon. Each member of a team must sweep the balloon around the course and back before the next member goes. The team to have every member finish the course first wins.

4 **PIN THE TAIL ON THE BLACK CAT.** Hang up a large picture of a black Halloween cat without its tail. Give each guest a tail with a piece of sticky tape on its base. One by one, blindfold the guests, turn them around, and then set them off toward the cat picture and see where they put the tail. The guest who gets the tail closest to its rightful place wins. A Halloween ornament (p. 230-231) makes a perfect prize.

5 **HALLOWEEN STORY GAME.** Include the beginning of a ghost story in your party invitations and ask each child to come to the party with an ending to tell. Hear all the endings and let the guests vote for the funniest, the weirdest and the spookiest, then hand out paper and markers and ask the kids to illustrate their stories. Give prizes for the most creative illustration, too.

6 **BUILD A SCARECROW.** Divide the guests into teams. Give each team a pile of old clothes (including hats), pillowcases for heads, newspapers for stuffing, ropes for tying, and markers for making faces. Give each team 15 minutes or 20 minutes to make a scarecrow. Give prizes for the silliest and the scariest and hang them outside or let the kids take them home as a special party favor.

PREPARE FOR A KIDS PARTY

- Send invitations that are colorful and enticing for the kids, but that also give thorough details to the parents. Make it clear if it is to be a costume party; whether kids need sneakers; whether a full meal, snacks or cake will be served; and if kids need to bring anything, like a gift or a trick-or-treat bag.

- Figure out a short parade route for the guests when all have arrived so that they—and you—can appreciate their costumes.

- Plan the games for outdoors if the weather is nice, but have a backup plan for the playroom or some other part of the house if the weather fades.

- To keep things happy, try to keep the number of guests fewer than the years in your child's age.

- Substitute craft projects for some of the games, such as painting small pumpkins with acrylics or decorating inexpensive masks with feathers, sequins, glitter and other notions.

- Have a teacher or performer come in costume and read a short ghost story. Check your local library for likely candidates.

- Don't plan to do everything yourself. Enlist a spouse or family friend or hire some older children to help.

CRAFTS & DECOR

Here, you'll find new takes on the classic Halloween crafts, like far-out jack-o'-lanterns and unique candy wrappers, but you'll also find creative twists on the traditional, like Halloween ornaments. Enjoy this spooky season making these simple, attractive, BOO-rific crafts.

Halloween Ornaments

Christmas isn't the only holiday you can use ornaments! Hang these from your mantel, in front of a window, or even from a coffee-mug rack!

BASIC SUPPLIES

Cardboard form or circle cut out from thick cardboard

Pencil

White paper

Scissors

White glue

Large needle or compass point

Liquid beads (beads floating in a glue-like gel medium) or microbeads (tiny plastic beads) and tacky glue in colors of your choice, see options for individual ornaments

Glittery string or thread

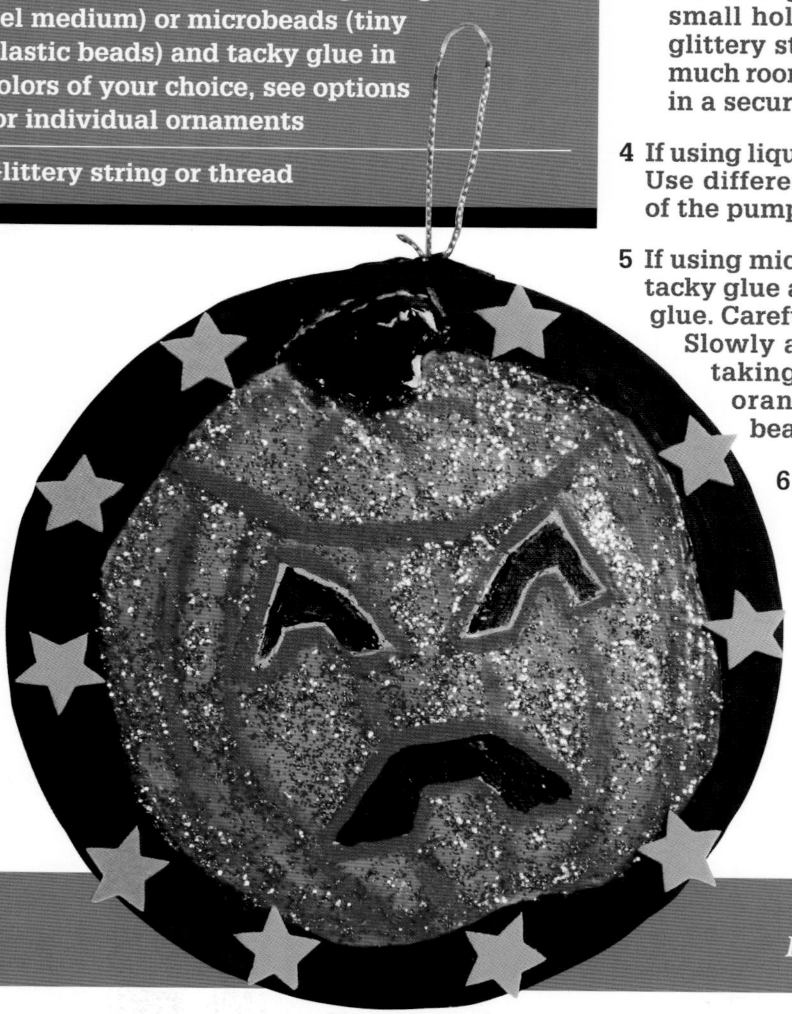

Jack o' Lantern Ornament

EXTRA SUPPLIES:

Black craft paint

Orange liquid beads or microbeads

Small, star-shaped stickers
(we used glow-in-the-dark ones)

1 To make a form, cut a circle shape out of thick cardboard. Paint it black.

2 Using a pencil, draw a pumpkin face onto a piece of paper at a size that will fit your ornament form. Cut it out and glue it to the form.

3 Use a large needle or compass point to punch small hole at the top of the form. Thread the glittery string through the hole, estimate how much room you'll need for hanging and tie ends in a secure knot or bow.

4 If using liquid beads, apply them to the pumpkin. Use different colors to depict the carved areas of the pumpkin.

5 If using microbeads, coat the pumpkin area with tacky glue and pour orange microbeads onto the glue. Carefully apply tacky glue to carved areas. Slowly add dark microbeads to these areas, taking care to avoid dropping beads onto orange sections. Gently tap off excess beads after the glue has dried.

6 Add stickers to the border if desired. We used glow-in-the-dark stickers for extra fun!

FUNNY BONE!
How much does a truck full of bones weigh? A Skele—Ton!

Spooky Witch Ornament

EXTRA SUPPLIES:

Colored construction paper of your choice

Liquid beads or microbeads in colors of your choice

1 Follow step #1 from Pumpkin Ornament.

2 Photocopy a drawing of a witch, ghost, skull-and-crossbones or any other Halloween image on colored paper at a size that will fit your ornament. (We copied our pumpkin carving template for the witch from page 242.) Cut it out. Glue it to the form.

3 Follow step #3 from Pumpkin Ornament.

4 If using liquid beads, apply them to the background around image. If using microbeads, coat the background area with tacky glue and pour microbeads onto the glue. Gently tap off excess beads after the glue has dried.

Spider Ornament

EXTRA SUPPLIES:

Orange and black craft paint

Two oval-shaped gemstones

White glossy *or* 3-D paint

Orange glitter glue

1 Follow steps #1 and #3 from Pumpkin Ornament, but do not paint black.

2 Paint the entire surface of cardboard form with orange paint. When it's dry, use a pencil to draw the spider and its web.

3 Use black paint to fill in the spider and legs. When it's dry, add tacky glue to the back of gemstones and position them on the spider.

4 Trace over the webbing lines with white paint. Add dots of glitter glue to intersections of the webbing and to spider legs.

Bat Ornament

EXTRA SUPPLIES:

Round gemstone

Liquid beads *or* microbeads in colors of your choice

Palette knife *or* flexible plastic knife

Sequins in colors of your choice

Orange and white craft paint

Glitter glue in colors of your choice

1 Follow steps #1 and #3 from Pumpkin Ornament, but do not paint black.

2 Using a pencil, draw an outline of a bat and moon (the same size as gemstone).

3 If using liquid beads, apply them directly to the background areas using a palette or plastic knife. If using microbeads, coat background area with tacky glue and pour microbeads onto the glue. Gently tap off excess beads after a few minutes.

4 Fill in the bat shape with tacky glue. Stack sequins into glue, beginning at the bottom of the wing and working upward.

5 Add two orange dots with orange paint for eyes. Allow to dry.

6 Glue gemstone into moon outline.

7 Use a dry brush and white paint to lightly apply highlights to ridges of the wings. Outline the bat figure and moon with glitter glue. Let dry.

Paper-Wrapped Vase

Top off your spooky decor with a few of these fun vases. They're easy to make, and you probably have the materials on hand.

- 1   12-inch x 12-inch piece of scrapbook *or* parchment paper
- 1   cylinder vase

Halloween stamps *or* motifs

Double-stick tape

Ribbon

Tea light *or* plumber's candle

Shallow bowl

Colored popcorn *or* Indian corn

1   Trim a 12-inch x 12-inch piece of scrapbook or parchment paper as needed to fit the outside of a clear glass cylinder vase.

2   Stamp or paste Halloween motifs around the top edge of the parchment paper as shown in photo.

3   Wrap the paper around a clear glass cylinder vase with the design at the top and secure it with double-stick tape.

4   Tie a coordinating narrow ribbon around the vase below stamped area.

5   Place a tea light or plumber's candle inside the vase.

6   Stand the vase in a shallow bowl filled with colored popcorn or Indian corn.

Halloween Movie Night

Grab the kids, turn off the lights, get into the Halloween spirit, but (thankfully) don't scare them out of their wits! Here is a collection of recommended Halloween and fantasy movies that will enhance the mood of the spooky season but won't give the kids nightmares.

For very young children:

- *Bedknobs and Broomsticks (1971—an oldie but a goodie)*
- *It's the Great Pumpkin, Charlie Brown (1966—the classic Halloween story)*
- *Mickey's House of Villains (2002)*
- *Pooh's Heffalump Halloween Movie (2005)*

For school-age children:

- *Scary Godmother Halloween Spooktacular (2003)*
- *The Corpse Bride (2005)*
- *The Nightmare Before Christmas (1993)*
- *The Simpson Trick or Treehouse (2000)*
- *Worst Witch: A Mean Halloween (2001)*

String of Paper Lanterns

Scare up some ambience at your next Halloween party with these lanterns. You can use any stamp design you'd like. Leave them up all season—they're so cute and fun!

- Parchment paper
- Decorative edge scissors
- Straight-edge scissors
- 1/4-inch round paper punch
- Halloween stamps *or* motifs
- String of orange mini-lights
- Double-stick tape

1 For each lantern, trace pattern at right onto parchment paper.

2 Use decorative-edge scissors and straight-edge scissors to cut out lantern from parchment paper as shown.

3 Use a 1/4-inch round paper punch or a straight-edge scissors to cut out a small circle where shown on pattern.

4 Stamp a Halloween design onto the cutout.

5 Wrap paper lantern around an orange mini-light, overlapping the straight edges. Use double-stick tape to hold the overlapped edges together.

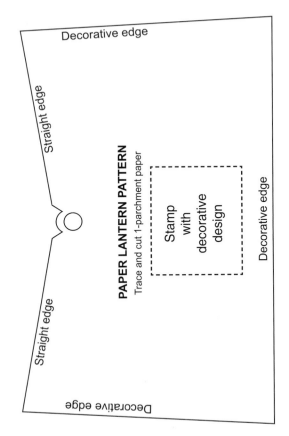

PAPER LANTERN PATTERN
Trace and cut 1-parchment paper

Decorative edge

Straight edge

Straight edge

Decorative edge

Decorative edge

Straight edge

Stamp with decorative design

Halloween Party Invitations

Here at Taste of Home, we all like to get in on crafting fun. Our dedicated Vice President, Executive Editor/Books, Heidi Reuter Lloyd, shares some of her creative, spooky-season party invitations, candy wrappers and scrapbook ideas on the next few pages.

Purchase a set of invitation stamps that contains a "You're Invited" stamp plus a second stamp that includes the date, time, place and occasion. You can use your computer instead of stamps to write the words. A black cat or bat stamp can be substituted for the spider. A patterned ribbon is an inexpensive way to add fun to the card.

9	sheets of 8-1/2 x 11-inch orange cardstock
18	pieces of 2-1/2 x 2-1/2-inch white cardstock
18	pieces of 2-3/4 x 2-3/4-inch black cardstock
1	spider stamp
1	black dye-based ink pad
1	set of invitation stamps
6-1/2	feet of thin decorative black ribbon, cut into 18 segments, 4-1/4 inches long *each*

Double-sided tape *or* Mono-Adhesive

1. Cut each piece of orange cardstock in half lengthwise, creating 18 pieces of 8-1/2 x 5-1/2 inches.

2. Fold each piece in half.

3. Stamp one spider on each piece of white cardstock.

4. Adhere white cardstock to black cardstock.

5. Adhere black cardstock to front of card.

6. Stamp "You're Invited" below spider.

7. Adhere black ribbon below "You're Invited" stamp.

8. Stamp inside of card with a single stamp that includes a line for the date, time, place and occasion.

Images copyright Stampin' Up!

Spider-Wrapped Candy

These easy treats are fun to hand out at classroom parties or to trick-or-treaters. For the simplest version, do black stamping on white paper (shown below left). To dress them up with color, use magic markers to fill in the spider's eyes and body, then create eye-catching borders with contrasting Halloween colors.

60	mini chocolate bars, such as Hershey Nuggets
2	sheets of 30 plain white 1 x 2-5/8-inch address labels
30	clear 2 x 3-3/4-inch plastic craft bags

White cardstock cut into 30 pieces of 1-7/8 x 2-1/4 inches

Black cardstock cut into 30 pieces of 2-1/2 x 4-1/4 inches

1	small spider rubber stamp
1	large spider rubber stamp
1	black dye-based ink pad

Double-sided tape *or* Mono-Adhesive

Stapler

Yellow, orange, purple and green markers, optional

1 With black ink, stamp small spiders lengthwise on white labels.

2 Remove outer wrapper from candy bars and replace with stamped labels.

3 Place two candy bars in each mini bag.

4 With black ink, stamp 3 large spiders on each piece of white cardstock.

5 Fold each piece of black cardstock in half.

6 Center white cardstock on black and adhere, with fold at top.

7 Place black cardstock around plastic bag and staple at bottom to hold.

8 If desired, use markers to color in spiders and/or add colored borders to edge of white cardstock.

Images copyright Stampin' Up!

FUNNY BONE!
Why was the skeleton afraid to cross the road? It didn't have the guts.

Halloween Scrapbook Page

To make a scrapbook page quickly, buy a group of Halloween images and a phrase or two at a craft store. Although this design features a stamped spider and bat, you could easily use another image or two from the self-adhesive Halloween grouping instead.

2	sheets of 8-1/2 x 11-inch orange cardstock
1	sheet of 8-1/2 x 11-inch white cardstock
1	scrap piece of black cardstock
8	black self-adhesive photo corners
2	Halloween snapshots
1	set of Halloween self-adhesive words and images

Spider and bat stamps, optional

1	black dye-based ink pad, optional

8-1/2 inch segment of decorative black ribbon

Double-sided tape *or* Mono-Adhesive

1 Tear white cardstock across top quarter for ragged-edge effect. Adhere smaller white piece to orange cardstock. Save larger white piece for another use.

2 Choose a headline from self-adhesive Halloween grouping and place on page.

3 Using a computer, write a caption and print it on orange cardstock. Trim around the caption forming a rectangle.

4 Cut a piece of black cardstock that is 1/4-inch bigger than the caption rectangle on all sides.

5 Adhere caption to black cardstock.

6 Adhere decorative ribbon to bottom quarter of page.

7 Position photos on page. Adhere photo corners where needed.

8 Adhere caption rectangle to page.

9 Add art elements from Halloween grouping or stamp spider and bat.

Images copyright Stampin' Up!

10 Candle Safety Tips

1. Never leave a burning candle unattended or even out of your line of sight.

2. Never place a burning candle on or near anything that can catch fire or where it can be knocked over.

3. Keep burning candles out of the reach of children and pets.

4. Use sturdy fireproof holders and containers made specifically for candles.

5. Trim the wick to 1/4 inch before each use. Extinguish and trim a flickering or high-flaming candle.

6. Burn candles in a well-ventilated room but away from drafts, vents and fans.

7. Don't touch or move a burning candle.

8. Stop using a candle when 2 inches of wax remains (1/2 inch in a container).

9. Keep matches, wick trimmings and debris out of the candle wax.

10. Never use a candle as a night-light.

FUNNY BONE!
What does a ghost get when he falls and scrapes his knee? A boo-boo.

Autumn Wreath

If you thought wreaths were only for winter holidays, think again. You can make a wreath that celebrates almost any holiday or season, and Halloween is no exception. And if you don't care for elaborate decorations, don't have the time to make them or don't have the space to display them, hanging a Halloween-themed wreath on the door is a subtle and elegant way to pay tribute to the holiday. In the wreath design here, various brightly colored items stand out in contrast to the traditional leaves and nuts of autumn. You can find the supplies you need to make a wreath at your local craft store.

Drying the leaves

Air-dry the oak, bay and other leaves following these steps:

1. Sort the leaves into small bunches and remove any excess foliage from the lower stems.

2. In a dry, warm, dark and airy place, either stand the branches upright in an empty container or secure the ends of the stems with string and suspend them upside down. Let them dry for a week or so; the time will depend on the size and moisture content of the individual pieces.

Making the wreath

1. Attach a length of wire across the back of the wreath base so that you can hang the wreath on a hook like a picture.

2. Start by filling in the background. Push small branches of salal leaves into the base. Intersperse them with oak and bay leaves. Make sure that the top and sides are covered and that the base is concealed. Allow some branches to hang into the center of the circle and some to overhang the outside edge. Once you are happy with the arrangement, glue the leaves into place using the hot glue gun.

3. Glue small groups of pinecones and Halloween items randomly around the wreath. If some of the Halloween items are too awkwardly shaped to glue, secure them with wire in the next step. Make sure that some of the groups are toward the inner side, some are on top, and some are toward the outer edge. Be sure to glue the pinecones and Halloween items to the base, not to the leaves. Turn the wreath as you work to ensure a balanced result.

4. Place groups of wired nuts close to the cones and fix them in place by pushing the wires through the vine base and twisting the wire around the vine at the back. Arrange the poppy seed heads, fanning them out around the cone groups, and when you are pleased with the result, glue them into place. Let the glue dry and hang on your door.

*To wire a nut, stand the nut on end in play clay and drill a small hole using a drill with a fine bit. Push a short length of thin wire through the hole.

FUNNY BONE!
What do you get when you divide the circumference of a jack-o'-lantern by its diameter? Pumpkin p

10 Tips for Perfect Jack-o'-Lanterns

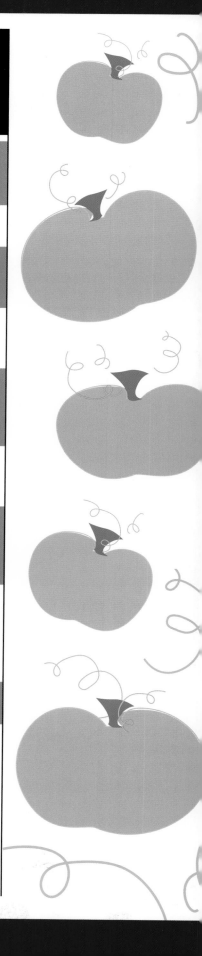

1 Never carry your pumpkin by the stem. It's part of the visual allure, and if it snaps, it can accelerate the pumpkin's rotting. Always carry the pumpkin from the bottom.

2 Store your uncut pumpkin in a cool, dry place. Once pumpkins ripen, they will deteriorate fast—heat and light speed up the process.

3 Wash the exterior of the pumpkin before carving. Use a solution of 1 gallon water and 1 teaspoon chlorine bleach. This will help prevent mold.

4 Draw your pattern on paper or use a pumpkin-carving template. (See pages 241-245 for ideas.) This is easier and cleaner than drawing right on the pumpkin and makes revisions a snap.

5 To transfer a template to the pumpkin, enlarge it, cut it out and adhere it to the pumpkin with masking tape. Then either use pin-pricks to mark the shapes and lines on the pumpkin or use a craft or utility knife and cut through the design to score it on the surface.

6 Don't just think of face designs. Moons, stars, cats and witches are all fun and easy to do. You can even use a drill to make patterned light holes.

7 Consider buying a pumpkin-carving kit. Often they can be found for just a few dollars. Kits usually contain small scoops and serrated saws that aren't commonly found in the typical toolbox. They're great for detailed carving work.

8 When cutting out your shapes, always use a sawing motion. Go slowly and gently. A small serrated saw is best for the detail work. Never try to forcefully cut your pumpkin with a straight-edge razor—you'll damage the pumpkin, hurt the knife and possibly cut yourself!

9 The more pumpkins in your display, the better. Four or five small pumpkins have much more visual impact than one large one.

10 If scraping out a pumpkin is too much hassle for you, consider buying a hollow acrylic or craft pumpkin. These are becoming increasingly popular, thanks to their realistic appearance and their ease in carving. Yes, you carve these soft plastic pumpkins just like a real one; most are made to be about 1/4 inch thick with inside colors that match a real pumpkin. And they last forever, meaning instant jack-o'-lanterns for next year!

Wicked Pumpkin Carving Templates

See next page for templates.

1 Boo!

2 Flying Witch

3 Starry Night

4 Hissing Cat

FUNNY BONE!
Where do fashionable ghosts shop for their clothes? BOO-tiques.

Enlarge any of these templates on a photocopier to the desired size, then follow the tips on page 240 for fantastic results!

1 Boo! Template

2 Flying Witch Template

3 Starry Night Template

4 Hissing Cat Template

Wicked Pumpkin Carving Templates

See next page for templates.

5 Who, Me?

6 Lopsided Grin

7 Cat's Whiskers

8 I'm Afraid, Too!

FUNNY BONE!
What do mummy children call their parents? Mummy and Deady.

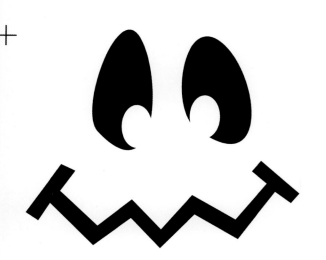

5 Who, Me? Template

6 Lopsided Grin Template

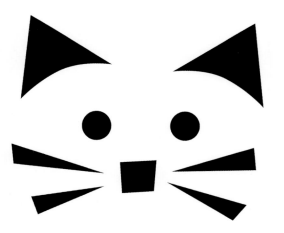

7 Cat's Whiskers Template

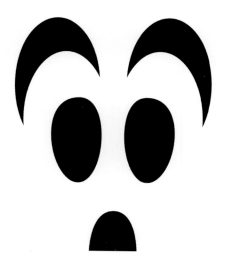

8 I'm Afraid, Too! Template

More Pumpkin Design Tricks

SECRETS TO SUCCESS

Think about light:

Part of the art of great pumpkin carving is thinking about shadows. Small designs in the back of the pumpkin can cast a wonderful shadow on a wall or door behind the pumpkin. Just remember to keep the design small, because the light that emerges gets magnified. If you are going to do this, be sure to scrape the inside of the back of your pumpkin to slightly under 1 inch in thickness.

The mouth:

When you are working on the mouth, you can make more realistic teeth by only peeling off the outer skin of the pumpkin within the mouth and leaving the pale flesh beneath. You can then carve lines between individual teeth. The candlelight will shine through the fleshy teeth, but you can also make an opening between upper and lower teeth for more light to come through.

Adding pieces:

You can use the pieces of pumpkin that you have carved out to fashion ears and fit them into slits that you have cut. Or you can use corks for ears (make holes and wedge them in). You can carve hair at the top of the pumpkin by scraping straight or curling lines all around the cap. Use a chisel or a linoleum cutter for this. Try a carrot for a nose or maybe a radish.

Finishing touches:

When you are finished, use a paper towel to rub petroleum jelly over all the cut surfaces, inside and outside the pumpkin. This will help preserve it for several days.

Create a Walkway

Why not light the path to your front door with a line of small pumpkins? Pick small pumpkins and prepare them as you would a jack-o'-lantern, except make the opening in the bottom instead of the top so that you can insert lightbulbs from underneath. Then run an outdoor string of lights (such as Christmas lights), and place several bulbs in each of the pumpkins. As long as you use approved outdoor lighting, they will be beautiful and safe.

Pumpkin Carving Fiesta

On the weekend before Halloween, invite friends and family to a BYOP (bring your own pumpkin) carving party. Dazzle your friends with a well-equipped outdoor workshop (or garage) for the task, with loads of space for people to work and all the tools you'll need. Add in fun music and finger foods appropriate for the messy fun, and it'll be like having two Halloweens in one week!

WHAT YOU'LL NEED

Several sturdy tables, each covered with newspapers or disposable plastic cloths

Pumpkin cleaning gear (paper towels, spray bottles of water, small container of baby wipes)

Old T-shirts, dress shirts or smocks

One pumpkin-carving kit for every three people:

> **Sharp kitchen knife**
>
> **Large, strong tablespoon or ice-cream scoop**
>
> **Sharp-tip marker (non-permanent)**
>
> **Electric screwdriver or drill with varying bit sizes**
>
> **Thin-blade serrated saws**
>
> **Bucket for seeds**

Decorating supplies for kids: paints, stickers, etc.

BYOP!
(Bring Your Own Pumpkin)

GETTING READY

The best place for your party is outdoors among the changing leaves and cool breezes of autumn. But have a backup plan for indoors, just in case of rain. Wherever you are, be prepared for a mess! If you can, collect all pumpkin waste for composting (or pumpkin seed roasting); also have garbage cans around for the soiled newspapers and paper towels.

Don't crowd your artists. You'll probably want no more than three pumpkins being worked on at any given table. So be sure to have ample folding tables, picnic tables and makeshift tables (plywood on top of sawhorses, for example) so everyone has a space to work.

Have music ready for outdoors. A boom box playing a collection of Halloween music will add perfect ambience.

Have diversions ready for the kids. It can take more than an hour to carve a pumpkin, and kids often get antsy before the work is complete. Have some mini-pumpkins available for painting, face-painting kits, scarecrow-building supplies and party games ready.

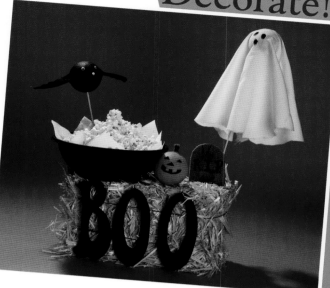

Decorate!

Decorate! Help create a Halloween mood by decorating your workshop with hay bales, finished jack-o'-lanterns, gourd displays and more.

ADD TO THE FUN

Want to give your guests extra creative opportunities? Put out a bowl of precut vegetables and toothpicks. Let them add pieces to their pumpkins—carrot antennae, broccoli ears, green bean whiskers and so on.

Make it a contest. When the carving is complete, line up the finished jack-o'-lanterns and either let people cast votes or have a "distinguished panel" make the decisions. Whatever the method, be sure to give out lots of prizes, including silly ones like "most crooked smile" and "pumpkin you'd least like to meet in a dark alley."

Make it a costume-making party instead. Like a pumpkin carving party, you want to provide your guests all the things they might need for a costume—old clothes, fabrics, scissors, construction paper, decorating supplies, lots of paper for stuffing things, wooden dowels—the list goes on. Or make it a scavenger costume party—once everyone arrives, give each person 1 hour and a budget of $20 to jump in the car, find or buy materials and return to make a costume. Don't forget your camera!

FUNNY BONE!
What is a witch's favorite subject in school? Spelling.

FACE PAINT & COSTUMES

Need some fresh, easy and inexpensive costume ideas? All you need is right here! Learn face-painting techniques from a professional makeup artist, then fashion a no-sew costume and your kids will haunt the streets in style. The best part—you'll save time and money when you follow our expert advice.

Scrappy the
Scarecrow, p. 255

Face Painting
MADE EASY

What makeup professionals know is no longer a secret: You can buy an inexpensive kit of safe, washable face paints and turn your Halloween child into whatever she or he fancies in a matter of minutes!

That's what we learned when we invited Broadway and television makeup artist Joel Mendenhall and his assistant Sadiya Sellers to our studios, along with some willing and curious children. We gave Mendenhall strict instructions: Spend less than $10 for makeup supplies per child (with all materials coming from an everyday drugstore), and take 20 minutes or less to apply the makeup.

The results were stunning. We learned that even the most basic and inexpensive face-painting kit allows you to create professional-level mustaches and beards, animal noses and whiskers, quizzical eyebrows and a scarecrow's face. You can paint on a pirate's bandanna that won't come off during the evening's activities. You can paint a panting puppy's tongue under a painted puppy nose.

Fairy princesses can be made more glamorous with fanciful painted eye treatments and glitter, reminiscent of New Orleans Mardi Gras masks (see p. 252). A clown is so adorable after a few simple application steps (see p. 251 and p. 254).

There's more to Halloween face painting than just fun and surprise. There's safety, too. Masks severely restrict vision, leading to accidents. There's also another benefit—with a well-painted face, the rest of the costume can be much less elaborate, saving time and expense.

If you finish off the makeup job with a dusting of powder, it will be less likely to rub off on clothes and upholstery. And at the end of the evening, removing the paint is simple: just start the cleanup process with commercial pre-moistened towelettes or a wet washrag with baby shampoo, and follow up with a scrubbing with soap and water.

GETTING STARTED

Buy a face-painting kit (from a craft or discount store) that contains the colors you want and has instructions for completing the design that you have in mind. Although most kits contain safe, washable paints, you might want to do an allergy test on your child. Dab some paint in the crook of the youngster's arm at the elbow. If no rash appears after 12 hours, you can proceed.

Sit your child in a chair that is high enough that you can work on the face without bending over. Tie the hair away from the face. Most kits come with applicators, but you may find that you are more comfortable working with your own. Soft sponges, like stipple sponges from an art store, are good for applying base paints.

Thin paintbrushes or makeup sticks or crayons from the kit are good for making lines. Your own powder puff is best for finishing off the face painting. You can use baby powder to set the paints and brush off the excess with a cosmetic brush.

A BASIC KIT

- **Foundtion makeup (often white, sometimes in a tube)**
- **Four or more colored makeups**
- **Black makeup pencil**
- **Paint sticks or crayons in various colors**
- **Application sponges**
- **Application brushes**
- **Step-by-step instructions with pictures**

FACE PAINTING 101

START FRESH: *Begin with a clean face. Pin a towel around the child's neck just in case the makeup drips.*

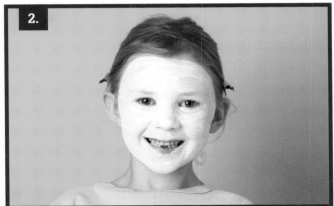

APPLY THE BASE: *Use a sponge and only dilute the paint if it is too thick to spread.*

ADD THE DETAILS: *Apply second and third colors. Here, blue goes around the eye in an inverted teardrop shape and red defines a large mouth.*

EMPHASIZE: *Outlining the new color areas with black makes them stand out. Use a paintbrush or makeup stick.*

ACCESSORIZE: *Props complete the image: a curly green wig, a fake red ball nose and an outrageous oversized bow tie are added.*

JOIN THE FUN: *The youngster from Step 1 is now a bona fide clown, ready for a night of trick-or-treating.*

PRINCESS GRACIE, A GOOD FAIRY

All the colors of her costume—lavender, pink, blue and white—are used in the enchanting design around her eyes. Paintbrushes and makeup sticks were the primary tools, starting with a pink line that defines her eyes and then spreads out toward her temples. Her cheeks and temples were painted lavender with a pad applicator. Blue squiggles were applied next with a paintbrush or makeup stick, which also made the white lines and white dots. Gossamer wings, a beribboned net skirt and a jewel-studded wand complete her costume.

THE MASKED GREEN GO-GETTER, SUPERHERO

The green mask that won't blow away in flight (and is much safer than a plastic one) was speedily applied with a sponge and outlined with a paintbrush. The eyebrows were made with a small pad applicator. A swishing cape attached behind his shoulders allows him to take off quickly.

NICKO,
THE CLOWN

Here is a very quick but lively clown makeup that doesn't use a base paint. His eyes are enlarged with white sponge-applied face paint, black paintbrush or makeup stick outlining, and green highlighter lines (also applied with a paintbrush or makeup stick). A big red mouth applied with a pad applicator is outlined in white and black, and black-rimmed white dimples dot both ends. A polka-dot hat, a big bow tie and curly green hair complete the silliness.

SCRAPPY,
THE SCARECROW

This happy face would hardly scare away a wren, but it will delight the hosts of Halloween parties. Her makeup starts with a yellow sponge-applied base. Black paintbrush or makeup stick lines, highlighted with white paintbrush lines sew up her mouth, make patches on her forehead and cheeks and extend her eyes. A straw-filled hat and a straw-stuffed flannel shirt are the perfect accessories.

Costumes!
low-sew, no-sew

"What are you going to be for Halloween?" It's the question that animates kids' conversations each and every October. Look no further for the answers!

When children's imaginations run too wild, it makes life tough for Mom and Dad. Do you rent, buy or spend weeks making an outfit from scratch? Isn't there a compromise that will thrill your child and be easy for you as well?

Absolutely! We asked Catherine Alston, a theatrical costume designer in Vermont, to create easy-to-make costume designs that would please children of all ages and be a relief for parents as well. She certainly delivered!

Catherine showed us that you can quickly improvise any number of wonderful costumes with a little fabric, some common accessories, a hot glue gun, some staples, or if you have a sewing machine, a few stitches.

In the pages ahead, we'll show you how to pull off five quick, inexpensive Halloween transformations.

The ideas will likely get your own imagination going, so that when your daughter wants to be an astronaut or your son wants to be Julius Caesar, you will know just what to do.

The tricks are simple. For example, start with a color scheme that will determine the base garments that you need. For example, witches usually wear black turtlenecks and black tights—unless they come from The Wizard of Oz and need colorful tights.

Once you determine the base clothing you need, think about the other pieces of the costume. Capes, hats, tails, ears and stripes are easily created from easy-to-find materials. Chances are, you can make a terrific costume in just 90 minutes! You'll save a fortune, thrill your child, amuse other kids and grown-ups and feel great that you made it yourself.

Popular Costumes

According to the National Retail Federation, the top five children's costumes in 2006 were: princess, pirate, witch, Spiderman and Superman. The top five for adults were: witch, pirate, vampire, cat and clown. Although traditional costumes never go out of style, current movie characters are often a popular choice, too.

GETTING READY

Once you have an idea for a costume, you might want to check a party store for components you will not have to make: a witch's hat, for example, or a knight's sword. Fabric and craft stores, particularly around Halloween, offer wide assortments of costume materials that won't ravel—like fake furs, felts and fleeces—and endless trimmings that can be sewn or glued on.

The first step in making a costume is to gather the various pieces together and check that you have everything you are going to need. Be sure the basic garments on which you plan to build are clean and pressed.

If you are making one of the costumes in this chapter, read the directions carefully. Check that your tools are ready: extra sticks for the hot glue gun, extra staples for the stapler, the correct color thread for your needles or sewing machine, and so on.

WHAT YOU'LL NEED

Here are nine items that are most often needed to make a costume:

- Base garments
- Cutting wheel and self-healing mat
- Fabrics
- Hot glue gun
- Needle and thread
- Patterns
- Scissors
- Sewing machine
- Staples

classic witch

You and your child can put together this smashing version of the classic costume in no time.

1	round black tablecloth, 84-inch diameter
1	yard elastic cord
1	yard 1/4-inch black elastic
1	roll electrical tape
1	black turtleneck
1	pair black tights
1	witch hat

1. Fold tablecloth in half, then in quarters, and finally in eighths, giving you a narrow cone of fabric. Measure 4 inches down from the peak and cut the peak off. Discard this fabric. Now measure 10 inches down from the cut and cut again (this will be the cape). The remaining 28 inches of fabric will make the skirt.

2. Open the cape and skirt pieces to semicircles and punch holes 1 inch apart on the inside edges of each. Thread the elastic cord through the holes. Gather the cape and tie it at the neck (see photo below). Shred the ends of the cape.

3. To make the skirt, thread 1/4-inch elastic through the waist holes and gather to fit the youngster's waist. Tie the ends. Shred the bottom. Add reflective tape detailing for nighttime safety.

4. Dress the child in the turtleneck and tights under the costume and add the hat.

snuggly lion

This furry lion costume feels soft and snuggly because it uses a thin, very soft type of fleece available at most fabric stores.

1/2	yard (18 x 60 inches) lightweight brown-and-tan-patterned fleece
1	yellow sleeper
1	yellow baby cap with ties
1	square (12 inches) brown felt
1	square (12 inches) tan felt
1	square (12 inches) yellow felt

1. To make the lion's mane, cut the fleece into three pieces, each 6 x 60 inches. Layer the pieces on top of each other and stitch or staple them together down the center of the 60-inch length. On both sides of the three-layer strip, make cuts at 1/2-inch intervals almost to (but not through) the 60-inch stitch line (see photo at right). Measure the neck of the sleeper and cut a piece of the three-layered, clipped mane to match. Attach this strip to the neck of the sleeper along the stitch line (see photo on p. 259, top). Use the remaining mane strips to trim the cap in three rows. Save an inch of the mane strips to finish off the end of the tail. Fold back and fluff the fleece strips.

2. Cut two outer ear pieces from the brown felt and two inner ear pieces from the tan felt, using the photo at right as a guide. Glue inner ear pieces to outer ear pieces and attach to cap with a glue gun, staple, or needle and thread.

3. Make the tail by cutting a 2 x 12-inch strip of yellow felt. Fold the strip in half lengthwise and staple or stitch together. Invert and attach fleece tassel to one end (see photo at right). Attach the other end to the back of the sleeper.

4. Dress baby in sleeper and cap.

lion's mane

lion's ear

lion's tail

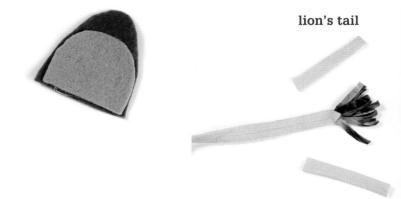

Kids' Costumes

Most adult and older kids' costumes have intricate detail and accessories that make them unique, but toddler costumes need to be simpler. Using a sleeper as the base and adding soft fleece not only makes this costume cute and comfortable, it keeps the baby warm and cozy, too.

attach mane to
neck of sleeper

attach flowers
to headband

bouquet of flowers

Turn your tiny trick-or-treater into a bouquet of flowers, and no one will be able to resist!

1	bunch fabric flowers from a craft store

Soft headband

12	yellow felt circles, 1/2-inch diameter (optional)
1	yard green yarn
1	yellow shirt
1	pair yellow pants
6	fabric leaves from a craft store

1. Remove as much plastic from flowers and leaf stems as possible to make them lie flat. Attach flowers to headband with stitching or hot glue until headband is covered (see photo on p. 260, top). Glue yellow felt circles to center of flowers if desired.

2. Cut 18 inches of yarn and place it on the front of the shirt in a flower stem pattern (see top photo on this page). Sew or glue it in place. Use the remaining yarn to continue the pattern down one pant leg, matching the overlap (see photo at left). Sew or glue in place.

3. Attach leaves along the stem.

4. Dress child in shirt, pants and headband.

flower stem pattern on shirt

flower stem pattern on pants

easy ladybug

Ladybugs are the one crawly creature most kids find fun, cute and friendly. Any child will feel the same wearing this simple, comfortable costume.

2	pieces (12 x 18 inches) stiff red felt
1	piece (12 x 18 inches) black felt
2	hook-and-loop stick-on buttons
2	large black chenille pipe cleaners
1	regular black pipe cleaner
1	square (12 inches) stick-on black felt
1	black headband
1	black turtleneck top
1	pair black leggings

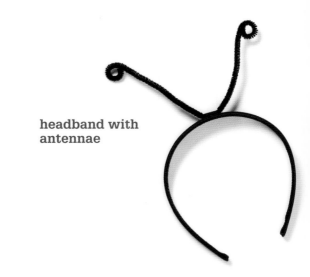

headband with antennae

1. To make the ladybug's wings, draw a semicircle on each piece of stiff red felt. You can attach a 12-inch piece of string to a pencil and, holding the string end midway on the 18-inch side of the felt, draw a semicircle by swinging the pencil in an arc. Curve the top of each wing as shown at right.

2. To make the yoke, fold the black felt piece in half lengthwise. At the center of the folded edge, cut a 5-inch, curved neck opening. Curve the outer edges of the yoke and cut the center open as shown in the photo at right.

3. Attach the top of the wings to the back of the yoke with glue or needle and thread. Add hook-and-loop buttons to either side of the yoke opening. Sew or glue the large chenille pipe cleaners to the outside joints between the yoke and the wings: these are the bug's extra legs.

4. Use a glass to trace 7 black dots on the stick-on black felt. Cut out the dots and stick them to the ladybug wings as shown at right.

5. Glue the center of the regular black pipe cleaner to the center of the headband. Reinforce it with a strip of black stick-on felt. Curl ends of pipe cleaner to complete the antennae.

6. Dress the child in the black turtleneck, leggings, wings with yoke and headband.

yoke with wings attached

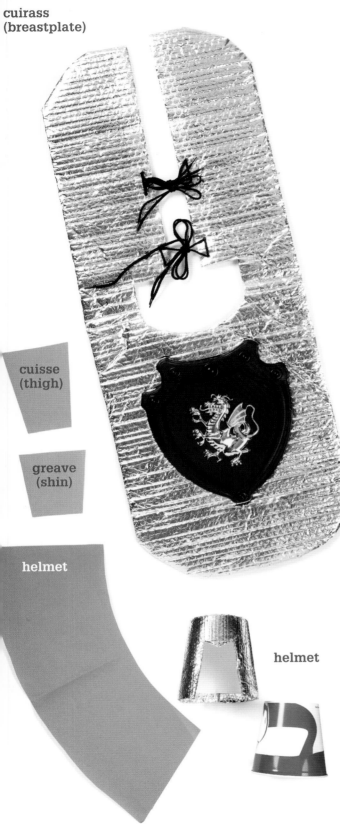

cuirass
(breastplate)

cuisse
(thigh)

greave
(shin)

helmet

helmet

silver knight

You'll need to visit a hardware store, a sports store and a party shop for the components of this costume unless, of course, you have items around the house that will do.

1	gray hooded sweatshirt
1	roll of silver insulation
2	foam kneepads with elastic holders
6	yards elastic cord
1	pair gray sweatpants
1	roll clear tape, 2 inches wide
4	black shoelaces, 27 inches each
1	paper paint bucket, 5-quart size
1	plastic or cardboard shield
1	plastic sword

1. To make the armor, start with the leg pieces. You need to cut out of the insulation two cuisse pieces to cover the thighs and two greave pieces to cover the shins. The kneepads will cover the knees. Measure your child's legs and cut pieces in the shapes shown at left.

2. Punch holes in the insulation pieces as shown in the photo on the facing page. Punch two holes in top of each kneepad and two holes at the bottom. Thread a 30-inch elastic cord through top of each cuisse piece and each greave piece. Tread a 24-inch elastic cord through one bottom and one top kneehole on the left side and then repeat on the right side. Use these cords to attach kneepads to cuisse and greave pieces as shown on facing page. Fit these pieces on the youngster over the sweatpants. Tighten the knee elastic and tie it off.

3. To make the breastplate, or cuirass, cut a piece of silver insulation 16 x 36 inches according to the photo above left. Fold under side edges 1 inch and tape down with clear tape. Curve bottom ends and tape down with clear tape. Cut center back opening and neck opening. Punch four holes on each side of back opening. Thread laces as shown in photo above left and tie. Glue shield to center of front.

4. To make helmet, trace sides and top of bucket on paper to make a pattern. Add 1 inch on each edge, cut out pattern, and use to cut out silver insulation. Cut face opening in bucket, according to photo at left. Carefully glue silver insulation all around bucket. Cut face opening in insulation, leaving 1 inch extra to fold back and glue. Turn under top and bottom edges of silver insulation and glue down. Glue round insulation piece to top.

5. Dress the child in the sweatshirt, cuirass, helmet, shield and sword.

making a mask

*Here's basic wisdom for fun
and effective mask making.*

1. Get a mask that—like a good pair of sunglasses—fits comfortably, can be worn for an extended length of time and complements your facial shape. If you are going to decorate the mask, make sure it has a surface that is easy to work with. Some masks are easy to draw on but don't hold glue well; others are the opposite.

2. Make sure there are extra-large holes for your eyes. They generally look better than smaller eye holes and are much easier to see through.

3. Be creative! Be prepared for the mask to take on its own life as you progress.

4. If you're a beginner, don't try to create a symmetrical design because it can be very hard to achieve. Asymmetrical designs are often more alluring and individualistic.

5. Less is more. Once the glue is pouring, it's easy to get crazy with glitter, stars and pompons. Then suddenly you're not a mysterious baroness but a circus clown!

6. If you paint your mask, shade it by making recessed areas darker and protruding areas lighter. This will immediately distinguish your mask from others.

7. Think about fun add-ons. Consider using feathers, fabrics, stones, ribbons, chain, beads and more. Add details that make the mask your own.

8. Reinforce the band that holds the mask to your face so you are assured it will withstand several hours of wearing. And just in case, keep extra elastic bands in your pocket or purse in case the mask band snaps.

9. Like any craft, you can take mask making to highly advanced levels. If you find that a craft-store mask is too simple for you, then explore the many books that teach the art of mask making for Mardi Gras or for specific cultures or religions. You may find yourself involved in a whole new hobby!

Mask-Making Lore

The wearing of masks dates back to primitive people, who most likely made and wore them to imitate game animals to improve hunts. Back then, masks weren't costumes or art, but functional objects that brought food, fertility or healing. Later on, the Greeks introduced theatrical masks for their plays, and the Halloween and Mardi Gras parties in New Orleans made the decoration of "false faces" both popular and fun! Today, masks are a central part of Halloween traditions all over the globe.

Creative Ideas for Mask Making

You can put whatever you want on your mask, and you'll find that the more personalized it is, the more you'll like it! You can add traditional decor, such as glitter, feathers and pompons (see the examples below), but you can also add individual flair, too. Add extra googly eyes, letters, stick-on metallic shapes, even small photos. Just remember to keep the design simple—the goal is to express yourself and have fun in the process!

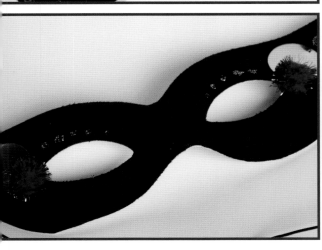

FUNNY BONE!
What is a baby ghost's favorite game? Peek-a-BOO!